# BEGINNINGS AND ENDINGS

Fethullah Gülen's Vision for Today's World

T0159368

# Beginnings
## and
# Endings

## Fethullah Gülen's
### Vision for Today's World

Walter Wagner

BLUE DOME

*Published by* Blue Dome Press
535 Fifth Avenue, Ste.601
New York, NY 10017-8019

www.bluedomepress.com

Library of Congress Cataloging-in-Publication Data Available

ISBN: 978-1-935295-31-0

*Printed by*
Çağlayan A.Ş., Izmir - Turkey

# Contents

# ACKNOWLEDGMENTS

Before a book reaches the stage of being published, an author relinquishes full control of his or her work. Many minds and hands are involved in the process of moving from manuscript to printed page. Those who proposed and approved the project, those who provided suggestions and critiques, those who checked facts and dates, those who copy-edited, and those who approved the final text form a community of supporters, guides, questioners, and, ultimately, colleagues with the writer. The published version takes on an existence of its own, for the writer and colleagues do not accompany the work in order to interpret it to readers or answer their questions or respond to their criticisms. Readers, too, become members of the community engaged in bringing the book to life. The members of that community deserve the writer's acknowledgment, respect, and gratitude.

I gladly give such recognition, respect, and appreciation to the literary midwives at Blue Dome Press and Dr. Huseyin Senturk, Yusuf Alan and their colleagues who accompanied this work from the delivery room to its walking into the world of readers and their audiences. I thank Dr. Heon Abdulhamid Kim and the other organizers of the 2010 conference "Making Peace In and With the World: The Role of the Gülen Movement in the Task of Eco-Justice" at Temple University, Philadelphia, PA. I presented some basic ideas that are present in this book in a paper titled, "End Times for These Times: Eschatology and Dialogue for Peace." Special thanks are expressed to Fatih Harpci for his advice, gentle and astute corrections, and patience in reading the manuscript. Still, I accept responsibility for what you are about to read and share.

The book is dedicated to the women and men of Hizmet, and M. Fethullah Gülen, the man justly called Hocaefendi, revered teacher.

Walter Wagner
Bethlehem, PA

# PROLOGUE

In the Name of God, the All-Merciful, the All-Compassionate.
All praise and gratitude...are for God, the Lord of the worlds,
The All-Merciful, the All-Compassionate,
The Master of the Day of Judgment.
You alone do we worship, and from You alone do we seek help.
Guide us to the Straight Path,
The Path of those whom You have favored, not of those who
have incurred (Your) wrath...nor of those who are astray.[1]

Surah *al-Fatihah* (The Opener)

**M**uhammad Fethullah Gülen is one of the most important Muslim leaders in the world. Born in the village of Korucuk in eastern Turkey in 1941, he now resides at the Golden Generation Retreat Center in Saylorsburg, Pennsylvania.[2] In spite of health issues, he continues to teach, write, and inspire thousands of

---

[1] The English interpretations of the Qur'anic verses are quoted from Ali Ünal's "*The Qur'an with Annotated Interpretation in Modern English.*" The ellipses here indicate my omitting the translator's parenthetical additions "whoever gives them to whomever for whatever reason and in whatever way from the first day of creation until eternity" and "punishment and condemnation." These expressions do not appear in the vast majority of the Qur'anic interpretations (though they are implied in the verses under discussion).

[2] Some sources give Gülen's birth as November 10, 1938 (see for example, the Introduction to Gülen's *Essentials*, p. vii). Given the chronologies related to his receiving his state license to be a preacher at the age of 18, the alternate and now accepted date is April 27, 1941. In 2012 he was cited as the tenth of 500 of the most important persons in the Muslim world. See Schleifer, p. 34. He was listed as the thirteenth most influential Muslims in both the 2009 and 2010 editions of Esposito and Kalin, pp. 18, 44–45 respectively. Schleifler considered him the fifteenth most important Muslim in the 2011 edition, see p. 59. In 2008, as a result of an on-line

people of different faiths and ideologies throughout the world. Yet he is unknown to many in the Western Hemisphere. One of the purposes of this book is to bring him to the attention of the wider public through examining what I consider to be at the center of his vision for a just, equitable, and peaceful world today. Perhaps this study will provide a unifying and theological perspective to other recent works noted in the bibliography that have focused on his educational, social, devotional, and literary contributions together with his writings on Islamic principles and spirituality.

The book contends that Gülen's views of the beginning and ending of creation determine his theological, anthropological, and social-ethical vision for a just and peaceful world in the here and now. He wrote, "After belief in God, belief in the Resurrection has the primary place in securing a peaceful social order."[3] His views of the beginning and the end provide the setting for his concentration on his vision for the present. This book seeks to show that Gülen's eschatology drives his thought and thrives as a dominant force among those affiliated with him. His Islamically-grounded eschatology envisions humans of different religious and ideological commitments cooperating and working together to promote harmony and peace within human society and the natural world in anticipation of the future end of the cosmos and start of the Hereafter. In addition and within the framework of Muslim traditions about the Prophet Muhammad's sayings, Gülen believes that the natural world will respond to that harmony and peace through yielding abundantly to support and enhance human development and life. During the course of the study, I quote extensively from Gülen's writings so that we may hear his voice expressing his understandings of this world, God's Plan for the whole of existence, and the vision he has for human responsibility in the present. This book may serve as a starting point that needs to be followed and amplified; it is an invitation for others to engage Gülen's contribution as well as the persons and the movement he inspires.

---

poll conducted jointly by the *Foreign Policy* and *Prospect* magazines, he was voted "The world's top public intellectual."

[3]   Gülen, *Essentials*, p. 131.

The Arabic word *al-'Alamin* is used for the whole spiritual and material cosmos while the word *ad-Dunya* refers to the present temporal world. Islamic eschatology is usually expressed in terms of *Ma'ad*, or the Resurrection, and is centered on the final state of the *Dunya* towards the fulfillment and how that involves the fulfillment of the whole *'Alamin*. While Gülen holds the traditional Sunni Muslim views of resurrection, judgment and afterlife, he realizes that those teachings impact life here and now. "Here and now" is the span of time and space granted by God for humans to fulfill their role of being God's vicegerents, or representatives, over the earth and their relationships with one another before the ultimate dissolution of *'Alamin*. One manifestation of that vicegerency is the movement known as Hizmet (Service). Gülen and the affiliates (or the participants and volunteers in the movement) clearly and consistently avoid speculations and activities associated in some Christian and Muslim circles with setting dates for the Day of Judgment, identifying evil and good forces, penultimate and final battles, violence in rhetoric and actions, and making conjectures about the afterlife of punishments and rewards. Gülen and those associated with Hizmet's activities and programs seek neither to establish theocracies nor to impose any type of religious law on any society nor to engage in proselytizing. His eschatology is rooted in a profound understanding of the Supreme Divine Being from Whom the entire existence comes into being, with Whom all existence subsists, and to Whom we all will return.

Hizmet already includes a spectrum of mostly, yet not exclusively, Muslims of different nationalities and races, most of whom are volunteers serving in current and planned institutions, organizations, schools, universities, refugee camps, relief societies, publishing houses, newspapers, television stations, and inter-religious/inter-ideological cultural and dialogue centers. Important terms linked to future developments are the New Man (using "man" to include women), the Golden Generation (*Altin Nesil*), the New Millennium, and Peace Islands.

Here, two Turkish words need clarification. First, *Camia*. Camia, spoken as *jamia*, is close to the Arabic root *jama*, that is, "gathering." The English renderings are often "organization" and "movement."

*Camia* does not signify a structured body, confederation, party, or specific group. It carries the meaning of affiliates, associates, individuals and/or groups that share some (not necessarily all) essential values and purposes. Affiliates who share some of Gülen's objectives and ideals may be Muslims, Christians, Jews, Hindus, and so on. They are Turkish, German, Korean, Senegalese, North Americans, and so on. There is no common headquarters, formal central authority, or central membership list. Affiliates are often volunteers who donate time, skills, and resources in enterprises that seek to carry out shared values and goals. Admittedly, a camia-style movement can bewilder Westerners who are likely to think in terms of organizations and corporate bodies. Gülen's characterization of his version of camia—community may be helpful:

> If a movement has started to produce its own models, and people have started to admire it, following its steps and devoting themselves to this cause, making it their ideal, or if they have accepted it as *mafkura* (lofty ideal), …then the person who seems to be at the front of this movement would not even be aware of what is happening most of the time. People would do similar things here and there, even if they didn't know about each other because they don't have any organic connection and because they have not been introduced to each other. But they are connected together by the bonds of a very serious thought and a lofty ideal.[4]

The second term is *Hoşgörü*. The standard and inadequate English translation is "tolerance." Hoşgörü means to regard someone else in the best and most accepting manner even though there may be differences and disagreements.

"Camia" and "Hoşgörü" are foundational factors in the manifestations and fulfillment of Gülen's vision for today's world and the realization of the Divine plan for existence. They are integral aspects of what is popularly called the "Gülen Movement," a prominent "Social Movement Organization."[5] Given that Hizmet's origins and outlook

4    Ibid, *Interview with Mehmet Gündem*.
5    Muhammed Çetin's work, titled *The Gülen Movement*, provides a sociological-political analysis of Social Movement Organizations with a focus on Hizmet. He noted, "The Movement originated in 1970s Turkey as a faith-inspired initiative to improve educational opportunities for a local community; over the three and a half decades since

derive from the inspiration and influence of Fethullah Gülen, Hizmet's vision and its components reflect those areas of Islamic faith and practice that encourage and mandate inter-religious and inter-ideological respect, understanding, and cooperation and which are open to and willingly include engagement and cooperation with the members of other religions and ideologies in the spirit of Hoşgörü.

This Prologue, the following chapters, and the Epilogue are prefaced and concluded with appropriate quotations drawn from the Qur'an, Gülen's writings, and other relevant sources. The first chapter introduces Fethullah Gülen through a series of ways in which he may be met with his thought, action, and services. Chapter Two, "A Sunni Muslim Narrative of This World's Beginning and Ending," provides a general Sunni position concerning the creation and termination of the world, which is broadly relevant to Gülen's positions.[6] I include references, as fitting, to Jewish and Christian analogues to Islam with distinctions within eschatologies that aid in understanding Gülen's intellectual and religious contexts. An essential point in the exposition is the distinction between "end" as fulfillment-consummation and "end" as termination. Chapter Three discusses Gülen's considerations about the present worlds' beginning, cosmology, and place of humanity in the present world of time and space. The fourth chapter presents Gülen's vision for the end in the sense of fulfillment in the present world as just and peaceful, followed by its final end and the new beginning of the Hereafter. Chapter Five considers Gülen's Islamic vision and exhortations as feasible and constructive ways to challenge other religions, contemporary social structures, and economic methods in order to develop a just, prosperous, and peaceful world. In the concluding Epilogue, I offer several reflections on next steps.

As we begin, I note some basic points about the man. Fethullah Gülen is a devout Muslim who stands within the mainstream Sunni Islamic theology and spirituality in the context of Turkish history and culture. He has been influenced by the Turkish perspective of the

---

then, it has grown into a transnational educational, social movement" advocating dialogue between the members of different cultures and faiths. (Çetin, p. xiv).

[6] Since Gülen is a Sunni Muslim, I limited the discussions to basic Sunni positions.

Naqshbandiyyah-style of Sufism as exemplified by one of his earliest spiritual teachers, Muhammad Lütfi Efendi (died 1956).[7] Gülen's spirituality encourages the use of God-given reason linked to faith so that he advocates dialogue and cooperation with a spirit of mutual respect while maintaining individual and communal integrity. His interpretation of Islam finds common ground between the followers of Islam and other religions, especially in efforts to achieve the social order of justice, compassion, and peace without having their followers surrender their distinctive ways of worshiping and serving God. His voluntary exile from his homeland to his current residence in the United States provides him with concerns and insights applicable to Turkey and, simultaneously, perspectives and experiences that address all societies. In brief, he is Muslim, Turkish, and a citizen of and for the world.

Although theological positions may be expressed in formal propositions, a theology that resonates with human minds and hearts can be a form of poetry about God, the world, and humans.[8] Theology's poetry sometimes will be astringent, direct, and logical, and at other times make use of allegory, metaphor, and ornate rhetoric. Muslim theology recognizes such language in the Qur'an (e.g., Surahs al-Baqarah 2:26 and Al Imran 3:7), and spiritual writers may employ enigmatic statements, word images, and figures of speech. Theology is also personal. A theologian expresses himself/herself in, with, and under the content, structure, and rhetoric of his/her oral and written word. Gülen is a prolific author whose works "interpret one another and gradually lead toward a main idea."[9] The main idea offered in this study is Gülen's vision for the present world in light of its beginnings and endings.

---

[7]   See Kim, *The Nature and Role,* pp. 119–120 for Gülen's words about and Kim's reflections on M. Lütfi's influence. The work is Kim's 2008 doctoral dissertation for Temple University (Philadelphia, PA) and has been published as a book available in part on-line through Pro-Quest UMI Dissertation Publishing in 2011.

[8]   See Robinson, p. 261. Petrarch, the early Renaissance poet-scholar wrote his brother, Gherado: "The fact is poetry is very far from being opposed to theology. Does that surprise you? One may almost say that theology actually is poetry, poetry concerning God."

[9]   See Gülen, *The Statue of Our Souls,* p. xiii. Muhammad Çetin translated the book and may have provided the Preface from which the quotation is drawn.

To understand Gülen, we need to meet him repeatedly in different yet unifying ways. I suggest that readers consider the meetings as a spiral that begins with general acquaintance and then goes deeper into who he is, what he offers, and what we may learn from him. It will be helpful to be alert to three Islamic metaphors that Gülen develops: Names, Seed-Growth, and Mirror-Reflection. Each derives from the rich traditions of Sufi spirituality.

Throughout our time together, I quote from Gülen's writings and from sources close to him. Gülen's published writings include transcripts of talks, interviews and speeches; articles; works intended for average Muslim and non-Muslim audiences; and books for persons who already have significant acquaintance with Islamic thought and practice. Because he speaks and writes in Turkish, many of his ideas and works are available only in translations. I have been limited to those which have appeared in English. The interpretation of the Qur'an used in our study was prepared by Ali Ünal, one of his frequent translators and close associate. It contains extensive notes and several appendices. Gülen provided the introduction to this interpretation of the Qur'an and accepted the notes as consonant with his views. Ünal also has reflected that he presented Gülen's positions in *The Resurrection and the Afterlife*.[10]

The Qur'anic passage that began this Prologue also ends the book. For Muslims, the entire Qur'an is God speaking to humanity. Surah *al-Fatihah* (The Opener) is a prayer that Muslims believe was given by the One-Only God to begin the Qur'an, to serve as the essence of that Holy Book, and to inspire faithful living. An observant Muslim memorizes it in Arabic and includes it in the five obligatory daily prayers. Its opening words, "In the Name of God, the All-Merciful, the All-Compassionate" known as the *Basmalah*, begins 113 of the Qur'an's 114 *surah*s (chapters) and serves as a dedicatory invocation for believers as they undertake God-acceptable activities, study, and even writing books.[11]

---

[10] Ali Ünal in an email posting to Huseyin Senturk, November 5, 2012. Ünal's book also relies on the views of Bediüzzaman Said Nursi (1877–1960). See p. viii.

[11] Qur'anic chapter of *at-Tawbah* ("Repentance") is the exception.

The opening Qur'anic chapter of *al-Fatihah* (The Opener) signals more than outward practice; it is the essence of the Qur'an and the epitome of Islamic intellectual activity, ethics, piety, spirituality, intra-communal relationships, and mission in the world. Convinced that God spoke these words, devout Muslims come to know and serve God as the All-Merciful and All-Compassionate Lord of all the spiritual and physical worlds. They believe that the present is the gateway to future realms of existence. The road to that gateway is the God-given Straight Path that leads from life now to the coming Day when the Master of all time and space will call all humans and other responsible beings to account for all their actions and deeds. The opening chapter of *al-Fatihah* stretches from beginnings to endings to new beginnings. By specifying the Straight Path, the Opener points to persons who are guides on that Way while it warns about the ways that end in destruction and those who bring doom upon themselves. *Al-Fatihah* (The Opener) expects humans to consider, envision, and act on what the Straight Way may be within the lives of individuals and this world.

Fethullah Gülen's vision for the present world resonates with this opening chapter, for he reaches back to the beginnings of all existence (*al-'Alamin*) through life in this world (*ad-Dunya*), and into the Here-after (*al-Akhira*). His belief that the Resurrection has a primary place in securing a peaceful social order reflects a conviction shared by many Jews, most Christians, and all Muslims: belief in God and expectations about the Hereafter are intimately and directly connected to transforming the present social order. Bundled into Gülen's reference to the Resurrection are events that started before the creation of all existence, lead up to the End Times, and point to the future that lies beyond current structures, institutions, ideologies, and religious teachings. Gülen points toward the core of beginnings and endings: the challenge of achieving and maintaining just, moral, and peaceful social order in the present time and world. Further, he recognizes a growing convergence of scriptural themes, theological views, historical currents, and awakened commitments among Muslims, Christians, and Jews. He is convinced that the "peaceful social order" is not only possible but inevitable for it is part of God's Plan for this world. Briefly stated, the bundle of End Time positions and expressions is essential as religiously committed and non-religiously committed persons seek to understand one another and labor to attain the goal of that society.

Some further introductory matters may be helpful. The Arabic word *Allah* is the regular word used for the One-Only God of Judaism, Christianity, and Islam. In a more developed sense, "Allah" is the fullest expression of the totality of what humans may express as God's essence and identity known through many Names and Attributes as well as Divine actions – all without compromising the absolute Oneness and Unity of the Unique-and-Only God. In that sense, "Allah" is God's personal Name.[12] While some may argue to the contrary, I assume that Jews, Christians, and Muslims worship the same God. Throughout the book, I use the Arabic "Allah" in direct quotations, but otherwise use "God" for the supreme Deity. The initial letters of pronouns and other terms referring to God are in upper case for the sake of clarity. Some translations of Hadith materials render *rasul* as "apostle." I altered those quotations by replacing "apostle" with the more Islamically accurate "messenger." I include Arabic and Turkish words, with translations, as necessary. Transliterations from those languages into English can be challenging; I use what are regarded as standard English renderings. English renderings of the Qur'an are from Ali Ünal's English translation. Note that Ünal supplied the words in parentheses in the Qur'anic quotations for the purpose of clarifying and sometimes extending the sense of the Arabic. References in the footnotes give an author's name, main words of a publication's title, and page numbers. The full citations are in the Bibliography. Muslims traditionally honor Prophets and Messengers when mentioning their names by adding "Peace be Upon Him," abbreviated PBUH. When speaking of God, they follow with the Arabic "Subhanahu wa Ta'ala" for "Glory be to Him, the Exalted," abbreviated as SWT. I acknowledge those uses here and ask readers assume their presence throughout the book.

For the purpose of full disclosure, I am an ordained Lutheran-style Christian clergyperson who is also an adjunct faculty member at

---

[12] Gülen, *Questions and Answers*, Vol. 1, p. 23.

the Moravian Theological Seminary (Bethlehem, PA) and the Lutheran Theological Seminary (Philadelphia, PA). My academic specialties include Church History and the New Testament. I have been teaching and writing in the area of Islamic studies since 1990. I have several connections with Hizmet and its affiliates. Those connections involve my having been the instructor and master's degree theses advisor for several Turkish Muslims who are students of Gülen. Through attending events at the Lehigh Dialogue Center in Bethlehem, I became acquainted with members of Hizmet and participated in two Hizmet subsidized trips to Turkey (2007 and 2011). In addition, I coordinate and often am a presenter at inter-religious dialogues between Muslims and Christians. Those dialogues are co-sponsored by the Lehigh Dialogue Center and Moravian Theological Seminary. I have been a guest and speaker at programs sponsored by the Golden Generation Retreat Center (Saylorsburg, PA where Gülen is in residence) and several dialogue centers. And I have met Fethullah Gülen.

Now, we begin:

In the Name of God,
the All-Merciful,
the All-Compassionate.

# CHAPTER ONE

## Meeting Fethullah Gülen

Fethullah Gülen is an authoritative mainstream Turkish Muslim scholar, opinion leader and educational activist who supports interfaith and intercultural dialogue, democracy, human rights and spirituality, and who opposes violence and turning religion into a political ideology. Gülen promotes not a clash of civilizations but cooperation of civilizations toward a peaceful world.[13]

I met Fethullah Gülen before I met Fethullah Gülen. That seemingly contradictory statement reflects my experiencing him through the women and men of Hizmet[14] and several institu-

---

[13] *Understanding Fethullah Gülen*, Istanbul: Journalists and Writers Foundation, 2012, p. 7. Gülen is the honorary president of the Journalists and Writers Foundation (GYV) that was founded on June 29, 1994.

[14] The "Movement" is called Hizmet, the Turkish term meaning "Service." When the word appears as "Movement" (initial letter capitalized), it refers to Hizmet specifically. According to Çetin, Hizmet is an international movement of persons who are dedicated to the ideals and example of Fethullah Gülen, regarding him as a spiritual guide and mentor. Each of the many Gülen-inspired groups, centers, schools, organizations and institutions functions fiscally, programmatically, and structurally independent of one another. Yet they share broad contacts. Çetin stated:

> [T]he Gülen Movement has not developed any aspirations to evolve into a conflictual movement, a political party or to seek political power. On the contrary, Gülen remains determinedly in the mainstream Sufi tradition of dealing with the spiritual needs of the people, educating them, and providing stability in times of trouble.... [It] aims to bring interior change in persons, in their mind-sets, attitudes and behavior. It teaches individuals to use their constitutionally given rights to contribute to and serve society positively. [T]he Movement is a form of collective, purposive, non-conflictual, apolitical, and organized social altruism that has arisen from civil society, which remains the boundary of its field of concern and action. (p. 285).

tions generated and sustained by his personal influence and writings. As with many in the United States, my initial encounters with him came through interfaith dialogue activities sponsored by area Dialogue Centers, starting with Iftar dinners and Ashura observances.[15] These programs lead, for those who desire further contacts, to developing personal relationships and opportunities to discuss mutual religious commitments, aspirations, anxieties about one another, and sincere friendships – all with respectful candor. The Centers sponsor partially subsidized tours to many of Turkey's tourist sites, several Hizmet-affiliated institutions, and meals with host families. In a number of instances, the Centers and affiliated individuals co-sponsor interfaith and intercultural dialogues with colleges, universities, and theological graduate schools. At times, Turkish Muslim students enroll in courses to study the Holy Scriptures, Christianity and other religions in order to deepen their understanding of those areas so that they may raise cultural awareness and better serve as future leaders at North American dialogue centers, and teachers in Canada, the United States, Turkey, and so on.

I admit to initial wariness. What were their motivations and agendas? Were any strings attached to what seemed to be their piety, generosity, and openness? Indeed, there are motives and agendas. One often repeated and urgent desire is to assure non-Muslims that Islam is a religion of peace, reconciliation, honesty, and morality. The 1998 bombings of the United States' embassies in Kenya and Tanzania, the attacks of September 11, 2001, and the conflicts in Iraq and Afghanistan have pressured many Muslims to probe themselves and to reach out to their broader communities. Another clear objective is to counter materialism with educational programs that promote a high regard for actualizing human potential in this world. Yet, questions linger. Does the

---

[15]   Iftar is the meal that breaks the day-long fast during the month of Ramadan. Gülen-inspired Dialogue Centers as well as many mosques sponsor a dinner during Ramadan for the general public. For Sunni Muslims, Ashura, the 10th day of the month of Muharram, celebrates the day Adam and his wife came to earth, Noah left the ark, and Jesus ascended to his heavenly place. Shi'ite Muslims mark it as the day Imam Husayn was martyred in 680 CE at Karbala (in present-day Iraq). For them it is a day of sadness and resolution to be faithful in spite of opposition.

Hizmet, or "Gülen Movement" as popularly known in the West, harbor radical elements that seek to infiltrate and subvert their host nations? To be sure, determined secularists in Turkey believe Gülen and those inspired by him seek to Islamize the Republic while Islamists who seek their version of a Muslim state reject his spirituality, and some Turkish ultra nationalists suspect he is in the pay of the United States' Central Intelligence Agency.[16]/[17]

The more that I came to know Gülen-inspired teachers, homemakers, engineers, teenagers, physicians, musicians, students, and business owners, the less wary I became. At the same time, my interest in Fethullah Gülen and Hizmet grew. Meeting, questioning and observing persons who are part of the institutions established by the Hizmet-linked Bosnians, Turks, Turkmens, and Azeris provided access to a consistent and variegated spectrum of approaches and activities. The consistency was in their dedication, while the variety was in their actions. The multi-racial staff of a television station in New Jersey; leaders of Turkish Cultural Centers in New York City and Houston; the heads of charter schools who inspire African-American and Lati-

---

[16] See *Ebaugh*, pp. xi–xiii, 1–11, 23–46, and 115–128.

[17] Gülen answered such baseless and contradictory claims in a recent interview: "Not even those who accuse us of all that really believe it. Equating the activities of the "Hizmet" with terms like "Islamism" is a clear sign of ignorance. Either wrong information is circulated intentionally or these people do neither know what Hizmet or Islamism really is. At the same time, other critics of the movement accuse us of treason to Islam, being slaves of the United States and Israel, making propaganda in favor of Christianity and Judaism, or cooperating secretly with the Vatican or other religious centers. How am I supposed to answer all of these inconsistent and self-contradictory accusations! I am 74 years old. My life and work are open for everyone to see. Nothing is kept secret. Up until now, I have never tried to bring a small village under my control, let alone states. Neither have I suggested or encouraged anyone to this end. The baseless accusations and the corresponding court rulings are well known. I do not even have the strength anymore to laugh about these fabricated accusations. I feel sorry for those who make up these things. The activities of the "Hizmet" are carried out in public with people from all walks of life, from all countries and religions. The activities have been approved by the public authorities and are checked by them. Activities outside the framework of the institutions which take place on the individual or social levels happen on the legal basis of the respective states which are informed about them. I would like to know what is not transparent about that." (Gülen, Interview with Rainer Hermann, "Do good and let it unfold").

no youth to go to college; the director and members of Kimse Yok Mu, an international disaster relief agency headquartered in Istanbul; the chief medical officer of Şifa Hospital in Izmir who spent weeks at his own expense in Haiti doing post-earthquake pediatric surgery; the exuberant children of a private elementary school in Konya, started and sustained by Hizmet-inspired donors; the men and women who serve as dormitory parents for university students from rural Turkey; and many more showed the depth of their commitment to their fellow humans, Islam, and Fethullah Gülen's ideals. Each person, even those who never saw him, evidenced that he is an extraordinary teacher and guide, a pillar of faith, and a steady optimist about the ability of humans to be just and compassionate. Throughout all of these experiences and research into Gülen's thinking and Hizmet's activities, I found a resolute avoidance of political controversies and steadfast rejection of any attempts to promote an Islamist or supposedly "Gülenist" social or religious agenda.

Almost finally, I met Fethullah Gülen at a dinner in the Golden Generation Retreat Center in Saylorsburg, Pennsylvania. Present at the dinner were Ali Ünal, several Turkish students and Dr. Muhammed Çetin. Because Gülen does not speak English, Dr. Çetin served as our translator.[18] Hocaefendi, as Gülen is respectfully called, is a soft-spoken, humble person whose presence is both gentle and impressive. During our conversation, he evidenced wide and deep knowledge of philosophy and literature, engagement with current events, and, naturally, knowledge of the Qur'an, Hadith, Islamic jurisprudence, and Sufism. All the while he drew out his table companions, attentively listening and quietly leading us to express ourselves more cogently.

---

[18] Çetin headed the dialogue center in Houston, Texas and was on the faculty of the University of Houston prior to becoming one of Gülen's translators of some of his works and sermons. In 2011 he was elected to the Turkish Assembly (Parliament). Gülen has been in residence at the Golden Generation Retreat Center in Saylorsburg, Pennsylvania since 1999. He entered the United States in order to receive medical treatment. He has a permanent resident visa in the United States. From another angle, he is in a self-imposed exile from Turkey. See *Harrington*. James Harrington recounts the nature of the accusations, the proceedings and the conclusion of the case.

On the surface it would seem that I met a mature, polite, scholarly leader who dealt courteously with his guest. My impression-intuition, however, was that there was much more to the meeting. That impression-intuition was put into perspective by the passage in one of Gülen's studies of Sufism in which he discussed *tafakkur*—reflection:

> *Tafakkur* literally means to think on a subject deeply, systematically, and in great detail. In this context, it signifies reflection, which is the heart's lamp, the soul's food, the spirit of knowledge, and the essence and light of the Islamic way of life. Reflection is the light in the heart that allows the believer to discern what it good and evil, beneficial and harmful, beautiful and ugly. Again, it is through reflection that the universe becomes a book to study, and the verses of the Qur'an disclose their deeper meanings and secrets more clearly. Without reflection, the heart is darkened, the spirit is exasperated, and Islam is lived at such a superficial level that it is devoid of meaning and profundity.[19]

He is a man of reflection.

To meet him is also to see him in the company of other Muslim scholars and spiritual leaders. Among these, he has mentioned several as being especially close to him: the four 12th–13th century Sufi masters known together as the Four Poles or Pillars (*Aktab al-Arbaa*) and several other Sufi masters from the 10th – 19th centuries.[20] He singled out for special mention Hamdi Yazir (1878–1942), Mustafa Sabri (1869–1954) and Muhammad Lütfi Efendi (1869–1956) as opening his mind and heart to the Sufi way and the love of learning. From the age of ten to sixteen, Gülen studied with Lüfti Efendi, and for a short

---

[19] Gülen, *Key Concepts in the Practice of Sufism*, Vol. 1, p. 10.

[20] Ibid, *Interview with Mehmet Gündem*, January 25, 2005. Accessed on August 24, 2012 from http://www.fgulen.com. The four *Aktab al-Arbaa*, or major Sufi saint-leaders, are Abd al-Qadir Jilani (1077–1166), Ahmad Badawi (1200–1276), Ahmad Rufai (1119–1183) and Ibrahim Dassuqi (1255–1296). Others mentioned by Gülen are: Abu'l Hasan al-Kharaqani (963–1033), Hayat ibn Qays al-Harrani, Aqil al-Manbiji, Muhammad Bahauddin (1317–1389), Imam Rabbani (1561-1624), and Mawlana Khalid (1779–1827). He reflected that the teachings and examples of Hamdi Yazir (1878–1942) and Mustafa Sabri (1869–1954) influenced him. He reserved special gratitude toward the Naqshibandi Sufi, Muhammed Lütfi Efendi of Alvar (1869–1956) whom, he said "nourished" him in the Sufi path.

time, with his grandson, Sadi Efendi. Gülen has had no further formal education. His thorough training in the religious sciences, wide and deep knowledge of languages, history, philosophy, literature, and other religions indicate that he is a man of constant study and significant intellectual abilities. At the age of eighteen, he scored one of the highest scores on the government's examination for the license to be an imam, and soon afterward, the state appointed him as a preacher. In the Turkish secular arrangement, the government provides the examinations and the assignments of imams and preachers. Preachers are to be thoroughly knowledgeable about the Qur'an and Hadith as well as eloquent in oratory and sermons. Gülen's lectures, conversations, and writings disclose a preacher's rhetorical style and awareness of his audiences. While Gülen is scholarly, he does not bolster his positions with copious footnotes or a plethora of citations. Two important points follow from this observation.

First and broadly speaking, we will encounter four types of the published materials of Gülen. Many of his published works began as sermons, talks, and *sohbet* discourses (responses to questions raised by students and visitors as well as his thoughts on various topics). These are intended to be accessible to listeners and, by extension, readers. A second type is that of articles in periodicals and interviews. These have a somewhat more formal flavor for he has the opportunity to read over the transcripts. A third type may be described as instructional materials about Islam and related issues in the tone of a preacher's exhortations. Finally, he covers complex spiritual matters that assume that readers are well-versed in Islamic theology and history. Naturally, these classifications are not rigid and the lines between them may blur. To understand him, it is advisable to be familiar with the full range of his works because he may express the same points from different angles, thereby providing fuller contexts and content to his views. Given the range of his thinking, breadth of his knowledge, the trajectory of his views, the venues he addresses, and the spectrum of his concerns, he brings together the contributions and insights of many thinkers, incorporating them and often integrating them into his own perspectives. As we read his works, we may recognize phrasings and

ideas encountered elsewhere, yet he transforms these past contributions and insights, harmonizing them with his positions for understanding them in the present and future. He told an interviewer:

> When a person spends a lot of time with certain people (or their
> works), they become an accumulation in the intellect. You express
> the same meaning with them, but in your own style, without being
> aware of it, perhaps you say the same things like *tevarud* in poetry.
> Sometimes you call this a "style" but you don't remember to whom
> it belongs, or you simply say "this is how it is in the words of this
> and that person."[21]

Second, Gülen's relationship to Bediüzzaman Said Nursi (1878–
1960) and the movements that derive from his thought, writings, and
influence call for comment.[22] Nursi was a Kurd, born in eastern Anatolia during the waning years of the Ottoman Empire. In the wake of
the establishment of the Turkish Republic in 1923, the government
came to regard Nursi with hostility, which led to his spending many
years in prison and internal exile. Under those circumstances and sur-
reptitiously, he wrote a multi-volume collection of interpretation and
commentary of the verses of the Qur'an known as the *Risale-i Nur*. It
is a wide-ranging work that includes discussions on cosmology, escha-

---

[21] Ibid, *Interview with Mehmet Gündem*. According to Gündem, *Tevarud* (or *tawarud*)
is the term used for the phenomenon that a line or couplet can be expressed by
two authors writing independently in precisely the same way (and possibly at the
same time). Meaning "coincidence of thoughts and expressions, *tevarud* implies two
authors or poets expressing the same ideas in very similar words without pre-knowl-
edge of one another. Gülen has been especially open to the great Sufi masters and
scholars, such as Abu Hamid ibn Muhammad al-Ghazzali (1058–1111) and Jalaluddin
Rumi (1207–1273).

    Rumi's followers founded the Mevlevi *tariqa* (Sufi "order" or brotherhood).
Technically, Gülen is not a Sufi if that is defined as a person who has a Sufi master
and is a member of an order (*tariqa*). If Sufism is considered to be a spiritual movement in which individuals dedicated to self-purification, overcoming all dualities
and passions that keep them from full obedience to the One-Only God, and to live
that obedience in the world, then Gülen lives in the Sufi way.

    In 1925, the Atatürk government banned all Sufi orders in the Republic.
Individual masters, such as Muhammed Lütfi Efendi, continued to teach and guide
interested persons. *Kim* (p. 121) holds that the main sources of Gülen's Sufi vision
can be traced to his time with Lütfi Efendi.

[22] See *Abu Rabi'* and also *Markham and Pirim* for studies of Nursi's theology.

tology, personal advice to his students, and interpretation and commentary on the Qur'an often with stories and anecdotal references to make his points clear and appealing. Nursi advocated bringing sciences and religion together as the work of the One-Only God, and he looked forward to a harmonious, prosperous, and peaceful world. Although he wrote under isolated and difficult conditions, his writings and spiritual bearing led to the development of what is called the "Nur Movement," which has a special meaning among Sufis, as *Nur* is the Arabic word for "Light" in the sense of Divine illumination. Following Nursi's death, the movement fragmented into different groups and approaches.[23] Gülen and Nursi never met, and Gülen was never part of the cluster of Nur movements. Nevertheless, Nursi was an important figure in Gülen's development. Gülen's views certainly are compatible with those of Nursi, yet Gülen differs largely in envisioning the world's transformations as starting in our present times and transforms his ideas and examples into societal expressions such as schools, media, hospitals, and so on, while both deliberately showed disinterest in all kinds of partisan political involvement. He urges persons to originate their own models and means of caring out God's will as long as these are Islamically compatible and are grounded in love and respect. With regard to his relationship to Nursi's ideas, Gülen said:

> What was essential for [Nursi] were the guidelines he proposed in his works that were devoted to the belief in taking action without disturbing anyone...If a person has benefited from any other person on matters like the truths of belief, the way of conduct, the priority of human values, then it would be ungrateful, disrespectful not to acknowledge this...If I was to disregard [my previous teachers] or undermine them, then that would be a demonstration of disrespect. But Bediüzzaman had a great influence on my ideas...Following their [earlier teachers] footsteps has been like walking behind the Messenger of God. The difference between them and Bediüzzaman, from my perspective, is that he belongs to the present age, an age for which he brought perfect interpretations.[24]

---

[23]  See Yavuz and Esposito, *Turkish Islam*, pp. 3–18
[24]  Gülen, *Interview with Mehmet Gündem*.

Gülen has listened to many voices. The highest priorities among those voices are the Divine Speech of God in the Qur'an and the Sunnah of the Messenger, followed by the voices of the sages who have preceded him. Yet he has his own voice, a voice that opens persons to seeing and hearing about God's Plan in our time.

I still keep meeting Fethullah Gülen. These encounters are through his writings that have been translated into English, through articles and books about him, and by way of continuing relationships with participants in Hizmet. I hear his voice as I picture him sitting in the Golden Generation Retreat Center's library discoursing in a *Sohbet*, when I sit at a table with affiliates and guests, and when Dialogue Center colleagues speak to me.

The statement about Fethullah Gülen that opened this chapter describes much about him. Yet it touches only the outer manifestations of his character and efforts. Although my period of wariness has ended, I still ask "Why? What is the inner motivation that frames his theology, energy, influence, and appeal?" My answer was given in the Prologue: Gülen's vision for the present and future makes Hizmet an essential part of his wider and urgent call for the formation of a community of religiously committed and non-religiously committed persons to work toward a just, equitable, and prosperous world now. That vision is grounded in his confidence that God wills such a "Golden Generation" to achieve a "New Millennium" before this world is terminated.[25] The stirrings of that Golden Generation are to be seen in Hizmet and in the welcome given to all who share, however generally, the same anticipations and goals. Gülen's Islamically-shaped understandings of creation, human nature, and the Hereafter are not literalistic repetitions of the Qur'an and Hadith. Nor are they derived from apocalyptic visions of a clash of religions and civilizations. "Islamically-shaped" means that his considerations on the origins and events leading up to the fulfillment of God's Plan and the Hereafter are faithfully consonant with the Qur'an and Hadith while inviting further inter-

---

[25] "Golden Generation" and "New Millennium" are terms covered in Chapter Four.

pretations and discussion directed toward ending poverty, ignorance, and disunity in the present.

Put succinctly: The ways in which one meets Fethullah Gülen may be ways to meet the future. To meet and begin to understand Fethullah Gülen means beginning with the Name of God, Who is the First (*al-Awwal*) and the Last (*al-Akhir*), and journeying again with and towards Him, that is, starting and ending with God.[26]

> Glorify the Name of your Lord, the Most High, Who creates and fashions in due proportions, and Who determines (a particular life, nature, and goal for each creature), and guides (it toward the fulfillment of that goal); and Who brings forth herbage, then turns it to dark-colored, rotten stubble. (For the guidance of humankind,) We will establish the Qur'an in your heart and have you recite (it to others), so you will not forget (anything of it), except what God wills. Surely He knows all that is manifest and all that is hidden (including your outward and inward states). We will guide you to the easiest path (in all your affairs). So remind and instruct (them in the truth), in case reminder and instruction may be of use. He who stands in awe of God will be mindful of the instruction.
>
> (Surah *al-A'la* [The Most High], 87:1–10)

---

[26] *Al-Awwal* (The First) and *al-Akhir* (The Last) are two of the Beautiful Names of God. Traditionally, God is said to have ninety-nine such Names. However, the Divine Names are not restricted to these ninety-nine Divine Names mentioned in the authentic Tradition reported by Abu Hurayra, one of the Prophet's Companions. There are many other Names of God mentioned both in Prophetic Traditions and in the Qur'an, both explicitly and by allusion. In addition, God Almighty has other Names which He mentioned in the other Divine Books or which He particularly informed some of His servants about or which He keeps concealed with Him.

# CHAPTER TWO

## A Sunni Narrative of the Worlds' Beginning and Ending

Say: "He Who produced them in the first instance will give them life. He has full knowledge of every (form and mode and possibility of) creation (and of everything He has created, He knows every detail in every dimension of time and space)." He Who has made for you fire from the green tree, and see, you kindle fire with it. Is not He Who has created the heavens and the earth able to create (from rotten bones) the like of them (whose bones have rotted under the ground)? Surely He is; He is the Supreme Creator, the All-Knowing. When He wills a thing to be, He but says to it "Be!" and (in the selfsame instant,) it is. So, All-Glorified is He in Whose Hand is the absolute dominion of all things, and to Him you are being brought back. (Surah Ya-Sin 36:79–83)

The essence of Islam is worship of, obedience to, and service for the One-Only God from Whom all humans come and to Whom they will return and be held accountable for their deeds. Islamic accountability is expressed not only in terms of belief and all the good or evil deeds one forwards to his or her afterlife while in the world but also with reference to this world's end, the resurrection of the dead, God's righteous judgment on individuals, and the entrance into the Hereafter each deserves.[27] Surah *al-Infitar* (The Cleaving Open) contains key Qur'anic elements about the Day of Judgment:

---

[27] See, for example, Surahs 8; 75; 83–89; 92 and 99–100.

When the heaven is cleft open; and when the stars fall in disorder
and are scattered; and when the seas burst forth (spilling over their
bounds to intermingle); and when the graves are overturned (and
pour out their contents)—everyone will come to understand all
(the good and evil) that he has forwarded (to his afterlife while in
the world), and all (the good and evil) that he has left behind
(undone). O human! What is it that deludes you concerning your
Lord, the All-Munificent? — He Who has created you, fashioned
you, and proportioned you (in measures perfect for the purpose of
your creation), having constituted you in whatever form He has
willed. No indeed! But (being deluded) they deny the Last
Judgment (in the other world). Yet, there are angel-guardians
(watching) over you—noble and honorable, recording—who
know what you do. The virtuous and godly ones will indeed be in
(the Gardens of) perpetual bliss; while the (disbelieving) shame-
less, dissolute ones will indeed be in the Blazing Flame. They will
enter it to roast (therein) on the Day of Judgment. They will never
be absent from it. What enables you to perceive what the Day of
Judgment is? Again: What is it that enables you to perceive what
the Day of Judgment is? The Day on which no soul has power to
do anything in favor of another—the command on that day will
be God's (entirely and exclusively). (82:1–19)

Events, warnings, promises and the standards of judgment concerning the End Times are part of God's immutable and eternal Plan
for the cosmos and all creatures.[28] Although the total Plan and some
of its portions are still known only to God, He has disclosed enough
of it through the structures and rhythms of the created order, human
nature and history so that no one can claim to be unaware of the One-
Only God's existence, will and coming judgment.[29]

Moreover, in the long course of human history, God raised numerous Prophets throughout the world and sent His Messengers with Books
for guiding humans to the Straight Way that leads to eternal life in
blessedness. In addition to belief in the coming resurrection of the dead

---

[28] See *Ayahs* 3:54; 7:34; 8:30; 68:45. Ünal translates "Plan" variously as "scheme,"
and "design."

[29] See, for example, Surahs 6:95–99 as one of many passages that describe God's using
creation from seeds to stars to point toward His Plan for the human journey to
eternal life.

and judgment, Muslims are to accept all these Prophets and Messengers of God and the Scriptures revealed to them prior to the Revelation of the Qur'an to Muhammad. Therefore, both the Qur'an and the Hadith[30] recognize persons and passages in the Bible as expressing God's will to some extent with the proviso that Jews and Christians over later eras have misunderstood, misinterpreted, added to, subtracted from, obscured, and corrupted the original revelatory Divine Speech given to those earlier Messengers of God. Christians and Jews lived in pre-Islamic Arabia, the Roman (Byzantine) Empire's Egypt, Palestine and Syria as well as the areas of the Persian Empire we now know as Iraq and Iran. Consequently, some among the early generation of Muslims were acquainted with the Bible along with Jewish and Christian developments. The Qur'an and Hadith, indeed, reflect such acquaintance.

Chapter Two centers on the main features of a general Sunni Muslim narrative of the world's beginnings and endings that takes into account two factors. The first and more important factor is the Chapter's serving as the framework for this study's three following chapters, that is, Fethullah Gülen's visions of the world's beginnings; its endings and new beginnings; and his challenges for today's world. The narrative, therefore, is not a complete exposition of Islamic views on the

---

[30] Hadith is a saying, action, or tacit approval of Prophet Muhammad transmitted outside of the Qur'an through a chain of known intermediaries. The Hadith collections are accounts concerning those sayings, actions, and tacit approvals of Muhammad as reported by his Companions and recorded by the early Muslim generations. Devoted scholars gathered these reports and accounts from the memories of the Companions, including the wives of the Prophet, then sorted and evaluated, arranged in categories and compiled in several collections.

There are two kinds of Hadith: Hadith Qudsi (Divine Sentence)—which is a direct Revelation in which God speaks in the first person by the mouth of the Prophet—and Hadith Nabawi (Prophetic sentence), which is an indirect Revelation in which the Prophet speaks as himself. The second type of Hadith is also called *Hadith Sharif* (Noble Hadith). The several collections are further arranged as Pure or Authenticated (*Sahih*), Good (*Hasan*), Weak (*Da'if*), and Fabricated (*Mawdu*). See Glassé, pp. 59–62. Sunni Muslims recognize as Sahih the collections by Muhammad ibn Isma'il al-Bukhari (died 870 CE), Abu'l-Husayn Muslim ibn al-Hajjaj (died 875), Abu Dawud as-Sijistani (died 875), Abu Isa Muhammad at-Tirmidhi (died 892), an-Nasa'i (died 915), and Ibn Maja (died 886). Some scholars also include the first written collection, *Muwattwa* of Malik ibn Anas (ca. 795).

world's beginnings, ending, and the Hereafter. The second factor is based on the Islamic teachings about the pre-Islamic Prophets, Messengers and Scriptures. The factor suggests that aspects of Biblical and post-Biblical Christian yet pre-Islamic elements may provide analogies and examples that are appropriate in considering the Islamic narrative and Gülen's visions as well as his urging that Muslims and Christians engage in interfaith dialogue for the sake of humanity today. The Chapter opens with descriptions of eschatology in general, Biblical analogues and examples related to eschatology, and a synopsis of relevant Islamic eschatological expectations. The Islamic narrative is structured through eight phases of God's Plan. The Chapter ends with a set of projections that inform Chapters Three and Four.

## ESCHATOLOGY: A GENERAL DESCRIPTION

Eschatology is a broad term that refers to the ends of time and space and deals with the circumstances leading to those conclusions. Nevertheless, eschatology is far more than the study of such endings and what might follow as a Hereafter. Considerations of the End Times are cosmic in scope, communal in nature, and individual in application. Eschatology embraces not only the essential religious teachings about death, resurrection, the following judgment, and the eternal life of the Hereafter, but also the tradition's understanding of beginnings, the meaning of history, and the direction and purpose towards which everything in creation moves.[31] End Time emphases involve preparing for the future through seeking to establish justice, equality, peace, and love in the present. As a result, eschatology provides a proleptic or forward dynamic that pushes present persons and proposals toward the future as well as an analeptic or retrospective perspective in which the future is presented as the vantage point to look back to the present and past. Eschatology, therefore, is deeply engaged with affairs in the present.

Furthermore, nature, events, and people are moving toward their divinely determined endings. Within the time span of the present, eschatological writings and portions thereof regularly call on the

---

[31] *Winter*, p. 308.

members of their communities to be patient, loyal, and morally pure as the cosmic drama unfolds around and within them. Descriptions of the events and conditions that lead to, will take place during, and that will follow the End Times are often expressed as disclosures from the Divine either directly and/or through angels to specially prepared humans who then convey the descriptions to others in symbolic as well as literal terms. Written versions of those descriptions, in whole or part, are termed "apocalypses":

> "Apocalypse" is a genre of revelatory literature with a narrative framework, in which a revelation is mediated by an otherworldly being to a human recipient, disclosing a transcendent reality which is both temporal, insofar as it envisages eschatological salvation, and spatial insofar as it involves another, supernatural world intended to interpret present, earthly circumstances in light of the supernatural world and of the future, and to influence both the understanding and the behavior of the audience by means of divine authority.[32]

Eschatological literature and particularly apocalypses are characterized by urgency; the End Times are imminent or already here, therefore be faithful, act according to God's will, and live in anticipation of the judgment. In sum, eschatological works call on those who are attuned to the End Times to live in expectation of God's judgment so that they are moral, faithful in times of persecution, and active in doing good works.

## ESCHATOLOGY: BIBLICAL ANALOGUES AND EXAMPLES

Traditional Christianity is profoundly eschatological. Jesus, for example, is presented as proclaiming the nearness of the Kingdom of God and the imminent judgment on the world. The apostle-missionary, Paul, told congregations that the End Times were already taking place. The author of the work called "To the Hebrews" wrote that this world was only a passing "city" and believers were longing to enter the eternal city. The Revelation (Apocalypse) to John is replete with visions of

---

[32]  Adela Yarbro Collins (ed.) *Semeia*. Vol. 36. Decatur, GA: Society of Biblical Literature, 986, p. 7.

conflicts, monsters, persecutions, and the descent of that city to a newly created earth.[33] The Old Testament, however, is a mixture of writings composed over nearly one thousand years. It, therefore, reflects different historical and cultural settings, concerns, literary genres, and perspectives coming out of the experiences and faith of the people of Israel but direct eschatological motifs are not central to it. Some passages in what is termed by Jews and Christians as the Prophets are clearly eschatological, the work called Daniel in the portion called the Writings is plainly apocalyptic. Traditionally, Christians interpret the Old Testament with Jesus-centered eschatological vision.

The literal meaning of the word "eschatology" derives from the Greek *eschaton* points to that which is the last, uttermost, and final. Yet "end" also connotes not only termination in the sense of being cut off or stopped. Another option is "end" in the sense of the Greek term *telos*, that is, completion, fulfillment. As a result, two eschatological models, termination and fulfillment, have emerged and may be seen as merging for Christians.

The termination model depicts a catastrophic annihilation of the present cosmos and its replacement by new heavens and a new earth with a marvelously peaceful and prosperous world for those blessed to live in it. In some versions, the new world may last forever, but individuals will reach ripe old ages and die serenely while in other versions they live forever.[34] The Christian missionary-apostle Paul seems to have expected a termination of the present world with eternal life for the faithful.[35] The New Testament's Revelation to John 21:1–22:7 reflects the same new heavens-new earth view with the citizens of the new world living forever in God's presence. The pseudonymous 2

---

[33]  See, for example, Mark 1:13–14 and 13:1–37; Matthew 25:1–48; 1 Corinthians 15:1–58 and Romans 13:11–14; Hebrews 13:14; and the whole of the Revelation to John.

[34]  Isaiah 65:7–25

[35]  See 1 Corinthians 15:12–58 and Romans 8:18–25. The latter passage, however, holds that the creation will be set free from the bondage to decay and will "obtain the freedom of the glory of the children of God" (8:21). That may be interpreted as a *telos* understanding of renewal and restoration under the New Adam, Jesus.

Peter clearly states that the present world will be dissolved by fire following the judgment and destruction of the "godless" (2 Peter 3–7).

Among the unique features of the Revelation to John is its inclusion of a thousand year interim between a preliminary imprisonment of the powers of evil and their release immediately prior to the climactic and final cosmic battles that precede the termination of this cosmos, the resurrection and judgment; the new creation; and the descent of the heavenly Jerusalem to that new earth:

> Then I saw an angel coming down from heaven, holding in his hand the key to the bottomless pit and a great chain. He seized the dragon, that ancient serpent, who is the Devil and Satan, and bound him for a thousand years, and threw him into the pit, and locked and sealed it over him, so that he would deceive the nations no more, until the thousand years were ended. After that he must be let out for a little while.
>
> Then I saw thrones, and those seated on them were given authority to judge. I also saw the souls of those who had been beheaded for their testimony to Jesus and for the word of God. They had not worshiped the beast or its image and had not received its mark on their foreheads or their hands. They came to life and reigned with Christ a thousand years. (The rest of the dead did not come to life until the thousand years were ended.) This is the first resurrection. Blessed and holy are those who share in the first resurrection. Over these the second death has no power, but they will be priests of God and of Christ, and they will reign with him a thousand years.
>
> When the thousand years are ended, Satan will be released from his prison and will come out to deceive the nations at the four corners of the earth, Gog and Magog, in order to gather them for battle; they are as numerous as the sands of the sea. They marched up over the breadth of the earth and surrounded the camp of the saints and the beloved city. And fire came down from heaven and consumed them. And the devil who had deceived them was thrown into the lake of fire and sulfur, where the beast and the false prophet were, and they will be tormented day and night forever and ever.
>
> Then I saw a great white throne and the one who sat on it; the earth and the heaven fled from his presence, and no place was found for them. And I saw the dead, great and small, standing

before the throne, and books were opened. Also another book was
opened, the book of life. And the dead were judged according to
their works, as recorded in the books. And the sea gave up the
dead that were in it, Death and Hades gave up the dead that were
in them, and all were judged according to what they had done.
Then Death and Hades were thrown into the lake of fire. This is
the second death, the lake of fire; and anyone whose name was not
found written in the book of life was thrown into the lake of fire.

Then I saw a new heaven and a new earth; for the first heaven
and the first earth had passed away, and the sea was no more. And
I saw the holy city, the new Jerusalem, coming down out of heav-
en from God, prepared as a bride adorned for her husband.
(Revelation 20:1–21:2)

Most Christian churches and scholars are Amillenialist, that is,
they do not accept the concept of a millennium. The passage has generated significant debate among those who have accepted the concept
of a millennium. The "Pre-Millennialist" position is that Jesus will
personally and physically return from heaven before the one thousand
year period and will rule with the martyred and then resurrected
saints. The Post-Millennialist position holds that Jesus will remain in
a heavenly position during the thousand years so as to influence the
persons and conditions on earth. In both interpretations, the millennium will be a time of serenity, joy, divine favor and peace. As the
millennial age entered its final days, all the faithful were to die or be
taken into heaven to be with Jesus, then the devil and his wicked
hosts were to be released for the final battles that would conclude in
God's victory, the final resurrection of the dead, the judgment, and
beginning of the new creation.

The influential Western theologian, Augustine of Hippo (354–
430) proposed that the millennium started when the Emperor Theodo-
sius I decreed that Christianity was the only legal religion in the Roman
Empire (381 CE). According to Augustine, the imperial and ecclesiasti-
cal rulers were purposefully, yet gradually, bringing about that time
when evil, vice and unbelief would be banished from the earth and the
world would become just, orderly, prosperous and peaceful.[36]

---

[36] Augustine, *The City of God*, Book 20, Chapters 6–9.

The second eschatological model envisions the End as *telos*, that is, the fulfillment of the present world through its transformation, by God's will, without wiping it out and starting all over again. Isaiah 2:2–5, for example, anticipated God's using Jerusalem and its Temple as the center for the transformation so that Mount Zion would be exalted above all other places, nations would turn their weapons into peaceful instruments, and all humanity would learn and keep the Law of the Lord. Isaiah 24:1–26:21 expected that after a period of international turmoil and Divine punishment of Judah for its disobedience, God would inaugurate a time of harmony and peace among humans and with God Himself.

A further factor related to *eschaton* and *telos* is whether or not God provides signs, omens, or signals that foreshadow the approach of the End. Whether or not God does so is not answered definitively in the New Testament. Old Testament prophets denounced the moral collapse and idolatries of leaders and people as preludes to God's punishing Israel and Judah defeats and exiles. In a parable concerning the Judgment, Jesus predicts that those who did not show compassion, give justice to and help the members of his community will be condemned in the final judgment (Matthew 25:31–46). He also told his followers that they would be subjected to persecution and martyrdom because they were faithful to him (Matthew 5:10–11 and Matthew 24:9–31). Jesus is reported to have said that the budding of trees and the hues of the sky can be interpreted by the wise as harbingers of the End, yet he is also remembered as stating that the End will come as unexpected as a thief in the night or the unanticipated arrival of a master who surprises his servants (Mark 13:28–37 and Luke 12:35–40). The image of the nocturnal thief was used by other New Testament authors (1 Thessalonians 5:2–5; 2 Peter 3:10; and Revelation 3:3 and 16:15). On the other hand, there will be signs as well as persons whose appearances indicate that the end is near. The author of 2 Thessalonians mentions an enigmatic "man of lawlessness who is in league with Satan and able to use power, signs and lying wonders" to deceive many (2 Thessalonians 2:1–12). The term "antichrist" appears only in the brief letters, 1 and 2 John.[37] In both instances it refers to persons who deny that Jesus had a real human body, claiming instead that he only seemed to be genuinely human. In the Revelation to John evil humans in league with Satan include a false prophet who deceived many through doing wonders yet speaking blasphemies (Revelation 16:13; 19:20 and 20:10). Over time, the term antichrist was fused with that of the false prophet and the man of lawlessness into a single diabolical figure, the Antichrist, whose appearance was taken as a sign of the End.[38]

Numerous passages in the Old Testament anticipate that humans, and especially the covenant people, ought be to aware that the Lord gives ample warning that decisive actions culminating in judgment are taking place in the present. Some of these are earthquakes, famines, victorious enemies, strange astrological portents, even monstrous peoples such as Gog and Magog, visions of strange women, and bizarre animals symbolizing formidable foes as well as warring angels.[39]

Pre-Islamic Christian eschatology with apocalyptic imagery may be seen as providing analogies and examples that contribute to understanding and employing Qur'anic and Hadith materials as we engage Gülen's visions.

## ANALOGIES AND EXAMPLES

1. This world will be both fulfilled and terminated. The fulfillment may be temporary as in the Millennium.
2. The termination will be prefaced by great moral decay; rampant evil generated by Satan; Satanically-allied human deceivers of humans and scoffers at God's truth; persecution and martyrdom of faithful believers; warring monstrous creatures; and colossal battles between God's and Satan's forces.

---

[37] 1 John 2:18–22; and 4:3; and 2 John 1:7.

[38] See especially Hippolytus (170–236), "Treatise on Christ and the Antichrist," in *Ante-Nicene Fathers*, Vol. 5, pp. 204–219.

[39] Although Amos' "Day of the Lord" refers to catastrophes and restoration for Judah and Israel, the imagery was expanded to cosmic dimensions in apocalyptic literature. See especially the biblical books of Joel, Zechariah, Ezekiel, and Daniel.

3. The termination will be anticipated by portents in the heavens such as eclipses and other astronomical signs; geological upheavals such as earthquakes; meteorological omens such as blazing heat and hail storms; and human suffering brought about by hunger and despair.

4. The termination will escalate when Jesus returns from his heavenly realm to defeat and destroy the forces of Satan just as those forces surrounded and threatened to overwhelm God's faithful remnant in Jerusalem.

5. The termination will reach its climax following the Divine victory over Satan and his minions, the resurrection of the dead and the judgment on those persons as well as those who are alive at the time will take place; those who are judged to have been wicked and unworthy in their lifetimes will be sentenced to eternal fiery punishment.

6. God will create a new heavens and new earth that will consummate God's will for humans to live eternally in joy, harmony, prosperity, worship and peace as they will be in God's loving presence and fellowship.

Details may vary, but the message is consistent: Christian eschatological thinking warns and promises believers to be alert, ready and morally and spiritually prepared for the End to come at any time; the Last Days, Resurrection, Judgment and New Beginnings are certain and coming soon.

## ESCHATOLOGY: A SYNOPSIS OF ISLAMIC EXPECTATIONS

### A. THE BACKGROUND

Islam is profoundly eschatological. Among the terms Muslims use to refer to eschatology are the overall destruction of the world and subsequent Resurrection and rebuilding of the world (*al-Qiyama*), the Hour (*as-Sa'ah*), and the Day of Judgment (*Yawm ad-Din*). More spe-

cific are the words *ma'ad* and its synonym *marja'*.[40] A complementary
term is *mabda'*—origin. The term *ma'ad* connotes both the action of
returning and the place and/or relationship to which one returns. The
cosmos' origin (*mabda'*) is from God and all will return to God. The
time between the beginning and the return is existence in *Dunya* (the
Here) in preparation for *Akhira* (the Hereafter). Humans are destined
not merely for limited life in Dunya but chiefly for eternal life in the
Hereafter. As noted previously, God has so arranged and covenanted
with this world and humanity that all have committed themselves to
serve God wholly and to reflect His Names and Light in worship and
conduct. God has also sent Prophets, Messengers and Books to rein-
force such awareness, obedience and accountability so that from the
Prophets, Messengers and Books people have warnings, encouragement and guidance as they trek the "Straight Way" to their meeting
with God in the Hereafter. There is, therefore, a direct link from the
One-Only God through the Prophets, Messengers and Books to the
Return and Hereafter. The pre-Islamic revelations and those who disclosed them spoke the Divine prescriptive commands that were appropriate for those earlier peoples and times.[41] The final Revelation-Scrip-
ture is the Qur'an and the ultimate Messenger who lived those commands is the complete, correct and confirmation of what God has
always willed in His mercy and justice.

The Qur'an as a whole and throughout its more than 6,000 ayat
is eschatological in that the Voice Who addresses humanity and the
Muslim community gives the prescriptive commands of the One-Only God summoning humans to the Day when the scales of judgment
will be set up to assess who will be welcomed into the Gardens of
eternal blessedness and who will be condemned to everlasting punishment. Since Muhammad is the human who is an *"excellent example to
follow"* (Surah al-Ahzab 33:21) and is of a *"sublime character and [acts]*

---

[40] See *Walls*, pp. 132–150. The article on Muslim eschatology is by William Chittick.

[41] *Walls*, p. 136. The prescriptive commands are those that humans are called upon
and are responsible to obey. The "engendering commands" (*takwini*) are those
from God that are immediately obeyed such as the commands that brought the
world into existence.

*by a sublime pattern of conduct*" (Surah al-Qalam 68:4), the Hadith are essential as means to grasp the spoken and as-yet-unspoken disclosures in the Qur'an. While the Qur'an is eschatological, it is not an apocalypse. Significant portions of the Hadith, however, reflect apocalyptic imagery and perspectives. The contours of the Islamic eschatological narrative are Qur'anic, while the Hadith and *tafsir*s furnish further information and detail.

## B. THE SYNOPSIS

### 1. Before Humans Began Their Caliphate on Earth

Everything exists because of God's engendering command, "Be!" and is ever-contingent for continued existence on the will of God. Whatever exists, whether or not it has free will, has covenanted to be obedient to God. God created Adam from matter, spirit and soul, breathing life into Adam. In His wisdom God has gifted the jinn and Adam with free will. Further, God has designated Adam to be His caliph, or representative, in caring for the earth, given him knowledge that not even the angels have, and called upon the angels and spiritual beings to acknowledge Adam's special status. Iblis refused and became a rebel who pledged to deceive Adam and his descendants so as to drag as many as possible to Hell with him in the Judgment. Adam and his wife were deceived, repented and were forgiven. They and Satan (previously known as Iblis) descended to the earth. God promised to guide humanity but it was a matter of free will for persons to accept such guidance in order to be granted eternal blessedness.

### 2. Humans on Earth

All humans were in some manner present within Adam. As each person is born, the soul enters into a covenant to be obedient to God. Humans are prone to ingratitude toward God and to being deceived by Satan. Nevertheless God is merciful and gracious. Through Prophets, Messengers, Scriptures, (the Divine signs throughout the entire book of) nature, and historical events that punish gross sinners, humans are confronted with and called upon to live their covenantal commitment and obey God. Each person is accompanied by the recording angels who tally good and bad deeds, the account books will be exposed on the Last Day. It is incumbent on humans to establish just and equitable societies. The Muslim community is to follow the prescriptive commands in their personal and communal relationships.

Hadith materials record that Muhammad anticipated problems, dissensions and defections within the Muslim community. God had assured him that while there might be such difficulties, God would not have the true religion be extinguished or corrupted. Within each century, God would raise up a "Renewer" who would influence Muslims so that many would return to spiritual and communal integrity.

## 3. Humans in the Grave

Those who die before the End will undergo a preliminary judgment through which they will know their ultimate destiny. Each person will be accompanied in the grave by angels who may comfort and assure the righteous and who will castigate the unrighteous.

## 4. Toward the Last Days and Ordeals (*Fitan*): Hadith-based

Although Muslims were to face opposition, hostilities and wars over the years, as the Last Days neared, excruciating spiritual and physical ordeals (*fitan*) would test their faithfulness to God. These were part of minor and major "signs of the End." Key Hadith collections catalogue a number of these events.[42] Among the signs are the appearances of antichrist *dajjal*s within the non-Muslim world and *sufyan*s within the Muslim world, the release of Ya'juj and Ma'juj (Gog and Magog), world-wide moral chaos and cruelty as well as wars involving Christians and Jews. A series of astronomical and geological disasters (falling stars, earthquakes, and so on) and strange events such as smoke and blazing fire and the rising of the sun in the west.

---

[42] See, for example, *Sahih al-Bukhari*, Vol. 9, Book 92, *The Book of the Fitan*; Sahih Muslim, Vol. 4, Book 39, *Book of the Turmoil (Fitan) and Portents of the Last Hour*; and *Sunan Abu Dawud*, Books 30–32. Note also *Dimashqi*; *Smith and Haddad*; *Cook and David*.

## 5. The Return of Jesus, the Mahdi and the Interim Period: Hadith-based

During the course of the Ordeals, the Dajjal will enter every place on earth except Mecca, Medina and Jerusalem, wreaking havoc, death and corruption. A remnant of faithful Muslims will be besieged in Jerusalem. They will be led by the Mahdi (Guide) during the Salat Prayer. Suddenly and with angels, Jesus will return first to Damascus, then Jerusalem. He will attack and kill the Dajjal whose armies will be defeated. The Mahdi and Jesus will inaugurate a period of justice, prosperity, right worship and peace. Jesus and the Christians will accept the Divine message to Muhammad and Jesus will perform the Hajj. After a period of time, he will die. The Mahdi will continue to lead the community apparently until his passing.

## 6. The Final Days, World's End and the Judgment: Largely Hadith-based

A gradually accelerating moral and spiritual deterioration will eventually mar the interim period. God will send a wind that will cause faithful Muslims to die peacefully so they will not experience the final catastrophes that will convulse the cosmos. The archangel Israfil will sound the first trumpet blast that will cause the whole of creation (including the angels) to die. After an indetermined period, God will create the conditions for Judgment and the Afterlife. The second trumpet blast will raise the dead from the graves, and they will proceed to the Judgment. The time taken by the Judgment, the thirst endured by those about to be judged, etc. are detailed in several Hadith collections. The Qur'an seems to indicate a brief period of time and direct conveyance to the eternal destinations.

## 7. The Entry into the Gardens or Hell Fire: Both Qur'an and Hadith-based

Following their being judged, all will cross a narrow bridge. Those whose destination is the eternal Gardens will cross quickly and without harm to be welcomed by angels and taken to their appropriate places. There they will enjoy prosperity and the fruits of being faithful to

God. They will greet one another with expressions of peace. Those whose destination is Hell will find the bridge to be razor sharp and will fall from it into the flames. They will be taken by angels to their proper places for the punishment they deserve.

### C. SUMMARY AND TRANSITION

The Qur'an emphasizes the inevitability of the End Times and Return so that men and women will repent of their ingratitude and sins, devote themselves to worship and serve God, seek justice in society and their personal lives, and give witness to the One-Only God, all the Prophets and Messengers, Muhammad, and the truths of the Qur'an. The Hadith may be seen as filling in the details and expanding the eschatological imperative to live Islamically in the present.

Islam and Christianity are profoundly eschatological in that both religions accept that God has a Plan for the whole creation and for what is beyond the present world. Both look forward to a completion and even termination of this world together with an opening of a new and fulfilling future. I suggest that some pre-Islamic analogies and examples from Christian sources will be helpful and even important in understanding Fethullah Gülen's visions and evidences for fruitful interfaith dialogue. We turn now to considerations of God's Plan.

### PHASE 1: THE PLAN – BEFORE CREATION TO ETERNITY

Islam's foundational and foremost teaching is belief in God. Having faith in God's Oneness and absolute Unity (*tawhid*) is contained within this essential belief in God. The Oneness and absolute Unity of God refers not only to His unique singularity, indivisibility, transcendence, and power, but also to the fact that none has the right to be worshipped save God, Who is One in His Self, Attributes, and Acts. God's Oneness and absolute Unity (*tawhid*) is, indeed, the key component of the testimony of faith (*shahada*), and of the entire scope of Islam: "I confess that there is no deity but God."[43] The proper response

---

[43] The usual English rendering makes use of lower and upper case conventions in English: "I confess that there is no god but God" where "God" is the Arabic word

to God by everything in creation is *taqwa*—full-hearted, total commitment in worship, intention, and servitude to Him. God transcends all in primacy and ultimacy. Surah *al-Ikhlas* (Purity of Faith) reveals:

> Say: "He – (He is) God, (Who is) the Unique One of Absolute
> Oneness. God – (God is He Who is) the Eternally-Besought-of-All
> (Himself in no need of anything). He begets not, nor is He begotten. And comparable to Him there is none." (112:1–4)

The absolutely transcendent One cannot be known by unaided human reason or experience but only as God revealed Himself either through the "revealed Books" (of the Torah, Bible, and the Qur'an) or through the "created book of the universe," that is, the entire creation and events in the universe. In this sense, every thing or event in the universe is a "sign of God" (*ayah*), pointing to its Maker and manifesting some of His Divine Names and Attributes. Indeed, what makes this entire "created book of the universe" manifest is nothing but the Names and Attributes of its Creator.

One of the primary revelatory ways for our consideration is, therefore, reading God's "created book" of the universe through His Names. Every creature is, in fact, a Divine art that reflect God's various Names; therefore, it is only through the Names and Attributes of God that we can truly understand the entire creation's true nature and purposes. In addition, while the universe is the collection of the manifestations of Divine Names and Attributes, human beings have a unique position in the entire universe since those manifestations are focused on the human, who is like an index for the whole universe as the most polished recipients and mirrors of those Names and Attributes. In one sense, God has no names such as Zeus, Astarte, or Ahura Mazda. In another sense, however, there are numerous Names and Attributes of God that are essential for one to be able to truly read this book of the universe, its functioning, and sustenance by the One and only God. There is no god other than Him; He is One, not in a

---

for "Allah." The Arabic for the complete Shahadah is "*Ashadu an lā ʾilāha ʾillallāh wa ashadu anna Muḥammadan abduhū wa rasūluh*," meaning "I bear witness that there is no deity but God, and I bear witness that Muhammad is His servant and Messenger."

numerical sense, but in the sense that He has no partner and nothing can be independent of Him. He is the All-Independent, Single One, Who is free from any equals or likes in His Divine Essence and Qualities. The Arabic proper name "Allah" is reserved for the supreme, One-Only God. This One-Only Allah (God) has made Himself revealed, or manifest, throughout the universe through His various Names and Attributes. When Muslims undertake prayers and activities "In the Name of God," they are responding to ways in which God has commanded, authorized, or given to them in order to place themselves under the scrutiny, protection, and will of the One they endeavor to praise and serve.

How believers employ the revealed Names expresses faith, commitment, and accountability. The Most Beautiful Divine Names (*al-Asma al-Husna*) derive mostly from the Qur'an and Hadith to express Divine sovereignty, majesty, compassion, mercy, knowledge, will, power, judgment, and so on.[44] For example, *al-Rahman* (the All-Compassionate) denotes a revealed Attribute of God while *al-Bari'* (the All-Holy Creator, who creates every thing or being and determines its nature according to His Knowledge and Wisdom) points to God's absolute sovereignty and action, making every being perfect and different from others. The Almighty God is always *al-Wahid* (the One and Only Divine Being) and *al-Ahad* (the Unique One of Absolute Unity), that is, God is beyond all kinds of human conceptions of Him and absolutely free from having any partners, likes, parents, sons or daughters; He begets not, nor is He begotten, and there is none comparable to Him.

The Divine Names associated with the making, sustaining, and ending of this world and those referring to opening the realm of the Hereafter are essential for spiritual and human beings to understand God's will in the present. These Divine Names include at least *al-*

---

[44] See *Glassé*, pp. 118–119, and *Muhaiyaddeen* (the book is an exposition of the Divine Names). Almost all of the Names are derived from the Qur'an while others are implicit in the Qur'an or are mentioned in the Hadith. Surah al-A'raf (7:179) holds that *"To Him belong the most beautiful Names."* *Glassé* notes that some categorize the Names into Names of the Essence and Names of the Quality of God. Others say that the categories may be expressed as Names of Mercy or Beauty and Rigor or Majesty. See p. 118.

*Khaliq* (Creator), *al-Mubdi* (Originator), *al-Qayyum* (the Self-Subsisting by whom all creation maintain their existence), *al-Awwal* (the First), *al-Akhir* (the Last), *al-Razzaq* (the All-Providing) , *al-Mu'id* (Restorer), *al-Ba'ith* (Resurrector, who restores life to the dead), *Malik-i Yawm ad-Din* (the absolute Master of the Day of Judgment), *al-Hakam* (the Judge, who settles the matters between people), *al-ʿAdl* (the All-Just), *Shadiydu'lʿiqab* (the One who Most Severe in retributing), *al-Ghaffar* (the One who forgives much), *al-Rahim* (the All-Compassionate One, who has particular compassion for His believing servants, especially in the Hereafter). All of the Divine Names are profound in meaning and open to interpretative expansion, spiritual deepening, and application in the lives of believers. From among the human beings—who are created potentially as the best recipients of the Divine Names and Attributes—the ones close to God are those believers who act not in their own name but "in the Name of God" and for His sake. While they possess and reflect the most, and best, of God's exalted Names and Attributes, they attribute every action or thing to God alone, including the accomplishments with which they are favored, and thus try to be perfect mirrors to numerous Divine Names and Attributes, to the best of their abilities.

Islam's second vital teaching is the belief in angels. Having faith in angels of God is the second article of Islamic faith after belief in God because angels are the means through which the revelations of God are conveyed. Therefore, the denial of the spiritual beings of angels results in the denial of not only the Holy Scriptures but also the Messengers to whom the angels conveyed Divine revelations.

Angels dwell in the spiritual realm beyond forms called the *Malakut*. Angels are the spiritual beings created from pure light and have intellects but neither free will nor carnal impulses. They are, therefore, ever-obedient to God. They have a great yet fixed knowledge of and access to God. Since they do not struggle with any inherent evil impulse, they cannot elevate their spiritual ranks; their stations are fixed. The angels near-stationed to God are called the Qaribiyyun (also as *Muqarrabin*), including the four greatest of these spiritual beings, who are the rough equivalent to archangels in traditional

Judaism and Christianity.[45] Angels are dutifully obedient to God, and along with bringing down the Divine Revelations to the Messengers of God, they are assigned to perform numerous other duties throughout the universe. Generally, the angelic beings are among those who link the heavenly and earthly realms although many are part of the heavenly court around the Throne of God. Numerous others are assigned to carry the Hidden One's (*al-Batin*) messages and will to other creatures, including humanity. Pairs of other angels accompany each person throughout his and her life to watch over and record their good and bad deeds. A number of angels have the duty to extract the souls of dying humans from their bodies, be present with the dead in their graves, blow the trumpet on the Last Day, and supervise and inflict the punishments of Hell.

Another separate class of spiritual beings is the jinn (singular *jinni*). They have started to inhabit the earth long before human beings were sent to the world. Unlike the angels who are created from the pure light, the jinn are created from smokeless fire. They have intellect and free will and are, therefore, accountable for all their acts and deeds, just like human beings. They can appear in the earthly realm in different forms or shapes. Some are beautiful and others grotesque. The original head jinni is Iblis (Satan).[46] Unlike angels, and similar to human beings, the jinn have free will to choose good or evil, they all will thus be judged on the Last Day.[47]

---

[45] See *Glassé*, pp. 49–50. The Arabic term "Qaribiyyun" is a cognate of the Hebrew *cherubim*. The four are Jibril (Gabriel) the revealer who is closest of all angels to God, *Mikail* (Michael), *Israfil*, the angel who will sound the trumpet on the Last Day, and *Azra'il*, the angel of death.

[46] See *Sakr* as a whole, especially p. 33; *Glassé*, pp. 241–242; *Smith and Haddad*, p. 153; Surahs 38, 55 and 72. *Smith and Haddad* list seven types of jinn: *ifrit, ghul, si'lat, ruh, shiqq, 'amr* and *shaytan*.

[47] Islam does not entertain the concept of "fallen angel." Although both the angels and the jinn are invisible spiritual beings, the jinn are a different creation of God. The Qur'an states that Satan was not one of the angels but *"of the jinn and transgressed against his Lord's command"* and were, therefore, casted out of the Divine presence. (Surah al-Kahf 18:50)

The Qur'an's cherished "Throne Verse" (*Ayatu'l-Kursiyy*) summarizes Islam's teachings as a whole as well as the first two articles of faith and serves as a transition to the Plan's purposes for creation:

> God, there is no deity but He; the All-Living, the Self-Subsisting (by Whom all subsist). Slumber does not seize Him, nor sleep. His is all that is in the heavens and all that is on the earth. Who is there that will intercede with Him save by His leave? He knows what lies before them and what lies after them (what lies in their future and in their past, what is known to them and what is hidden from them); and they do not comprehend anything of His Knowledge save what He wills. His [Throne] embraces the heavens and the earth, and the preserving of them does not weary Him; He is the All-Exalted, the Supreme. (Surah *al-Baqarah* [The Cow] 2:255)[48]

## PHASE 2: THE PLAN – CREATION OBEYS AND TESTIFIES TO GOD

The Qur'an declares that upon creating the earth and the heavens, God asked the spiritual and material worlds if they would be willingly obedient to their Maker. The response was a joyful "*We have come in willing obedience.*"[49] All that exists and all that happens, therefore, starts as "islam," that is, in joyful and voluntary obedience to the One-Only God.[50] The same question is directed to every human soul before it is joined to a physical body, and each responds that it will be in "islam," obedience, worship and service. Moreover, the obedience from all existence makes everything that is visible and invisible a network of "pointers" (*ayat*) directing humans to worship and serve the Creator. This ceaseless testimony given by the whole of creation about the One-Only God is matched by the internal covenant every person's soul makes with God before it enters this world:

---

[48] The brackets indicate my substitution of the traditional "Throne" in place of Ünal's "Seat (of dominion)."

[49] Surah Fussilat 41:11.

[50] I use the term "islam" to indicate the obedience-service of all creation, angels, spiritual beings, and humans before the Revelation to Muhammad. I use the term "Islam" for the same but after the Revelation.

And (remember, O Messenger,) when your Lord brought forth from the children of Adam, from their loins, their offspring, and made them bear witness against themselves (asking them:) "Am I not your Lord?" They said: "Yes, we do bear witness." (That pledge was taken) lest you should say on the Day of Resurrection, "We were indeed unaware of this (fact that you are our Lord)." (Surah *al-A'raf* [The Heights] 7:172)

Every human being in every culture and in every time has confirmed this pledge of faith in their Lord before they were sent to this world for trial and is challenged here to be in an obedient, worshiping, serving relationship with the Creator.

Following the creation of the realms of the angels, spiritual beings, and the material world, God announced to the angels and jinn that the next step was to make the human being, Adam, from lifeless clay.[51] Indeed, humans are the pinnacle and purpose of God's Plan. The Maker proclaimed to the heavenly beings that Adam, and, implicitly, his descendants, were to be God's vicegerents, that is, *khalifah* (caliphs), over the earth:

It is He Who (prepared the earth for your life before He gave you life, and) created all that is in the world for you (in order to create you—the human species—and make the earth suitable for your life); then He directed (His Knowledge, Will, Power, and Favor) to the heaven and formed it into seven heavens. He has full knowledge of everything. ... I am setting on the earth a vicegerent. (Surah *al-Baqarah* [The Cow] 2:29–30)

## PHASE 3: THE PLAN – DISOBEDIENT JINN, DECEIVED HUMANS, LIFE ON EARTH

God's Plan included Divine foreknowledge of the disobedience of many jinn under the leadership of Iblis (Satan);[52] the subsequent deception of Adam and his wife; the expulsion of the rebelling Satan and the

---

[51] See, for example, Surahs 2:30; 7:12; 17:61 and 18:50.

[52] The Qur'an uses the name "Iblis" for Satan in eleven different places where it mentions about his rebellion against the Divine order to bow down to God's new creation—Adam, the forefather of humanity. Following this defiance, Iblis is called "Shaytan" in the Qur'an.

primordial human couple from the heavenly Garden; life in this transient world (*dunya*) until the Day of Judgment; and the eternal life of the Hereafter. Not knowing the Plan, the angels asked the All-Subtle One (*al-Latif*) Whose eternal Knowledge and Power penetrate all things and times, *"Will You set therein one who will cause disorder and corruption on it and shed blood…?"* only to receive the answer, *"Surely, I know what you do not know."*[53] Following that exchange, the All-Knowing God (*al-Alim*) instructed Adam in "the names." Muslim tradition holds that these "names" were of all creatures, objects, and even of the angels themselves as well as Adam's own descendants, and that they are indicative of the superior potentiality of Adam and his descendants for various kinds of knowledge and sciences. After the angels admitted that they did not know all the names, God presented Adam to the hosts of angels and jinn, instructing him to recount to them the names. The father of all humanity complied and passed this initial test, thereby convincing them that humans indeed possessed the requisite knowledge to fulfill their role as God's vicegerents, or caliphs, over the earthly realm, and that God-instructed humans were superior in knowledge even to the angels. God then tested the heavenly beings by instructing them to show their obedience to God through prostrating themselves before Adam. Naturally, the angels complied. Iblis, however, refused. His arrogant retort disclosed that while he acknowledged God's Divinity and Power, he rejected His Lordship, and thus disobeyed to his Lord, *"I am better than he, for You have created me from fire, and him You have created from clay."*[54] Obstinate in his rejection of being in "islam"—of submitting to the Lord, Iblis accepted his imminent expulsion from the heavens down to his temporary residence on earth. That residence, Iblis and his aides from among the jinn knew, was a way station to their eternal destination: Hell. Iblis realized that God included his disobedience as part of the Divine Plan, discerned his further place in God's Plan, and announced his plan for humanity:

---

[53] Surah al-Baqarah 2:30.
[54] See Surahs 15:26f; 17:61; and 18:50.

(God) said: "O Iblis! What is the matter with you that you are not among those who have prostrated?" (Iblis) said: "I am not one to prostrate myself before a mortal, whom You have created from dried, sounding clay, from molded dark mud." (God) said: "Then get you down out of it; surely you are one rejected (from My mercy). And cursing is upon you until the Day of Judgment." (Iblis) said: "Then, my Lord, grant me respite till the Day when they will all be raised from the dead!" (God) said: "You are of the ones granted respite, (but) until the Day of the appointed time known (to Me) (i.e. the Last Day)." (Iblis said:) "My Lord! Because You have allowed me to rebel and go astray, I will indeed deck out as appealing to them on the earth (the worldly, material dimension of human existence and the path of error), and I will surely cause them all to rebel and go astray, except Your servants from among them, endowed with sincerity in faith and Your worship." (God) said: "This (path of sincerity in faith) is a straight path that I have taken upon Myself (to lead to Me). "My servants – you shall have no authority over any of them, unless it be such as follow you being rebellious (against Me, as you are)." And for all such (rebellious people), Hell is the promised place. (Surah al-Hijr 15:32–43)

Following his defiance and rebellion, Iblis becomes known as Shaytan (Satan, the adversary), for he and his ilk are sworn enemies to human beings and set about to deceive people in order to lead them away from the obedience of "islam," that is, to trap them in sin, disbelief, and Hell. The first target was Adam and his wife. The couple was still in the original presumably heavenly garden. The Qur'anic text tells the next stage of the Plan. God said:

"O Adam! Dwell you, and your spouse, in the Garden, and eat (of the fruits) thereof to your hearts' content where you desire, but do not approach this tree, or you will both be among the wrongdoers." But Satan (tempting them to the forbidden tree despite Our fore-warning,) caused them both to deflect therefrom and brought them out of the (happy) state in which they were. And We said, "Go down, all of you, (and henceforth you will live a life,) some of you being the enemies of others. There shall be for you on the earth a habitation and provision until an appointed time." (Aware of his lapse and in the hope of retrieving his error, rather than attempting to find excuses for it,) Adam received from his Lord words that he perceived to be inspired in him (because of his remorse, and he pleaded through them for God's forgiveness). In return, He accepted his repentance. He is the One Who accepts repentance and returns it with liberal forgiveness and additional reward, the All-Compassionate (especially towards His believing servants).

We said: "Go down, all of you, from there!" (and executed Our order). If, henceforth, a guidance[55] comes to you from Me, and whoever follows My guidance (and turns to Me with faith and worship), they will have no fear (for they will always find My help and support with them), nor will they grieve." But those who disbelieve and deny Our signs (the verses of the revealed Book of guidance, as well as the signs in both their inner world and the outer world establishing My Existence and Unity and other articles of faith), they will be the companions of the Fire; they will abide therein. (Surah *al-Baqarah* [The Cow] 2:35–39)

Another passage describes the crucial scene in greater detail and focuses on the couple's nakedness, thereby setting a precedent for later Muslim modesty:

(To Adam, He said): "O Adam! Dwell, you and your spouse, in the Garden, and eat (of the fruits) thereof where you desire, but do not approach this tree, or you will both be among the wrongdoers." Then Satan made an evil suggestion to both of them that he might reveal to them their private parts that had remained hidden from them (and waken their carnal impulses), and he said: "Your Lord has forbidden you this tree only lest you should become sovereigns, or lest you should become immortals." And he swore to them: "Truly, I am for you a sincere adviser." Thus he led them on by delusion; and when they tasted the tree, their private parts (and all the apparently shameful, evil impulses in their creation) were revealed to them, and both began to cover themselves with leaves from the Garden. And their Lord called out to them: "Did I not prohibit you from that tree, and did I not say to you that Satan is a manifest enemy to you?" They said (straightaway): "Our Lord! We have wronged ourselves, and if You do not forgive us and do not have mercy on us, we will surely be among those who have lost!" He said: "Go down, (all of you,) (and henceforth you will live a life,) some of you being the enemies of the others. There shall be for you on the earth a habitation and provision until an appointed time." He said: "You will live there, and there you will die, and from it you will be brought forth (on the Day of Resurrection)."

---

[55] I have deleted Ünal's parenthetical addition "(like a Book through a Messenger)."

O children of Adam! Assuredly, We have sent down on you a
garment to cover your private parts, and garments for adornment.
However, (remember that) the garment of piety and righteousness
– it is the best of all. That is from God's signs, that they may
reflect and be mindful. Children of Adam! Never let Satan seduce
you (and cause you to fail in similar trials) as he caused your (ances-
tral) parents to be driven out of the Garden, pulling off from them
their garment and revealing to them their private parts (and the
carnal impulses ingrained in them). He sees you, he and his host
(see you), from where you do not see them. We have made satans
the confidants and fellow-criminals of those who do not believe.
(Surah *al-A'raf* [The Heights] 7:19–27)

The time and place for humans to begin their vicegerency had
come. Although the circumstances were less than auspicious with Satan
and his aides lurking in this fleeting world and whispering their deceitful suggestions, humans have what angels do not have: free will to
obey or disobey God. In Islam, no blame or guilt is attributed to the
woman, neither is there a lingering distortion of the human will that
is passed on to the children of the first couple. While Adam and his
progeny might have prodigious capacities for knowing creatures, things,
and even spiritual "names," they need further awareness, instruction,
discipline, and, above all, revelations about the Names and Attributes
of the God Who creates, sustains, and summons them to obedience.
To be sure, all existence is a network of signs and pointers, signaling
that all are to worship and serve the One-Only God. Satan smugly
assaults humans through the twin tactics of forgetfulness about and
ingratitude toward the Creator. Through these deceptions, evil powers pervert the worship of the true God by means of idolatry and thus
to greed, immorality, and violence. Yet not all jinn are deceived, for
there are those who remember and live thankfully to the Source of all.
Nevertheless, the Qur'an reveals that the Day is coming when all will
be gathered for judgment and recompense.

Still, God is not only the Judge (*al-Hakam*). God is the Forgiver
(*al-Afuww*) and—as the Opener (*Surah al-Fatihah*) signaled—the All-
Merciful (*al-Rahim*) and All-Compassionate (*al-Rahman*). From the time
of Adam to the End of the time, God is the All-Loving (*al-Wadud*)

and the All-Guiding One (*al-Hadi*), encouraging jinn and humans to walk the Straight Way. To show that Way, God's Plan called for further revelation.

## PHASE 4: THE PLAN – REVELATION THROUGH PROPHETS, MESSENGERS AND SCRIPTURES

That further revelation is expressed through Islam's third and fourth essential teachings on Prophets-Messengers and Scriptures. The first is belief in all the Prophets and Messengers of God. The One-Only God raised up countless numbers of Prophets and Messengers across the ages and throughout the world who proclaimed and advanced the message of God's will, mercy, and judgment. God adapted the revelations to the capacity of humans in particular places and times to comprehend, accept, and enact the basic message that would guide them as they walked on the Straight Way.[56] For example, the Prophets and Messengers who spoke to tribal people in Mongolia in the 5th century BCE were matched by other Prophets and Messengers who proclaimed the same core message at the same time in Athens, each using the intellectual and cultural terms suitable to those audiences. The essential proclamation called then and still summons humans to testify to the One-Only God through worship and service, seeking God's forgiveness and rejecting polytheism, infanticide, immorality, and greed while caring for the orphaned and poor and maintaining ethical relationships and fidelity in marriage. The exhortations link promises of prosperity and peace in this life and in the Hereafter with warnings of punishments if not now, certainly in the life to come. God prepared and purified the Prophets and Messengers so that they could speak and act fearlessly and faithfully, yet sinlessly, to their own people. When they summoned their compatriots to worship and serve the One-Only God, they were mocked, rejected, and threatened by most who heard them. The Qur'an reports that occasionally God, the Righteous Avenger

---

[56] See, for example Surahs 10:48, 13:36–40 and 14:1–4.

(*al-Muntaqim*), destroyed communities that rejected the message and sought to harm those who brought it.[57]

Both Prophets and Messengers of God receive Divine revelations and have the duty of conveying it to people. In a more particular sense, however, a Prophet (*al-Nabiyy*) who receives Divine revelation follows the Book and the Law that the Messenger (*al-Rasul*) prior to him brought or follows a contemporary Messenger, without himself having received a separate Book. Every Messenger is also a Prophet, but not every Prophet a Messenger (who is given a Scripture). In this sense, Messengership is included in the meaning of Prophethood. All Messengers were, therefore, Prophets gifted with two enhancements. First, every Messenger restored the religion to its original purity and God revealed through them further developments of the eternal message. Messengers were enlightened by God to advance the basic proclamation by including clearer positions and by adding or altering earlier conditions that were consonant with the core proclamation. For example, the consumption of alcohol was gradually forbidden by revelation in Muhammad's Madinah.[58] The second enhancement was that all Messengers came with Divinely bestowed Books that were to guide the communities to which they were sent. In the Islamic tradition, Moses, David, and Jesus had such books. Tragically, these Scriptures were not preserved as they were revealed but misinterpreted, corrupted, or distorted in time by the Jews and Christians.

God's Plan took into account the Prophets, Messengers, and Books prior to the revelation to Muhammad. From before the beginning, God determined to raise up Muhammad to be the Prophet-Messenger for the Arab people and the Prophet-Messenger for all humanity and spiritual beings for the rest of the world's existence. Muhammad is the complete, ultimate Prophet-Messenger for all times. Likewise, the Book given to him, the Qur'an, is to be regarded as the fulfilled and final Book, the last and perfect revelation of God's Plan and Will.

---

[57]  See, for example, Surahs 7, 11, 22 and 71.

[58]  See, for example, Surahs 2:119 and 5:90.

## PHASE 5: THE PLAN – THE RELIGION COMPLETED

According to Sunni Muslim tradition, two crucial events occurred on or around March 6, 632 CE as Muhammad completed the Hajj subsequent to the victorious Muslim return to Makka, the Holy City.[59] Following the Hajj rituals of the requisite circumambulation of the Ka'ba, the striding between the hillocks of Safa and Marwa, the stoning of the representational demons at Mina, and the sacrifice after the standing at the plain of Arafat, Muhammad took an elevated position and began to speak to a throng of fellow believers from the Mount of Compassion.[60] Muslims call this speech the "Farewell Sermon."[61] Traditional texts of the sermon vary, yet the content is clear.[62] All agree that he foretold his impending death, and he died seventy-two days later in Madinah. Ever practical, he gave the Muslim community advice about maintaining their property, replacing blood vendettas with regular laws, keeping business contracts, prohibiting usury, and warning about the danger of relapsing into the polytheist practices of the pre-Islamic era.

Another portion made plain that all Muslims were equal; that is, no ethnic or racial group was superior to others. The superiority of

---

[59] An approximate date. In the Muslim calendar, the 9th day of the lunar month of Dhul Hijjah, 10 AH. Others cite the date as February 23. For the Farewell Sermon, see www.worldislamday.org accessed August 5, 2011.

[60] Some traditions report that he was standing on a prominent place at the Mount of Compassion while others report that he was seated on his camel.

[61] The Hajj, pilgrimage to Makka, was made obligatory in the last period of the Prophet's life. Although this was the Prophet's first hajj, it was called the *Hajj al-Wada*—the Farewell Pilgrimage, which was, indeed, the first and only pilgrimage performed by the Prophet after it was enjoined as one of the five essentials of Islam. During the Hajj rite of standing at Arafat, which fell on a Friday, the Prophet delivered the Farewell Sermon and bade farewell to his community, saying: "O people, listen to me well, for I do not know if I will be amongst you again after this year. Therefore, listen to what I am saying very carefully and past these words on to those who could not be present here today." On Saturday, the following day of the Eid, he once again said: "Learn your rituals (of Hajj) from me. I do not know—maybe I will not be able to perform any other Hajj after this year" (Muslim, Hajj, 310, 2197; Abu Dawud, Manasik, 78, 1970).

[62] The majority of Muslims hold that Ibn Hanbal has the most accurate text of the Farewell Sermon. (*Musnad*, Hadith 19774). See *Ibn Ishaq*, pp. 651–652.

persons was to be judged according to their superlative piety and good, righteous deeds. In the same context, he went through what later Muslims call the five pillars of required forms of worship: faith in the One-Only God, the daily obligatory Prayers, the *Zakat*, or annual purifying alms given for the relief of the poor and needy, fasting in the month of Ramadan, and the Hajj (pilgrimage to Makka) if they could afford it physically and financially. After warning the assembled believers that they and those who came after them would one day stand before God to answer for their deeds, he advised them not to stray from the path of righteousness that God had commanded. As Muhammad neared the conclusion of his sermon he said:

> O People, no Prophet or Messenger will come after me and no new faith will be born. Reason well, therefore, O People, and understand words which I convey to you. I leave behind me two things, the Qur'an and my example, the Sunnah, and if you follow these you will never go astray.

As his human words concluded, Muhammad entered a revelatory state. From God to Gabriel thus through Muhammad and to Muslims and the world ever after, God gave instructions concerning diet, unlawful activities such as idolatry and forms of divination, and then ended with what now is part of Surah *al-Maedah* (The Table):[63]

> This day, those who disbelieve have lost all hope of (preventing the establishment of) your Religion, so do not hold them in awe, but be in awe of Me. This day I have perfected for you your Religion (with all its rules, commandments and universality), completed My favor upon you, and have been pleased to assign for you Islam as religion.—Then, whoever is constrained by dire necessity (and driven to what is forbidden), without purposely inclining to sin—surely God is All-Forgiving, All-Compassionate. (5:3)

---

[63] I assume the generally accepted Sunni tradition that this verse is the final revelation. Other passages have been proposed as the last disclosure. These are Surahs 2:278–282; 3:195; 4:93; 4:167; 9:128–129; and 18:110. See Louay Fatoohi's discussion and citation of the sources in al-Bukhari, Muslim, an-Nasa'i, at-Tabari, as-Suyuti, Ibn Hanbal, and at-Tabarani.

For our purposes, the following five points are relevant. First, the sermon and the last revealed passage are cast in the context of the coming judgment and the Hereafter. The Judge, however, is also the All-Forgiving and Compassionate One to the believers. Second, the Plan has reached a crucial high point, not its termination. The millennia of preparation through the sending of Prophets, Messengers, and Scriptures are over. The revelation has been given fully and finally. The entire religion (*din*, also transliterated as *deen*) has been conveyed. The term *Din* involves rituals, teachings, judgment, inner consciousness of what is rightfully God's will, and a way of life.[64] All the principles, prescriptions, and rules have been brought together, clarified, and expressed in their final form in the Qur'an and further elucidated and practiced by its first and foremost interpreter and practitioner Muhammad. While there will be no new revelations, not everything in the Qur'an can be known fully by all human beings:

> God, there is no deity but He, the All-Living, the Self-Subsisting (by Whom all subsist). He sends down on you the Book in parts with the truth, confirming (the Divine origin of, and the truths still contained by) the Revelations prior to it; and He sent down the Torah and the Gospel, in time past, as guidance for the people; and He has sent down the Criterion to distinguish between truth and falsehood, and the knowledge, and power of judgment to put it into effect. Those who disbelieve in the Revelations of God, for them is a severe punishment. God is All-Glorious with irresistible might, Ever-Able to Requite. Surely God – nothing whatever on the earth and in the heaven is hidden from Him. It is He Who fashions you in the wombs as He wills. There is no deity but He, the All-Glorious with irresistible might, the All-Wise. *It is He Who has sent down on you this (glorious) Book, wherein are verses absolutely explicit and firm: they are the core of the Book, others being allegorical.* Those in whose hearts is swerving pursue what is allegorical in it, seeking (to cause) dissension, and seeking to make it open to arbitrary interpretation, although none knows its interpretation save God. And those firmly rooted in knowledge say: "We believe in it (in the entirety of its verses, both explicit and allegorical); all is from our Lord"; yet none derives admonition except the people of discernment. (They

---

[64] *Glassé*, p. 118; *Esposito, Dictionary*, p. 68.

entreat God:) "Our Lord, do not let our hearts swerve after You have guided us, and bestow upon us mercy from Your Presence. Surely You are the All-Bestowing. Our Lord, it is You Who will gather humankind for a Day about (the coming of) which there is no doubt. Surely God does not fail to keep the promise." (Surah *Al Imran* [The Family of Imran] 3:2–9)

Diligent and pious study and interpretation within the parameters of the Qur'an's own hermeneutical principles based in God's Oneness and absolute Unity (*tawhid*), the coming judgment, faith in the Divine origin and truth of the revelation, and the goodness of its prescriptions for human life are needed because of the changing circumstances of human life.

The Qur'an, however, contains allegorical verses the full and true meanings of which are known only by the All-Knowing God (along with those verses that are explicit and clear in meaning). In this sense, the verses of the Qur'an are divided into two groups that are known as *muhkam*—or *"absolutely explicit and firm,"* ones and *mutashabih*, or *"allegorical,"* ones. The second group contains verses that have rich and profound meanings and need exegetical effort for elucidation as well as those ones whose true nature cannot be conceived by mere reasoning or narration. Therefore, certain profound meanings of such allegorical verses could only be grasped by those who are *"firmly rooted in knowledge"* while the full and true meanings of such verses are only known by the All-Knowing God.[65]

Accordingly, it is possible to derive meanings even from the verses about God's Divinity and His Attributes, which are in the category of "allegorical verses." Obviously, as we cannot grasp His Attributes in all their reality, we abstain from likening God to His creatures. For this reason, the interpreters of the Qur'an refer the full and true

---

[65] There is a narration, for instance, that when preaching from the pulpit, Caliph Umar recited a Qur'anic verse containing an uncommon word whose meaning was unknown to the people of the Hijaz region at that time. Recognizing his limited knowledge in the face of the eternal Divine Knowledge, the caliph went on to say, "Look into what is explained in the Qur'an and act in accordance with it; leave whatever you do not understand to (the All-Knowing) God. (For more details see Akgul, *The Qur'an in 99 Questions*, Tughra Books, 2008, pp. 56–57).

nature of "Divine Attributes" to God Himself—since such Attributes do not refer to God's Self, who cannot be known in His Essence or Self—while interpreting such attributive words only in ways that fit God's Divinity.[66] The Qur'anic verses under discussion warn us against those in whose hearts there is doubt or perversity and who delve into the meanings of such allegorical verses to *"seek (to cause) dissention"* among the believers although they do not possess even the necessary preliminary qualifications so as to interpret and expound such verses. Such an attitude of the people *"in whose hearts is swerving"* would lead to divisions and hostility in the Muslim community and rejection of the Qur'an and Islam itself – exactly what Satan wants. In the words of God, however, *"those who are firmly rooted in knowledge"* totally submit themselves to God and His entire commandments in His Book, saying, *"We believe in it (in the entirety of its verses, both explicit and allegorical); all is from our Lord'; yet none derives admonition except the people of discernment."* Being aware of the necessity to interpret such allegorical verses extremely carefully, such exegetes of the Qur'an know how to approach and benefit from the allegorical verses of the Qur'an but refer the full meanings and nature of their truth to God. Regardless of how much they are endued with knowledge, they always keep

---

[66] For instance, in connection with the attributive word of *"Hand"* used for God in the verse, *"Those who swear allegiance to you (O Messenger), swear allegiance to God only. God's "Hand" is over their hands…"* (Surah Fath 48:10), some interpreters of the Qur'an asserted that it is possible to interpret such attributive words so long as one can ascribe a sound meaning to these words that is both reasonably appropriate to the Almighty God and which is in accordance with Islamic Law. Accordingly, they give two important meanings to this Qur'anic verse.

One meaning they give to the allegorical word of *"Hand"* is that the Messenger's hand is over the hand he grasps in allegiance as it represents God's *"Hand"*; that is, obedience to the Messenger means the same as obedience to God. The other meaning is that God helps those who swear allegiance to the Messenger. So, here *"Hand"* signifies "Power," just like the verse given at the very beginning of this chapter, *"…All-Glorified is He in Whose Hand is the absolute dominion of all things, and to Him you are being brought back."* Similarly, the "Throne of God," the exact nature of which we cannot know, signifies God's absolute authority over the universe. Therefore, such terms as God's *"Hand"* or *"Throne"* that are used in various verses of the Qur'an are allegorical and their true nature is known by God alone. (For further details see Akgul, *The Qur'an in 99 Questions*, Tughra Books, 2008, pp. 58–60).

in mind the fact that *"Above every owner of knowledge, there is (always) one more knowledgeable"* (Surah Yusuf 12:76), and that "God knows best!" Considering also the Prophetic interpretation as well as the classical and contemporary commentaries of allegorical verses, they interpret such verses extremely carefully, and finally refer the truth of everything to God by saying, "While the absolute knowledge is with God, an interpretation of the verse is this!"

In this sense, the Qur'an is universal, speaking to all people to come until the End of the World. Such addressing to all the people (with different understanding levels) with the very same words is secured and maintained by the existence of the allegorical verses. Through these allegorical expressions the Qur'an becomes the source of countless meanings. People of all times can, therefore, perceive different implications of the allegorical expressions used in the Qur'an to the degree of comprehension that they have reached at the time in which they live.

> [It is through the allegorical verses in the Qur'an that] God has kept the doors open for the human mind and intellect to exercise personal efforts and judgment (*ijtihad*) so that we can benefit from the blessings of the God-given faculty of understanding and perception. As a result of this incentive to study the Qur'an, people are invited to reflect on the Book and scholars are prompted to discover the hidden beauties of the Qur'an.[67]

The Qur'an is also the Criterion (*al-Furqan*) that distinguishes truth from falsehood, faith from blasphemy, goodness from evil, and the lawful from the prohibited clearly and in their finality. As the final, fullest, and truest scriptural revelation, the Qur'an exposes the errors, misinterpretations, and corruptions that have crept into the Tawrah revealed to Moses and the Injil revealed to Jesus as well as into Judaism and Christianity as a whole. Biblical accounts and themes may help Muslims understand the rest of God's Plan but are to be considered judiciously and Qur'anically. The Plan is still unfolding.

Third, while the Qur'an and Muhammad's sermon state clearly the six Teachings and the five Pillars, the sermon mentions what became

---

[67] Akgul, *The Qur'an in 99 Questions*, 2008, p. 63.

the second portion of the testimony of faith, that is, Muhammad is the servant and Messenger (*Rasul*) of God. Prophetic statement about being the final Messenger and the explicit Qur'anic passages such as Surah Muhammad (47:33) make clear that he has the ultimate position among the other Prophets and Messengers.[68] The Teachings, or Six Articles of Faith, require assent, trust, and sincere commitment. The five Pillars of Islam provide the external manifestations that the person who does them can be identified as a Muslim. On these grounds, Surah al-Maedah (5:3) and the sermon preclude the addition of anything essential to be believed or practiced by Muslims.

Fourth, the sermon cited two standards for the believers and for future generations to follow. The first is the heaviest, that is, the greatest factor, the Qur'an as the World of God. The second is Muhammad and his Sunnah (tradition, customs, words, and example). Islamically understood, Muhammad is more than a heroic figure or captivating leader. He is the paragon embodiment of Islamic faith, thought, obedience, worship, service, life-style, and action. While the Qur'an is the written revelation, Muhammad is the living embodiment of the revelation. As Adam was the first human to be addressed by God, given special knowledge and to whom the angels bowed, so Muhammad is the human who journeyed above the angels and into the presence of God, received special instructions, and then returned to earth to share that knowledge and instructions with the human community. The Night Journey (al-Isra) and Ascent into Heaven (al-Mi'raj) are hinted at in the Qur'an (see Surah *al-Isra* [The Night Journey] 17:1–2) and amplified further in the Hadith collections.[69]

Fifth, the sermon and the Qur'an describe and prescribe the equality of all peoples before God and in the umma. Arabs, for instance, are not granted special status because of God's use of their language, land, and the Messenger's ethnic origin. At the same time, the sermon recognized that equality was not sameness. Women and men have mutu-

---

[68] *"O you who believe! Obey God (in all His commandments and obey the Messenger (in his execution of God's commandments and in his own directive), and do not let your deeds go to waste."* See also for example, Surah *al-Ahzab* (the Confederates) 33:40.

[69] See Wagner, *Opening the Qur'an*, pp. 126–127 and "Journeying to God."

al responsibilities to one another that fit their respective natures and roles in God's Plan. In this regard, Muhammad's example as a husband and father may offset Qur'anic passages such as Surah *un-Nisa* (Women) 4:34. Racial, ethnic, and class bias have no place in the umma. All people are God's people, persons whose angels busily record their deeds as every person and jinni hurry toward the Last Day.

The Book that began to be revealed in 610 CE was completed shortly before Muhammad's death (632) and collated *circa* 650. His words and example, as remembered by devout followers, formed the corpus of his *Sunnah* or Tradition. From the 7th through the 9th centuries scholars collected, checked, sorted through, and set down in writing several versions of the Prophetic Traditions. These are termed the hadith, literally, reports or accounts (in Arabic, the plural is *ahadith*). References in our study will be made chiefly to the Hadith collections by the imams al-Bukhari, Muslim, Abu Dawud, and at-Tirmidhi. These Hadith masters were active in the last half of the 9th century CE.

The Hadith collections show Muhammad speaking substantively and figuratively about the Plan's stages leading up to, including, and following the End Times and about the Hereafter. The Hadith, therefore, are important for Muslims generally and Gülen specifically.

## PHASE 6: THE PLAN – LIVING ISLAMICALLY AND EXPECTANTLY

As important as March 6, 632 CE was in the Plan, the worlds did not end then. Life went on and continues to the present. Muhammad died,[70] and his Muslim community and the *Din* he conveyed contin-

---

[70] While the death of Muhammad was, indeed, a shock to the Muslim community, his closest Companion Abu Bakr calmed down the people by saying: "If you worship Muhammad, know that he is dead; if you worship God, then know that He is Ever Living and will never die." He then continued: "God says: '*Muhammad is but a Messenger, and Messengers passed away before him. If, then, he dies or is killed, will you turn back on your heels? Whoever turns back on his heels can in no way harm God. But God will (abundantly) reward the thankful ones.*'" (Surah Al Imran 3:144). This short but significant speech of Abu Bakr was, indeed, nothing but a reminder of the basic monotheistic message of Muhammad: "There is nobody worthy of worship but God."

ue. The challenge and opportunity for Muslims is to live Islamically each day until the end of the worlds. The Qur'an indicates that non-Muslims, especially Jews and Christians, can live what I term "islamically." For instance:

> Those who believe (i.e. professing to be Muslims), or those who declare Judaism, or the Christians or the Sabaeans (or those of some other faith) – whoever truly believes in God and the Last Day and does good, righteous deeds, surely their reward is with their Lord, and they will have no fear, nor will they grieve (Surah *al-Baqarah* [The Cow] 2:63).[71]

The conditions are plain, and the way is left open to consider when and how those who live Islamically and those who live "islamically" may join together before, yet certainly on, the Last Day.[72] We will return to ways Gülen handles that possible eventuality and consider its importance in his views of the fulfillment of God's Plan.

When Muslims invoke a Divine Name, they realize that they and all humans are humble creatures who begin as physical embryos and may yet be spiritual embryos who need to grow and learn as they are summoned to live in God's Way until they reach full term in the Resurrection. The very first verses revealed to Muhammad starts with the command to begin to "read" in the Name of God. This initial revelation of the Qur'an expresses the beginning of the human situation clearly, leaving open for persons to accept the complete meaning of living to and for God:

> Read in and with the Name of your Lord, Who has created – created human from a clot clinging (to the wall of the womb). Read, and your Lord is the All-Munificent, Who has taught (human) by the pen – taught human what he did not know. (Surah *al-Alaq* [The Clot] 96:1–5)

The Lord and Creator (*Rabb* and *Khaliq*) is also the All-Munificent (*al-Mukrim*) Who teaches humans what they are yet to learn. The Originator of all that exists is also the One to Whom everything

---

[71] See also Surah 5:82–85.
[72] See also Surah 18:87–88.

and everyone who has ever lived will return on the Day of Judgment.[73] Each person, Muslim and otherwise, and every spiritual being is responsible for her and his beliefs, intentions, and actions. The account books will be weighed on the scales at the Resurrection when judgment will be rendered:[74]

> Then We will surely narrate to them (the full account of their worldly lives) with (full, accurate) knowledge; We were not absent (while they were doing their deeds, and so we have a perfect record). The weighing on that Day shall be the truth (complete and accurate), and those whose scales (of good deeds) are heavy – they will be the prosperous. And those whose scales are light (because they have no acceptable good deeds) – they will be those who have ruined their own selves because they were unjust to Our Revelations and signs (in both the universe and themselves). Indeed, We have established you on the earth (O humankind, endowed you with great potential) and arranged for your livelihood in it. Scarcely do you give thanks! (Surah *al-A'raf* [The Heights] 7:7–10)

Living Islamically entails keeping the duties stated clearly in the Qur'an and summed up in the Teachings and Pillars.[75] The principles undergirding individual ethics, family relations, and communal life are part of the faith in the One-Only God and worship as well as service to *al-Majid*—the All-Glorious and Majestic One. Although peo-

---

[73] For example, see "To God is your final return (*marji'ukum)*" Surah Hud 11:4.

[74] See also Surah Qaf 50:17–18:

> Assuredly, it is We Who have created human, and We know what suggestions his soul makes to him. We are nearer to him than his jugular vein. Remember that the two recording angels (appointed to record his speech and deeds), seated on the right and on the left, receive and record. Not a word does he utter but there is a watcher by him, ever-present. And the stupor of death comes in truth (being the established decree of God for life). That is, (O human,) what you were trying to escape. And (in time) the Trumpet will be blown. That is the Day when God's threat will be fulfilled. And every person will come (before the Supreme Court) with one (angel) driving, and one (angel) bearing witness. "Indeed you were in heedlessness of this, and now We have removed from you your veil, so your sight today is sharp." And the one (the witnessing angel) who accompanies him says: "This is (his record) that I keep ready with me."

[75] See Surah al-Kahf 18:54.

ple may live for decades, the time in this world is but a moment when compared to eternity. Life in this fleeting world (*dunya*) is a test of faithfulness to God. The Lord has made the world a glittering display to test humans concerning proper worship and good, righteous deeds as contrasted with wealth and greed.[76]

> For thus it is: all power to protect belongs to God, the True. He is the Best for reward, and the Best for the outcome. And strike to them a parable of the present, worldly life: (it is) like water that We send down from the sky, and the vegetation of the earth mingles with it (flourishing abundantly). Then it turns into dry stubble which the winds scatter about. God is absolutely able to do all things. Wealth and children are an adornment of the present, worldly life, but the good, righteous deeds (based on faith and) which endure are better in the sight of your Lord in bringing reward and better to aspire for. (Bear in mind) the Day when We set the mountains in motion, and you see the earth denuded, and We raise to life and gather them together (all those who are content with themselves, deluded by the charms of the world), leaving out none of them. They are arrayed before your Lord (Whom they disregarded in the world), all lined up (without discrimination of wealth or status as in the world, and they are told): "Now, indeed, you have come to Us (divested of all worldly things) as We created you in the first instance – though you used to suppose that We had not appointed for you a meeting with Us." And the Record (of everyone's deeds) is set in place; and you will see the disbelieving criminals filled with dread because of what is in it, and they will say: "Alas, woe is ours! What is this Record? It leaves out nothing, be it small or great, but it is accounted!" They have found all that they did confronting them (in the forms thereof particular to the Hereafter). And Your Lord wrongs no one. (Surah *al-Kahf* [The Cave] 18:44–49)

In the midst of graphic passages about the looming judgment, the pain of Hell fire and the delights of the Gardens, God, speaking through the Qur'an, repeatedly emphasizes His gracious forgiveness to those who repent and do good, righteous deeds. God is *al-Ghafur* (The Much-Forgiving), the Compassionate and Merciful Master of all existence. The offer of eternal life in harmony and peace is present for

---

[76] See Surah al-Kahf 18:7.

those who seek to live on the Straight Way. God is also *al-Hadi*, the All-Guiding to that way.

The Qur'an mentioned the roles of pious persons who had insights into the meanings and applications of the texts and traditions. The first generation of Muhammad's close associates along with later devout and knowledgeable persons provide the basis for interpreting and applying the Qur'an and the Hadith traditions in an ever-changing and challenging world. Over time, Muslim scholars formed law schools that developed the sciences or bodies of knowledge of the Qur'an and the Hadith. The general expression for commentaries on the Qur'an is *tafsir*. Most often the commentaries are closely tied to the text while some venture into engaging inner and spiritual meanings.[77] Gülen, as will be seen, combines comments on the Qur'an in both manners, that is, to probe literal meanings and spiritual interpretations.

God's Plan for the worlds of angels, jinn, and humans was built into the order and relationships of every aspect of those worlds. The angels came to know the Creator's will for humans as the angels carried out their assignments of praise, recording, revealing, and preparing for the Last Day. The jinn knew what prices Satan and his minions would pay and what blessings awaited those who sought the Way of obedience to God before the Judgment.[78] All the worlds form a network of signs pointing to the One-Only God. That "pointing" involves directing humans to proper worship and God-obedient ethical conduct in the present as preparation for the resurrection and the Hereafter.[79]

The Qur'an emphasizes the revelations proclaimed by Prophets and Messengers sent to all peoples before the final Revelation to the Last Prophet. These purified, inspired, and divinely guided and protected humans testified to coming events, gave warnings and assurances, and forecast the dénouement of God's Plan as far as humans were shown such mysteries:

---

[77] See Wagner, *Opening the Qur'an*, especially pp. 180–184, and *McAuliffe*, pp. 181–207.

[78] See Surah 72:1–17.

[79] See, for example, Surahs 10:1–10; 16:48–49; 21:16–23; 74:32–56; 80:17–42.

> We have revealed to you (O Messenger) as we revealed to Noah, and the Prophets after him; and We revealed to Abraham, Ishmael, Isaac, Jacob, and the Prophets who were raised in the tribes, and Jesus, Job, Jonah, Aaron and Solomon; and We gave David the Psalms. And Messengers We have already told you of (with respect to their mission) before, and Messengers We have not told you of; and God spoke to Moses in a particular way. (Surah *an-Nisa* [Women] 4:163–164).

The Islamic understanding of God's Revelations through Prophets, Messengers, and Scriptures before the beginning of the Qur'anic Revelation and the beginning of Muhammad's Prophethood includes the belief that the Prophets and Messengers constitute a guild or brotherhood in which they may be regarded as one body.[80] Along with many Prophets and Messengers cited above, the Qur'an and Hadith also mention approvingly the following Biblical persons: Enoch, Saul, Elijah, Elisha, Joseph, John the Baptist, Lot, Zachariah (Gospel of Luke), Mary, Moses' mother and wife, pharaoh's wife, the Egyptian official's wife who repented of her failed attempt to seduce Joseph, the Queen of Sheba, and Jesus' disciples. A reference to Ezra is ambiguous (See Surah *at-Tawbah* [Repentance] 9:30). The angels Gabriel and Michael are accorded special mention. On the other hand, Goliath, Gog and Magog are negative figures. As the titles "Messiah" and "Christ" are given to Jesus in the New Testament and later Christianity, these titles are also attributed to Jesus in the Qur'an. Muslims are, indeed, required to believe in all the Prophets and Messengers of God without making any distinction between them, and a person cannot be a Muslim if he does not believe in Jesus as one of the greatest Messengers of God. The title and figures "anti-christs" from 1 and 2 John, false prophets and "false messiahs-christs" (Mark 13:21–22) are mentioned in the Hadith as well. Muhammad mentioned about two anti-christs; one to appear in the Muslim world (a.k.a. "Sufyan") and the other in the non-Muslim world (a.k.a. "Dajjal") toward the End Times.

The Qur'an refers to the Scriptures of the Jews and Christians and reflects portions of the Pentateuch, Psalms, and perhaps some prophet-

---

[80]   See, for example, Surahs 2:136, 285; 4:152.

ic and wisdom sections in the Old Testament. It is, therefore, a Book confirming the Divine origin of and the truths revealed in the earlier Scriptures. Similarly, in the Abrahamic line, Moses came with the Torah, and then Jesus with the Gospel, which confirmed the Torah in the essentials of faith, worship, and morality. The Qur'an confirms many truths of faith and morality in the canonical Gospels of the New Testament and several accounts from Gospels that were used among some Christians but rejected from the canon by church authorities around the mid-4th century. These rejected Gospels continued to circulate as part of popular Christian piety. It is likely that Surah 9:30 refers to the 1st century Jewish apocalyptic called 2nd Esdras. As a partial summary and as a forecast of what follows, I offer the following six points regarding shared eschatological and other beliefs among Muslims, Jews, and Christians:

1.  Muslims shared with Jews and Christians similar beliefs in God's Divine Plan for the world and its endings as well as a Hereafter that involved places and types of reward and punishment.

2.  Muslims, Jews, and especially Christians shared, although often with significant differences, a reservoir of symbols, expressions, and expectations about the End of the world and the Hereafter.

3.  Muslims shared with Jews and Christians scriptural and traditional accounts about numerous persons who were regarded as inspired by God and others who were evil.

4.  Muslim anticipations of the signs of the coming End, the End itself, and aspects of the Hereafter mentioned in the Qur'an and Hadith as well as their interpretations have analogues and precedents in the Bible and Christian developments.

5.  Muslims living in the 7th–9th centuries had substantial knowledge about Judaism and Christianity, including popular and sometimes seemingly heterodox views and writings. Christians, however, seemed to have had little knowledge of Islam.

6.  Muslims and Christians were apt to regard contemporary social–political events as immediate preludes to the End Times of God's plan and included one another in those speculations.

## PHASE 7: THE PLAN – BIBLICAL AND
## CHRISTIAN PRECEDENTS

With these points in mind, let us turn to positions among Jews and Christians that are relevant to Gülen's Islamic vision of the ends and the present. For this study's purposes, I present Jewish and Christian precedents to the Plan, that is, in Christian terms God's *oikonomia*.[81] Since eschatology and apocalypticism have been considered earlier, we will deal with two major heads: Messiahs-Christs-Renewers and Anti-Christs and Millennialisms.

### MESSIAHS-CHRISTS, ANTIMESSIAHS-ANTICHRISTS, GUIDES-RENEWERS

While Judaism contained messianic speculations, one or more such figures was not essential in the Hebrew Bible or later forms of Judaism. On the other hand, eschatological savior-rescuer figures play a necessary role in traditional Islam and Christianity. Both Islam and Christianity also feature evil counter-saviors.

First, messiah-christ. The Hebrew word "messiah," translated as the Greek "christos," means someone who is anointed. Psalm 2, probably an Israelite coronation hymn, calls God's anointed king, the "son of God" (Psalm 2:2, 7). In Isaiah 45:1–19, the author quotes the Lord calling the Persian king Cyrus His anointed (messiah in Hebrew, *christos* in the Septuagint). The book of the Old Testament (Prophet) Zechariah indicates that there will be an anointed kingly and an anointed priestly leader.[82]

A messiah-christ can also be a high-ranking angel. In the Jewish portions of the early first century CE work, 2 Esdras, two figures are called "messiah."[83] One is a human from the family of David and the

---

[81]    See, for example, Ephesians 1:3–14.

[82]    Zechariah 4:1–14. The two figures are probably the restored high priest, Joshua, and the Persian-appointed Zerubbabel. Zechariah 3:1–10 has an angel rebuke Satan in the process that restores the purified Joshua and the priesthood to leadership and honor.

[83]    2 Esdras was included in some printed Bibles as an appendix. Surah at-Tawbah (9:30) appears to reflect the position of 2 Esdras 14:9 that the scribe was raised to

other an angelic being. The human messiah will be kept hidden by God until God reveals him at the God-appointed time. He will defeat evil, liberate God's elect within the borders of the holy land, then head a temporary, bountiful, just and joyful kingdom for four hundred years before he dies. Following his death, the world will be turned back to its pre-creation "primeval silence" until a new creation is roused into existence by God. The human messiah is not mentioned as being among the resurrected dead or having any role in the new creation. The initial stages of that new creation will involve judgment, rewards, and punishment. The second messiah is an angelic figure who appears as the "man from the sea" and destroys evil forces, liberates God's people, and make them joyful until the judgment day (13:1–52). Note that in both instances, the absolute final day will be prefaced by a period of joy, prosperity, and peace headed by a Divinely-appointed leader.

Both Islam and Christianity have traditions about false or counter-messiahs or antichrists. According to the synoptic Gospels, Jesus warned his followers that prior to the Last Days, pseudo-christs will appear to deceive many on earth, some claiming to be the returned Jesus.[84] As indicated earlier, the writer(s) of 1 John and 2 John use the term "antichrist" in the singular and plural. The singular antichrist is yet to come, but there are many antichrists in the present and who have been members of the author(s)' congregations.[85] The antichrists were members of the Johannine community in name only and had separated from it. They did not confess that Jesus is the Christ–Son of God. 2 John 7 further defines anyone who denies the humanity of Jesus as the antichrist. The Revelation to John features an evil beast who transitions into being a false prophet who deceives many with

---

angelic or even higher divine rank (2 Esdras 7:26–41, 11:36–12:36 and 13:1–52). Surah 9:30: "And those Jews (who came to you) say (as did some Jews who lived before: 'Ezra (Uzayr) is God's son'; and (as a general assertion the Christians say: 'The Messiah is God's son.' Such are merely their verbal assertions in imitation of the utterances of some unbelievers who preceded them. May God destroy them! How can they be turned away from the truth and make such assertions?"

[84]  E.g., Mark 13:21–23 and Luke 21:7–8.

[85]  1 John 2:18–23 refers to a single *antichristos* who is yet to come and *antichristoi* active in the present.

signs and wonders, seals the deluded with the mark of the beast, then organizes the kings of the earth to fight God at Har-Megiddo only to be defeated and thrown alive into the lake of burning sulfur.[86] Beginning in the second century, the Markan false christ, Johannine antichrist, and the Revelation's false prophet came to be understood as a devil-inspired and empowered human being who was amalgamated into a singular figure: the Antichrist.[87] The theme of deceivers, false teachers, deceitful doctrines, immorality within the religious community, dissension, lust, etc. became a common eschatological trope in 1 and 2 Timothy, Titus, Jude, 2 Peter, and the Revelation to John as well as in the Gospel of Matthew. Believers were to be disciplined and on guard against those who would lure the faithful from the road to salvation.

Christians also had extra and post-biblical traditions concerning End Time figures. Two merit comment. The first was Alexander the Great. The originally pre-Christian story known as the *Romance of Alexander* was re-worked and essentially "Christianized" by the fourth century.[88] The various versions present the Macedonian conqueror as a mighty sage, warrior, and defender of what became Christian virtues. A fourth-century CE version describes an enemy host being driven off by Alexander's forces. He prayed to the God of gods and Lord of all creation who made everything by God's word, noting that the Creator made him the king of all the human realms. His prayer was answered by God's moving two mountains together, thereby blocking twenty-two kings and their armies from attacking the peaceful world on Alexander's side of the mountains.[89] Alexander installed bronze gates to further thwart the enemy. The blockaded kings and their people became foul and vengeful. These foes of humanity re-appear in Christian expectations of the End when they break through the mountains as Gog and Magog. A similar account featuring an

---

[86]   Revelation 13:11–18, 16:12–16, 19:17–21.

[87]   See *Roberts and Donaldson*, Vol. 5, Hippolytus, "Treatise on Christ and Antichrist," pp. 204–221 and *McGinn, Antichrist.*

[88]   *Stoneman* translated the extant texts.

[89]   Ibid, pp. 186–187.

enigmatic person called Dhu al-Qarnayn[90] appears in the Qur'an with the explicit mention of Gog and Magog, who are to burst forth near the End of Time to wreak destruction.

The other figure is the Last Emperor of the Roman Empire. The complex historical setting of Syria is beyond the scope of our study, yet because of this figure's role in Muslim-Christian relations in the seventh and eighth centuries, some explication is appropriate. Western Asia (modern Iraq, Turkey, Syria, Lebanon and Palestine-Israel) were usually part of the Roman Empire. A series of natural, human, theological, and military catastrophes struck from the mid-500s through the mid-800s. Plague caused a demographic collapse, famine raged, earthquakes devastated urban areas, and eclipses were taken as signals of Divine disfavor. Ecclesiastically, tensions between Rome and Constantinople widened into occasional breaches, and further schisms split Syrian Christians both from Rome's and Constantinople's jurisdictions. Following the Council of Chalcedon's Christological decrees (450) and shifting imperial loyalties to those decrees, a Syrian Orthodox Church emerged in Edessa (modern Urfa, Turkey) in 543 to rival the Constantinople-based Greek-speaking Orthodox Church. Occasional pressures and persecutions of the Syrian Church's clergy and laity made reconciliation unlikely. The Syrian side fragmented further as those who were considered heretics by Constantinople's standards entered Syria, and some established themselves in Mesopotamia.[91] Accusations about false teachers and corrupters of the faith were common and vituperative. Several high level palace maimings and murders in Constantinople's royal family fostered the valid impression that the foundations of the Christian state were shaking. Fourth and fifth century Barbarian pressures led to significant Byzantine defeats in Anatolia and Greece. Then the Persians attacked. Serious warfare in western Asia led to rapid Persian campaigns that captured Damascus and Jerusalem in the late 620s. Constantinople was under siege

---

[90] Dhu'l-Qarnayn is mentioned in the Qur'an as a beloved servant of God who made great conquests in His name. It is not certain whether he was a Prophet or not. (See Surah al-Kahf 18:83–98).

[91] For example, those who claimed to follow the teachings of Nestorius.

from the west by the Avars and Bulgars and from the east by the Persians. The Persians and the western foes were beaten back and territory re-taken just in time for the Arab incursions into the territory of the Roman and the Persian Empires. Religiously, the Arabs were motivated by the message of Islam. All these factors caused Christians from Greece to Mesopotamia to think that the signs of the times were pointing to the coming of the End. Lost in that volatile mix, some Christians identified Muhammad as the Antichrist and Islam as the deception of Satan.

In the middle of the seventh century, a Syriac document known today as the Revelations of Pseudo-Methodius gained wide circulation and credibility.[92] Christian contemporaries believed it was written by a fourth-century bishop, Methodius. Beginning with the creation of the world, Pseudo-Methodius built a case for the Plan of God involving Alexander's earlier mountain joining and gates being breached by Gog and Magog. The anti-God forces were abetted by the rise of the Ishmaelites (Arab Muslims). The document predicted that the Empire's Last Emperor and his forces would defeat all enemies and enslave God's opponents (including the Ishmaelites!). Then "the earth will sit in peace and there will be great peace and tranquility upon the earth such as has never been nor ever will be any more, since it is the final peace at the End of time." The Emperor's final acts were to provide for the end. The "son of perdition" would appear:

> The earth which they destituted will then be at peace; each man will return to his own land and to the inheritance of his fathers— Armenia, Cilicia, Isauria, Africa, Greece, Sicily. Every man who was left captive will return to the things that were his and his fathers, and men will multiply upon the once desolated earth like locusts. Egypt will be desolated, Arabia burned with fire, the land of Ausania burned, and the sea provinces pacified. The whole indignation and fury of the king of the Romans will blaze forth against those who deny the Lord Jesus Christ. Then the earth will sit in peace and there will be great peace and tranquility upon the earth such as has never been nor ever will be any more, since it is the final peace at the End of time.

---

[92] See *Palmer, Brock, and Hoyland*, pp. 44–51.

Finally, [the Emperor] will go to Jerusalem... After this the king of the Romans will go down and live in Jerusalem for seven and half-seven times, i.e., years. When the ten and a half years are completed the Son of Perdition will appear....When the Son of Perdition has arisen, the king of the Romans will ascend Golgotha upon which the wood of the Holy Cross is fixed, in the place where the Lord underwent death for us. The king will take the crown from his head and place it on the cross and stretching out his hands to heaven will hand over the kingdom of the Christians to God the Father. The cross and the crown of the king will be taken up together to heaven. This is because the Cross on which our Lord Jesus Christ hung for the common salvation of all will begin to appear before him at his coming to convict the lack of faith of the unbelievers....When the Cross has been lifted up on high to heaven, the king of the Romans will directly give up his spirit. Then every principality and power will be destroyed that the Son of Perdition may be manifest.[93]

The absolutely final end was expected to come with the return of Jesus and his angels to destroy all evil. Note that a period of peace and prosperity preceded the last battles. The Last Emperor was a renewer of the rule of God. The interim period of joy, peace, and prosperity on earth seems to combine the End of *telos* with *eschaton*. And that prepares for considerations of the third biblical Christian precedent for consideration, the Millennium and Millennialisms.

## MILLENNIUM AND MILLENNIALISMS

The prior presentation on the millennium in the New Testament's Revelation to John quoted the relevant passage, cited Augustine's application of the thousand year period during which Jesus was expected to influence human leaders and societies from his heavenly position, and described the interpretation of Post-Millennialism. Although the term "millennium" refers literally to one thousand years, it has come to connote "any period of great happiness, peace, prosperity, etc."[94] In that sense, expectations for a millennium fits well with the fulfillment model of eschatology. Post-Millennialism provides the opportu-

---

[93] *Palmer, Brock, and Hoyland*, pp. 49–51.

[94] *Webster's New World College Dictionary*, p. 914.

nity and context for religious social movements to develop and implement activities and programs that aim at achieving millennial-style goals. When coupled with an Augustinian-based perspective, a Post-Millennial approach is able to engage persons and groups that have differing ideologies in efforts intended to promote and realize as far as possible the conditions of stability, prosperity, happiness, and peace under the spiritual guidance, leadership and influence of Jesus without Jesus' being physically present.

Among applicable Biblical analogies are the Old Testament's Genesis 2 and Isaiah 11:1–16 as well as passages in the New Testament. The Genesis account describes human life in the Garden of Eden as a time of harmony between humans and nature, meaningful work, abundance, peace and fellowship with God as long as humans obey and serve God. Eschatological visions often see the new heavens and new earth as recapitulating that primal time. The Isaiah passage looks forward to the peaceable kingdom when ferocious predators and their prey will live together in amity, safety and harmony while God liberates exiled persons so that they will return to their homelands. In that time, "the earth will be full of the knowledge of the Lord as the waters cover the sea."

Whether or not Christians are Amillennialists or Post-Millennialists, the traditional Christian interpretation of the Old Testament as predicting God's will being fulfilled through Jesus, such passages are readily applicable to the fulfillment model of eschatology. The analogous application of a Post-Millennial optimism that societies can be reformed and transformed provides incentives for Christians to work together and to join persons of other religious commitments to realize the common goals of the peaceable kingdom. Nevertheless the millennium so depicted is temporary and not eternal. The millennium will pass, the human condition will deteriorate and God will bring the whole cosmos to its termination so as to have the new beginning of the Hereafter.

The analogy sketched above resembles the interim between Jesus' return to defeat the Dajjal and terminal End Times. Is it possible for Muslims and Christians to employ their different positions so as to understand one another and work together for the resent world? We will return to that question when we meet Fethullah Gülen again.

## PHASE 8: THE PLAN – MOVING TOWARD AND INTO JUDGMENT AND THE HEREAFTER

> Surely your Lord is God, Who has created the heavens and the earth in six days; He established Himself on the Supreme Throne, dictating all affairs....There is none to intercede with God unless He grants leave. That is your God, so worship Him....To Him you are all bound to return; a promise from God in truth....He originates creation, then He brings it forth anew....To the end that He may reward with equity those who believe and do good righteous deeds. Whereas for those who disbelieve, there is a drink of boiling water and a painful punishment because they persistently disbelieve. (Surah *Yunus* [Jonah] 10:3–4)

The Plan's final stages started with the Farewell Sermon and last Revelation. The creation continues to point to the One-Only God; the Prophets and Messengers have delivered the promises, instructions, warnings, and books; the umma has been established on Divine Principles; the Final Messenger has given his Sunnah (or Practice); and the Religion has been pronounced complete. Satan and his aides know that their days are numbered because the world's Last Hour is coming and so is the time when they will be cast into Hellfire. These aides of Satan from among the jinn and human beings will multiply their efforts to delude as many humans as possible in order to drag them also into Hell. Time is short for humans to accept, believe, obey, and practice the Pillars and the Teachings, even if in fumbling, partial ways. The All-Forgiving God (*al-Ghafur*) will understand and accept those who are sincere and who do good works as long as they do not reject Him, the Ultimate Truthful One (*al-Haqq*) and do not despise the angels, Prophets, and Messengers. Time is running out, and all will soon be summoned for the great Return to God—the Originator (*al-Mubdi*).

People who rejected the Divine Principles that their souls covenanted to accept before birth, principles that were revealed in nature and disclosed by God's emissaries before and after the Last Messenger and the Revelation, would be held accountable for their beliefs and actions. The Qur'an notes that many, such as the Arabs in the pre-Islamic Age of Ignorance and since then, might have believed in a distant, vague

Allah who had little or no direct involvement with the world. Such a deity, they believed, had partners, including daughters, who were to be honored and worshiped as local gods and patrons. As long as the rituals were performed properly, the believers were free to engage in activities that they found pleasurable, profitable, or at least possible. Any notion that conduct and intentions would be judged and recompense assigned after a person died threatened the social-political hierarchies and traditions of polytheistic society. The claim that the dead would be reassembled and raised from their graves prior to such a judgment was considered ridiculous. The beliefs in the supreme power of only one God and the derogation of the traditional deities or their demotion to deceitful jinn compounded the polytheists' rejection of the Qur'anic message, the Messenger, and those who accepted Islam.

Nevertheless, the teachings of the resurrection-Divine judgment and Divine Destiny (*Qadar*) were the logical and necessary results of the other four Islamic teachings (Articles of Faith).[95] Islam is geared to

---

[95] As has been discussed throughout Chapter Two, the future events or appearance of certain figures towards the End of Times (which are described mostly in the Traditions) are not counted among the "Six Articles of the Islamic Faith." With respect to this fact, Bediüzzaman Said Nursi states in his *Rays* that "[t]he future events that are not part of the truths of belief were unimportant in the sight of Prophethood" (p. 353). Similarly, Gülen explains this matter as follows:

> The issue [of the coming of the Messiah and Mahdi towards the End of Time] is not dealt and explained in the works of such leading imams of the *Ahl al-Sunna* as al-Maturidi and al-Ash'ari. In addition, this issue is a secondary matter of the Islamic jurisprudence, and the related reports reach us through the *Ahad* Hadith (which is reported at any stage of its chain by a small number of reporters that is less that the number of reporters of a *Mutawatir* Hadith—a hadith which is reported in each stage of its chain by a large number of reporters and is thus authenticated). Therefore, the issue was not dealt in the early books of Islamic creed (*aqa'id* that explain all the aspects of the articles of Islamic faith) because their denial will not lead one to unbelief. In all the branches of the Shiite schools, however, the Mahdism is an important matter, and the anticipation of Mahdi is always kept alive in minds....

> The issue is not one of the matters for Muslims to believe with certainty just like they believe in the six indispensible Articles of Faith. The Six Articles of Islamic Faith are to believe with certainty in God, His angels, His Books, His Prophets, the Resurrection and the fol-

and moves toward the goal of the Straight Way. That goal is the end

lowing Day of Judgment in the Hereafter, and the Divine Destiny and
Decree. Thus, neither the appearance of the Mahdi nor the descent of
the Messiah is among these Six Articles of Faith. If they were also to
be believed in as one must believe with certainty in those essential
articles of faith, and if non-belief in them would lead one to unbelief,
then the Prophet to whom the Sharia was sent would certainly count
them among the essentials of faith. There is, however, no mention of
Mahdi or the Messiah in those hadiths where the articles of faith were
declared. And if they were mentioned, the imams of the *Ahl al-Sunna*
would certainly cite them among the articles of faith....There is no
verse in the Qur'an that has an overt reference to them; the hints
about them are given in Mutashabih verses. Since it is not overtly and
decisively stated, it is not necessary to believe with certainty in one of
the many possibilities or comments....The belief about [the anticipation of] the Messiah and Mahdi has been exposed to many abuses
throughout the history, and it can still be used wrongly now; there
may appear false prophets as well as those pretending to be the Mahdis
or the awaited ones. (Gülen, "Mehdi Kim? Mesih Nerede?", in *Yeni
Ümit*, January–March Issue, 2007.)

In one of his recent sermons, titled "Balance and Moderation," Gülen further
elucidates the issue. Under the subtitle of "An inflation of the 'Divinely-guided
Saviors in an Age of Arrogance," he gives examples of such "Divinely-guided saviors" and "some false prophets—such as Aswad al-Ansi and Musaylima the Liar—
appearing even at a period when the true light illuminated everywhere. Those poor
people became victim to certain gifts they saw in themselves and perished in the
claws of pride and egotism." He further states:

Surely such cases of deviation and misguidance are not limited to a
particular period in history. Almost every period witnesses such events.
Today, as well, you can see some people who can talk or write impres-
sively or have taken a few steps on the spiritual path, who lose their
balance and seek to become an idol and display due arrogance. When
they display themselves and when a circle of naïve ones begins to form
around them, they start seeing themselves like a bright star immediately. For this reason, there is an inflation of Mahdis—the so-called
"Divinely-guided" people, today. Even a humble servant like myself
knows five or six such "saviors" who have appeared in Muslim community....In fact, one of them came here recently....I tried to remind
him of some points about humbleness and modesty. I tried to tell him
that the sign of worthlessness in worthless ones is their assuming
greatness, virtually standing on their toes to look greater than they

of this world in Resurrection and Judgment and the opening of the Hereafter. When challenged by unbelievers who mocked him for proclaiming the imminence of the Resurrection and Judgment, Muhammad was given a revelation that echoed biblical precedents:

> Let them know that God never fails to fulfill His promise; but a day with your Lord is like a thousand years in your reckoning. (Surah *al-Hajj* [The Pilgrimage] 22:47)

The length of time from 632 to this world's end is a matter of God's planning. Surah as-Sajdah 32:5, as did 2 Peter, indicates that God's time can be measured in thousands of years of human terms, *"He directs the affair from heaven to the earth; then the affair ascends to Him in a day the measure of which is a thousand years of what you reckon."* The Last Day of the world and the Day of Judgment may then be understood in human terms as extended periods in which numerous events take place. I offer four angles through which to understand traditional Muslim views as background to Gülen's positions. The angles are: Death and Existence in the Grave; Signs; Events and Figures Prior to the End; and Aspects of the Hereafter.

### FIRST ANGLE: DEATH AND EXISTENCE IN THE GRAVE

First, death. God alone is the Ever-Living One (*al-Hayy*); all other beings and things will taste death, for another of God's names is *al-*

---

really are; and the sign of worth in truly worthy ones is their humbly curved stature, in order to look lesser than they really are. After I spoke to him, I thought that he was convinced. To my surprise, the last thing he said before leaving was: "All right sir, but what can I do if I have [been divinely chosen and appointed and thereby] not been given a right to choose at this issue?" However, there is no spiritual rank or title in Islam—including the imamates of the Sunni schools of thought (Hanafi, Shafii, Maliki, and Hanbali) or being the Mahdi— that puts one under obligation of proclaiming it to others, except for Prophethood. However, it is very difficult to tell anything to those who are obsessed with such a thought. May God guide all of the egotist and arrogant ones obsessed with a claim of being Mahdi to the Straight Path. (http://www.herkul.org/weekly-sermons/balance-and-moderation/ accessed on June 07, 2013.)

*Mumit*, the One Who Causes Death. In itself, death is neither a punishment for sin nor an enemy to be conquered. It is part of God's Plan for individuals and the universe. Further, God's knowledge, power, and mercy include God's setting the exact moment for an individual's birth and death.[96] Moreover, death is not extinction but rather the state in which the soul retains consciousness, emotions, and feelings. While God has made the decision about the time and knows the manner of a person's death, humans are responsible for their roles in their own deaths and the deaths of others. Further, death and sleep are related to the End. During sleep, a person's soul leaves the body and hovers between life and death. God takes some souls into the state of death, and others God returns to their bodies for continued life in this world (Surah az-Zumar 39:42). In that manner, sleep is a rehearsal for dying with dreams sometimes providing intimations of the Judgment and the Hereafter.

Death ends an individual's abilities to act anymore in this world although the person's past actions will continue to have good and bad results. Each person is responsible for her or his thoughts, intentions, and actions. Nothing escapes or can be hidden from God. The account books kept by each person's recording angels will be opened and placed in the balance scale when he or she is judged at the Resurrection. God, who alone knows everyone's intentions, will include the intentions when rendering the verdict. That verdict will be just and as merciful as possible but will not come as a surprise or shock, for the soul will know its eternal future even before the Resurrection Day.[97]

---

[96]  Surahs 4:78–79 and 56:60.

[97]  The dead are, indeed, exposed to a life resembling either Paradise or Hell in their graves until the Resurrection. It is reported in the Hadith that "The grave is either a garden of the gardens of Paradise, or a pit of the pits of Hell." (Tirmidhi, Qiyamah, 26) "When one of you dies they are exposed to their abode in their graves morning and evening. If they are among the residents of Paradise, they will be exposed to their abode in Paradise. If they are among those of Hell, they will be exposed to their abode in Hell and be told: 'This is where you are to remain until your resurrection on the Day of Judgment.'" (Tirmidhi, Janaiz, 70). Similarly, the Qur'an mentions, for instance, the punishment of the Fire for the Pharaoh and his court in the grave in the form of being exposed to it in the morning and evening: *"The Fire: they are exposed to it morning and evening; and when the Last Hour comes in*

When 'Azra'il, the Angel of Death, and his assistants come to extract the souls from the bodies of those who will be accounted righteous, those souls will slip out gently and gladly from their bodies. Angels will process joyfully with those souls through the heavens into the near-presence of God. The souls will be returned to their bodies to rest in their graves until the last day. In the time between death and the Resurrection, two angels will stay with the righteous persons, encouraging and assuring them of God's faithfulness. Those who will be condemned will have the opposite experience. 'Azra'il and his associates will be met by those souls with fear and resistance. These souls will cling desperately to the body but will be torn out. The journey will be accompanied with beatings and accusations from angels along with visions of Hell's punishments. When such souls are returned to their bodies in the graves, two angels will be there in this intermediate realm of the grave to punish and denounce the person until the full extent of misery and pain starts at the time of the Resurrection. The Messenger advised that when living persons pass cemeteries, they ought to listen carefully. The men of perception may hear the conditions, joys, laments, praises, and groans of the dead. The living, therefore, have added incentives to deepen their faith in and obedience to God and to strive to increase their good works while in this world.[98]

## SECOND ANGLE: SIGNS ANTICIPATED
## BEFORE THE END OF THE WORLD

The second angle covers the signs anticipated before the world's end. Distinctly Islamic signs and descriptions of the steps leading to the End are supplemented by Biblical precedents and perhaps from 2 Esdras as well. Jesus is an essential figure in the Muslim narrative of the last stages of God's Plan. A quick summary of his roles include:

---

*(and the Judgment is established, it is ordered): 'Admit the clan of the Pharaoh into the severest punishment.'"* Therefore, the Pharaoh and the relentless enemies of God from his clan will be exposed to the Fire in their graves morning and evening before their punishment in Hell.

[98] See Surahs 79:1; 8:50–51; and 29:56–64, Wagner, *Opening*, pp. 231–239; al-Ghazali, *Remembrance*, pp. 97–158.

his virgin birth, his mission as Messenger, his designation as the Messiah, his station in one of the seven heavens, his promised descent at the right time in God's Plan to destroy the evil Antichrist, and his presence during a period of prosperity and peace before his death and prior to the ultimate End of the world.

According to the Qur'an and the Hadith, 'Isa has not died yet. In somewhat greater detail, 'Isa (Jesus) is Muhammad's immediate predecessor-messenger and was sent to the children of Israel. He, like Adam, was fully human but did not have a human father. God simply said "Be," and the virgin named Maryam (Mary) conceived and bore him. As a newborn, he spoke clearly about his mission. His messengerhood included healings, raising persons from the dead, caring for his mother, clairvoyance, and testifying to the One-Only God. His disciples proclaimed proudly that they were Muslims.[99] Opposed by the Jews, 'Isa only seemed to have been crucified. His opponents' boasts about killing him was based on an error either through someone else being executed or God's veiling the perceptions of the onlookers from what actually occurred.[100] In any event, according to the Qur'an, 'Isa was taken by God and is in a celestial place or dimension. During Muhammad's Night Journey and Ascent into heaven, he met John the Baptist and Jesus in the second heaven.[101] Jesus recognized Muhammad as a fellow Messenger, and Muhammad later referred to Jesus as his brother in Prophetic Revelations.[102] Jesus is in close proximity to the earth, that is, close enough, if God wills, to exert salutary influences on persons and communities in the present.

Compared to the Hadith, the Qur'an is modest in describing the signs that foreshadow the world's end. The Makkan surahs usually

---

[99] Surah Al Imran 3:49–53.

[100] See Surahs Al Imran 3:55 and an-Nisa 4:156–159. Some Christians held that Simon of Cyrene or another disciple or Judas was the victim. Some others insisted that only the fleshly body of Jesus was killed while his "Christ-power" was unscathed by the crucifixion.

[101] See Wagner, *Journey* and numerous Hadith such as *Sahih al-Bukhari*, Vol. 1, Book 8, Item. 349 and Vol, 4, Book 59, Chapter 6, Item 3207; and *Sahih Muslim*, Vol. 1, Book 1, Chapter 75, Item 309.

[102] *Sahih al-Bukhari*, Vol. 4, Book 60, Chapter 48, Item 3442.

describe the events of the world's last Day rather than the signs that lead up to it. The Overwhelming Event will be a calamity filled with noise and disorder that scatters persons and mountains, (Surah al-Qari'ah 101:1–5), on which there will be a great fire and earthquake (e.g., Surahs al-Layl 92 and az-Zilzal 99). The sky will be torn apart, the stars will fall, the sun will fold up, the crumpled mountains will disappear, the seas will boil over and the earth will be flattened as the dead are raised from their graves (Surahs at-Takwir 81, al-Infitar 82, and al-Inshiqaq 84). The Hadith collections are more fulsome in recalling what Muhammad said to those around him. Some Muslim scholars discern him enumerating as many as fifty-two minor signs along with ten major signs that precede the Day.[103] Some of these will occur before the Last Day. The ten major signs listed by Imam Muslim are the appearance of Dajjal (Antichrist); the Smoke; the Beast; the Sun rising in the West; the outbreak and attacks by Gog and Magog; three Landslides in the East, West and Arabia; Fire from Yemen, and Jesus' Descent.[104]

## THIRD ANGLE: EVENTS AND FIGURES ANTICIPATED BEFORE THE END OF THE WORLD

The Islamic term *fitna* characterizes much of the Hadith descriptions of events that build up to the termination of the world. Ali ünal's definition of *fitna* fits the eschatological context:

> Disorder and corruption rooted in rebellion against God and recognizing no laws. It denotes associating partners with God and adopting that as a life-style, spreading unbelief and apostasy, committing major sins with willful, insolent abandon, open hostilities

---

[103] *al-Awalki*, Tapes 3–5. The minor signs include wars between the Muslims and Jews and between Muslims and "Greeks" (the Byzantine Romans), and between Muslims and polytheists in the west.

[104] *Sahih Muslim*, Vol. 4, Book 39, chapters 1202–1203, items 6931–6935, pp. 1503–1505. In *Sahih Muslim*, Book 39, Chapter 1212, saying 7040, p. 1525, Muhammad said six signs were to come: the rising of the sun from the west, the smoke, the Dajjal, the moving beast, death of one of his listeners and "the general turmoil."

to Islam, destroying the collective security or causing public disorder, and oppression.[105]

The authentic Hadith materials describe two *fitna*s. The first
involves a grotesque human figure, the Dajjal, also called the Antichrist (*Masih al-Dajjal*). Secondary Hadiths, such as Ahmad ibn Hanbal's *Al-Musnad*, report that Muhammad spoke of a lesser Dajjal, the
Sufyan. The authentic Hadiths focus on the Great Dajjal, describing
him as the false or imposter messiah whose appearance is one of the
major signs that the Last Day is drawing near. *Dajjal* connotes covering as in coating a cheap object with a precious metal or covering the
defects of a product in order to cheat a buyer. Yet it is possible that
the term may also refer to a wide number of mighty deceivers.[106]
Imam Muslim's sources described the Dajjal as a misshapen man of
great power who is chained in a cave in the east. Sometime before the
cataclysms of the Last Day, he will burst from his cave to attack and
deceive the inhabitants of the world.[107] He will travel throughout the
world except for Makka, Madinah, Jerusalem, and Damascus. He and
his armies will slaughter those who resist his claims for divinity. He
will perform great wonders (*istidraj*), produce illusions that deceive
many, and attack the remnant of the faithful Muslims. He and his
forces will besiege the remnant of faithful Muslims in Jerusalem and
be on the verge of total victory when Jesus will return from his heavenly place, kill the Dajjal (Antichrist) near Jerusalem, and destroy the Dajjal's forces. Jesus will then inaugurate a period of prosperity, joy, true
religion (Islam), and peace. According to Bukhari, Abu Hurayra
reported that Jesus went further:

> God's Messenger said, "By Him in Whose Hands my soul is, son
> of Mary (Jesus) will shortly descend amongst you people (Muslims)

---

[105] Ünal, *The Qur'an with Annotated Interpretation*, p. 1337. Except for the reference to
Islam, the same description fits 2 Thessalonians 2:1-12; 1 Timothy 6:4–6; Jude 17
and 2 Peter 3:1–7 as well as Mark 13 and parallel passages.

[106] According to a Hadith recorded in *Sahih al-Bukhari*, about thirty Dajjal will appear, each
claiming to be a Prophet. *Sahih al-Bukhari*, Book 92, Chapter 25, saying 721 (2).

[107] See *Sahih Muslim*, Book 92, Chapter 1207–1212, sayings 7005–7041, pp. 1515–1525.
The actions and illusions of the Dajjal are given in some detail in *Sahih Muslim*.

as a just ruler and will break the Cross and kill the pig and abolish the Jizya (a tax taken from the non-Muslims, who are in the protection of the Muslim government). Then there will be abundance of money and nobody will accept charitable gifts.[108]

In other words, Jesus will bring forth the needed corrections to Christianity and lead the Christians into Islam. At the end of that period, Jesus will die.

Ibn Hanbal's report of the Hadith on the Sufyan introduced a distinction in the nefarious work of these two deceivers.[109] According to Hanbal, Muhammad said that the Dajjal would be a non-Muslim, and his attacks would be directed against those who were not in Islam. The Sufyan, on the other hand, would be the deceiver, that is, the Dajjal of Muslims. He would not be as crass and vicious as the Dajjal of the unbelievers. Nursi quoted Hanbal's description and continued:

> "The *Sufyan* will be an eminent scholar, and he will fall into misguidance on account of his learning. Numerous other scholars will follow him." While the *Knowledge is with God*, an interpretation is this: Although contrary to kings, he has no sovereignty such as power, tribal or racial support, courage, and riches, the *Sufyan* will win his position through cleverness, skilled conspiracies, and political acumen; with his intelligence he will bewitch the minds of many other scholars, causing them to confirm and support his ideas and actions. He will transform numerous teachers into his supporters and try vehemently to establish an education system that is bereft of religious instruction.[110]

---

[108] *Sahih al-Bukhari*, Vol. 3, Book 34, item 425.

[109] See Nursi, *The Rays*, Fifth Ray Eighth and Ninth Matters, pp. 360–361, footnote 79. Note also Ünal, *Resurrection and Afterlife*, pp. 169–171.

[110] Ahmad ibn Hanbal (780–855) was caught up in the controversy concerning whether the Qur'an as a Book (*Mushaf*) was created or uncreated. He held the former position (which became the orthodox view). In his time, the "created" view gained the support of many scholars and the government. The orthodox view is that the Qur'an is the Divine Word, and therefore, eternal, and it was not created. However, it is not eternal as a book composed of letters and words and binded between covers, recited, listened to, and touched.

The second, positive, and faithful figure, the Mahdi, is often associated with Jesus in the struggle against the Great Dajjal (Antichrist).[111] Some Sunni positions stress the Mahdi as the one who will introduce a golden age as a glorious time between a first and second *fitna*. The latter will lead to the Last Hour. The *Sunan* of Abu Dawud expanded on the Mahdi for Sunni Muslims.[112] He is mentioned as coming in the aftermath of twelve caliphs who guided the Muslim community properly, but then great turmoil will roil the Muslims and the world. God will raise up the Mahdi from the family of Muhammad. He will reign "with equity and justice" for seven or nine years.[113] Neither number needs to be taken literally. The Mahdi will be a spiritual leader. When the remnant of true Muslims will be besieged by the Dajjal and his army, the Mahdi will lead the faithful in the Prayer as Jesus returns. The Mahdi will continue the Prayer as Jesus proceeds to annihilate the Dajjal and his forces.

A third set of positive figures is mentioned by Abu Dawud. He reported that "Abu Hurayra reported the Messenger of Allah (pbuh) as saying: Allah will raise for this community at the end of every hundred years the one who will renovate its religion for it."[114] This is "Centennialism," that is, a periodic renewal of Islam through a *Mujaddid*, or Renewer, every 100 years.[115] The Renewers are understood to be scholars and figures not involved in political affairs or struggles. They are spiritually oriented educators who correct and influence the umma, and, through the umma, the world. In this sense, the *Mujaddid*s contrast with the Mahdi traditions and expectations. Belief in the periodic rise and influences of Renewers may help explain how many Muslims are able to cope with disasters, defeats, and divisions without

---

[111] Mahdism is vital to Ithna Asheri Shi'ia (Twelvers) views of the Imamate and eschatology.

[112] *Abu Dawud*, Vol. 3, Book 31, chapter 1586.

[113] Forms of Mahdism may trigger actions intended to hasten the apocalyptic signs of the coming golden age. Note the seizure of the Grand Mosque in 1979. See *Trofimov's* account of the event.

[114] *Abu Dawud*, Book 32, Chapter 1587, saying 4278.

[115] See *Winter*, p. 316.

resorting to despair, apostasy, or violence; they believe God will restore the umma to God's righteous way.

Abu'l-Fadl Jalal al-Din al-Suyuti (850/1445–911/1505), a Sunni scholar in the Shafi'i legal tradition living in Cairo during the late Mamluk period, expanded on the Centennialist view of Renewers.[116] In his "Epistle of the Sharp and Glistening Sword to the Shi`i People of Opposition," Suyuti used the Hadith and tradition that is ascribed to Muhammad that the world and Muslim community would deteriorate. People are fallible and will fall away from what is true and good for them. Conduct will worsen, worship will become distorted and lax, ignorance and wickedness will grow. Each century will have to cope with its own *fitna*. Yet every 100 years, God will send at least one Mujaddid to renew and restore the Muslim community to what God intends it to be. The concept of the Renewers will give hope and patience to Muslims. They know that the present disorder in which they live will end, but they will have to figure out where and when within the centennial timeframe the Renewers live. Suyuti developed a century-by-century table of persons whom he considered to be the Renewers of their times. He included himself for his own century.[117]

## FOURTH ANGLE: ASPECTS OF THE HEREAFTER

The Qur'an and especially the Hadith give ample, often graphic descriptions of the times and places of the Hereafter. The path taken by the resurrected dead and righteous to the place of judgment and the subsequent punishments inflicted on the condemned together with details concerning the passage of the righteous to the Garden (*Jannah*) are important in Islamic eschatology. They are, however, not germane to our present study. Three aspects of the Hereafter are particularly relevant for understanding Gülen. Each is linked to and foreshadowed in the Qur'anic view of God's Plan: the nature of creation, human account-

---

[116] *Poston*, "The Second Coming of 'Isa: An Exploration of Islamic Premillennialism" in *The Muslim World*, Vol. 100, Number 1, January, 2010, pp. 100–116. Suyuti is also known as Abu al-Fadl 'Abd al-Rahman ibn Abi Bakr Jalal al-Din al-Suyuti.

[117] *Poston*, pp. 104–106.

ability structured into the purpose of humanity, and the joys of the righteous in the Hereafter.

First, the will of God manifested in creation testifies to God's bountiful care, and the tapestry of relationships with creation are signs to lead humans to confess faith in and to worship the One-Only God. The connections and inter-dependencies of all elements in the Dunya are provided for human existence and point to the Resurrection and the Hereafter. Natural events that people consider as catastrophic are actually evidences that humanity and all else are contingent, that is, dependent on God's will. What and who have been created do not endure forever, but all hasten to their fulfillment, termination, and judgment. Past and present are aimed inexorably to the future:

> He it is Who has made the earth subservient to you (as if a docile animal), so go about through its shoulders (uplands) and eat of His provision, but (be ever mindful that) to Him will be the Resurrection. And yet, are you secure that He Who is above everything will not cause the earth to swallow you up then, when it is in a state of commotion? Or are you secure that He Who is above everything will not send against you a deadly sand-storm? Then you will know how My warning is. Indeed, those before them denied (the truth and were destroyed). So (reflect on) how awesome was My disowning them! Have they never considered the birds above them, flying in lines with wings they spread out and fold in? Nothing holds them up except the All-Merciful. He indeed sees everything very well. (Surah *al-Mulk* [The Sovereignty] 67:15–19)

Second, the Qur'an enjoins all persons, especially Muslims, to care for the poor, widowed, orphaned, and strangers. Such efforts are not options; they are commanded by God. The injunctions are based in the ways God has arranged the world and placed humans in it to be God's *caliphs* (vicegerents who improve the world and rule over it according to His commandments). Obviously there are disparities of wealth and possessions among individuals and communities. Nevertheless, God has so arranged the earth's fecundity and human abilities to provide for human flourishing so that through cooperation, justice, mercy, and generosity those who have more than they need are able to share with those in need. In actuality, all that every person has is a loan from God to be used to give glory to the One-Only God through gratitude, aiding fellow humans, and caring for God's world.[118] According to the Qur'an, the poor have a God-recognized right to be given adequate provisions from the wealthy whether or not the indigent ask for such assistance.[119] Differences in social and economic status are part of God's Plan, as is the obligation for people to respond to those differences in order to build human harmony and community through which God will be honored and served. The fulfillment of the material part of God's Plan will be weighed, revealed, and recompensed at the Judgment:

> Say: "Am I, then, to seek after someone other than God as Lord when He is the Lord of everything?" Every soul earns only to its own account; and no soul, as bearer of burden, bears and is made to bear the burden of another. Then, to your Lord is the return of all of you, and He will then make you understand (the truth) concerning all that on which you have differed. He it is Who has appointed you vicegerents over the earth (to improve it and rule over it according to God's commandments), and has exalted some of you over others in degrees (of intelligence, capacity, and then wealth and status): thus, He tries you in what He has granted you. (Always remember that) your Lord is the most swift in retribution (when it is due), and assuredly, He is the All-Forgiving, the All-Compassionate (especially toward those who turn to Him in repentance as His believing servants). (Surah *al-An'am* [Cattle] 6:164–165)

Third, this world (*dunya*) and the Hereafter (*al-Akhira*) are directly and analogically bound to each other. As the direction of time in this world moves toward the next world, the Qur'anically promised light from the Hereafter shines into the present to disclose through signs and foreshadowings the coming eternal realities. On the one hand, thorny trees, bitter liquids, and pain experienced before death

---

[118] See, for example, Surah 7:10.
[119] Note Surah 70:24–25.

are harbingers of the punishments waiting for the unrighteous.[120] On the other hand, those admitted to the Paradise will have abundant food and drink, clothing, and companionship. To their surprise and delight, they will recognize the perfect fruits of Paradise as resembling what they now realize were prefigured during their earthly lives:

> Give glad tidings to those who believe and do good, righteous deeds for them are Gardens through which rivers flow. Every time they are provided with fruits (of different color, shape, taste, and fragrance, and that are constantly renewed) therefrom, they say, "This is what we were provided with before." For they are given to them in resemblance (to what was given to them both in the world, and just before in the Gardens, familiar in shape and color so that they may not be unattractive due to being unknown). Furthermore, for them are spouses eternally purified (of all kinds of worldly uncleanliness). They will abide there (forever). God does not disdain to strike any parable – (that of) something like a gnat or something greater or lower than it. Those who have already believed know that it is the truth from their Lord. As to those whose unbelief has long been established in their hearts, they say, "What does God mean by such a parable?" Thereby He leads many astray, and thereby He guides many. He thereby leads none astray save the transgressors. (Surah *al-Baqarah* [The Cow] 2:25–26)

Further, life in Paradise is such that the righteous will live in profound and eternal peace. The angels who open the gates to the Garden will bid them enter, greeting them with the salutation, "Peace!"[121] In the Garden, they will continue to worship and praise the One-Only God, engaging with one another in consummate joy and peace in the midst of prosperity:

> But those who believed and did good, righteous deeds are admitted to the Gardens through which rivers flow, therein to abide by their Lord's leave. Their greeting therein (among themselves and from God and the angels) will be "Peace!" (Surah Ibrahim 14:23)

In the beginning of the worlds and beyond the worlds' end are the Gardens. The primal Garden contained the seed of the promise that

---

[120] See Surah 88:1–7.
[121] See Surahs 13:23–24; 16:32; 39:73.

is fulfilled in the final Garden: glory to the Creator, prosperity and joy among the righteous who will dwell in peace. God's Plan stretches between the beginning and the consummation, giving humans the signs and guidance they need to know and serve God, thereby fulfilling God's loving, compassionate, and gracious will.

## CONCLUSION AND PROJECTION

Chapter Two serves as the framework and background for Fethullah Gülen's thought and influence. Through that thought and influence, he animates Hizmet and opens ways for inter-religious and inter-cultural dialogue and action. Because Gülen is a knowledgeable and deeply spiritual Muslim, readers may anticipate his thinking to be rooted in the Islamic understandings and narratives presented in this chapter. Moreover, since Islam is an eschatologically-oriented religion, Gülen's theology, spirituality, and perspectives are imbued with eschatological perspectives even when not stated directly.

Although Chapter Two as a whole informs Chapters Three and Four, particular points will recur in what follows:

1. The importance of names, especially those of God;
2. The linkage between Primal Time and Endtime–Hereafter;
3. Proximate views shared by Judaism, Christianity, and Islam;
4. Understanding eschatology as connoting both Fulfillment and Termination;
5. Millennial perspectives during which the world and its inhabitants will be at peace;
6. The roles-presence of Jesus during the millennial interlude;
7. Centennialism and the expectation of Renewers;
8. The Divine commands that humans are to share God's bounty with one another and to care for the creation;
9. The worship, joy, abundance, companionship, and peace predicated of life in Paradise being anticipated in the present world and human relationships; and
10. The Qur'anic-Islamic confidence that God's Plan shall be accomplished, that humans are capable of uniting and accountable

to carry forward their roles in fulfilling their God-mandated responsibilities in this world.

With all that in mind, we move forward to meet Fethullah Gülen again.

> (The truth is that) whoever submits his whole being to God and is devoted to doing good, aware that God is seeing him, he has indeed taken hold of the firm, unbreakable handle. With God rests the outcome for all matters....To God belongs whatever is in the heavens and on the earth (over which He has full and exclusive authority; and, therefore, He alone is to be worshipped and none other). God is He Who is the All-Wealthy and Self-Sufficient (absolutely independent of the whole creation), All-Praiseworthy (to Whom all praise and thanks belong and are due). If all the trees on the earth were pens, and all the seas (were ink), with seven more seas added thereto, the words of God (His decrees, the acts of all His Names and Attributes manifested as His commandments, and the events and creatures He creates) would not be exhausted in the writing. Surely God is the All-Glorious with irresistible might (Whom none can frustrate, and Whom nothing can tire), the All-Wise. (Surah Luqman 31:22, 26–27)

## CHAPTER THREE

---

# Gülen's Vision of
# the Worlds' First Beginning

The universe, which has been ornamented with every sort of art, is like an endless parade or exhibition designed to attract us and make us reflect. Its extraordinary diversity and magnificent adornment, the sheer abundance and flow of events, present a certain reality to our senses and minds. This reality indicates the existence of an agent who brings it into being. Through the reality of His works and deeds, we come to know the Doer, and so His Names. Through these Names, we try to know His Attributes. Through the channels and prayers opened to our hearts, we strive to know Him in Himself. This raising up of our being is inspired across a wide domain of reality – things, events, the vast realm of humanity's stewardship, as well as the relation or connection between us and the universe and the realm of God's Names and Attributes.[122]

Beginnings and Endings are linked to each other through events in time and through those who are involved in those events until nothing further transpires and nothing is any longer present. Likewise, Above and Below, that is, the realm of the Transcendent and the realm of this world, are bound to each other. Their relationship is determined by the ways in which each is known to the other and by whom such awareness is disclosed. The plurals Beginnings and Endings are deliberate. The first Beginning concerns the creation and its aftermath in present existence. The second Beginning starts with the eternal Hereafter.

---

[122] Gülen, *Questions and Answers*, Vol. 1, pp. 17–18.

Chapter Three ventures a basic description of Gülen's vision of the worlds' beginning. In the next Chapter, the discussion continues, focusing on the two forms of eschatological Endings. The time span between the First Beginning and its final End as well as the space span of Above and Below constitute the worlds in, with, and under which all exists, yet whose existence is contingent on the will, power, and authority of the One who is Self-Subsistent (*al-Qayyum*) and All-Living (*al-Hayy*), the One Who is the Absolute Eternal Authority (*as-Sultan*). As Gülen wrote:

> Now, as it is the All-Living, All-Subsisting One Who gives existence and subsists, who can have the right to claim self-existence? Everything's existence depends on His Existence and Knowledge; whatever exists is a mirror in which His Names manifest themselves as being ultimately responsible for anything that occurs in it. Humanity is the most comprehensive and polished of these mirrors, and the Master of creation, upon him be perfect blessings, is the most perfect and complete of these.[123]

God's purpose in creating the universe with human beings and everything therein is to know and worship Him while in this world and thus prepare its creatures, especially humans, for eternal life in the Hereafter.[124] Time and space will come to their God-appointed dissolutions. The entire cosmos will participate in that final dénouement. Using the Qur'anic image of the scroll, again, in Gülen's words:

> The Qur'an likens the universe to a book unfolded. At the end of time, its destruction will be as easy for God as rolling up a scroll. As He unfolded it at the beginning, He will roll it up and, manifesting His absolute Power without any material cause, will re-create it in a much better and different form:
>
> On that day We shall roll up the heavens like a scroll rolled up for books. As We originated the first creation, so We shall bring it forth again. It is a promise (binding) upon Us. Truly We shall fulfill it (as We promised it). (al-Anbiya 21:104)

---

[123] Ibid, *Sufism*, p. 83.
[124] See especially Surahs 51:56; 21:16; 378:27 and 44:38–39.

> Have they not seen that God, Who created the heavens and the
> earth and was not wearied by their creation, is able to give life to
> the dead? Surely He has power over everything. (al-Ahqaf 46:33)[125]

Following another meeting with Gülen and through the opening
Qur'anic chapter of *al-Fatihah*, we are guided first into an exploration
of the All-Beautiful Names of God with references to the Divine Attributes of Will and Power and the Divine Attribute of Speech. In a sense,
this entire universe is, in the words of Gülen, "a Divine Book of Creation issuing primarily from the Divine Attributes of Will and Power"
—a book that "reads and interprets" its counterpart of the "revealed"
Books issuing from the Divine Attribute of Speech. These will bear
on Gülen's vision of the beginnings and endings of the worlds. The
balance of the Chapter is arranged around the theme of God's three
"books," that is, the Book of the Creation or Worlds, the Qur'an, and
the Book of Humanity. The Chapter concludes with a summary that
also serves as a transition to Chapter Four, titled "Fethullah Gülen's
Vision of the Worlds' Endings and New Beginning." The exposition
shows Fethullah Gülen as an eschatological thinker but not in the sense
that he is fixated on the standard apocalyptic despair over the corruption and evil in the present world. He is in full accord with the Qur'anic
insistence that God always is the sovereign Lord and never cedes
power to any other being. His eschatological view is consonant with
the Qur'anic expectation that believers will say, "*Surely we belong to
God (as His creatures and servants) and to Him we are bound to return.*"
And then their actions will reflect their declaration so that they gain
the New Beginning of eternal blessedness and peace.[126]

## MEETING FETHULLAH GÜLEN AS A GUIDE

The Qur'an's opening chapter of *al-Fatihah* ("The Opener") instructs
believers to pray for Divine guidance as they seek to live on the Straight
Path—the Path of those whom God has favored. We meet Gülen now
as one who is on that Path as a fellow traveler and guide. Our guide

---

[125] Gülen, *Essentials*, p. 139.
[126] Surah al-Baqarah 2:156.

seeks to bring wisdom about the worlds through a spirituality that may draw persons closer to God.[127] His thought, influences, and practices, including his eschatology, grow out of his Sufi-oriented disciplines that render him as one who is spiritually qualified to show others the way to live:

> A guide is one who has sufficient knowledge of the relationship between God, humans, and the universe, and the matters concerning this sphere of religion....A guide is a hero of spirituality, one who is a careful student of the Qur'an and the book of the universe, and one who has an inquiring mind which has an acquaintance with existential mysteries. A guide is also a sagacious insightful one with eyes that are observant of things, a tongue busy with reciting the Qur'an and ears that listen to it. With sound and accurate sense perceptions, profound and comprehensive observations, and powerful reasoning, a guide is distinguished with the manners that are found in a Prophet at a perfect level. Such a person has a universal viewpoint in dealing with matters, is careful of the intersecting points of the revealed rules and commandments of the Divine laws of creation and life. These individuals seek only God's good pleasure and approval in conveying and in communicating whatever is inspired into them to needy souls, thereby considering His nearness in whatever they do and say.[128]

## GÜLEN'S VISION OF THE WORLDS' BEGINNING

> In the Name of God, the All-Merciful, the All-Compassionate.
> All praise and gratitude…are for God, the Lord of the worlds,
> The All-Merciful, the All-Compassionate, the Master of the Day of Judgment.
> You alone do we worship, and from You alone do we seek help.
> Guide us to the Straight Path,
> the Path of those whom You have favored,

---

[127] See *Albayrak* as a whole and especially pp. 66–68. Albayrak posits that Gülen is eminently qualified to be a *mujtahid,* that is, a recognized scholar-jurist who is able to use his reason in making legal-ethical decisions (*itjihad*) and Qur'anic interpretations (*tafsir*). In his youth Gülen was influenced significantly by the Hanafi school of legal and scriptural interpretation.

[128] Gülen, *Sufism,* Vol. 3, pp. 4–5.

not of those who have incurred (Your) wrath ... nor of those who are astray.

(Surah *al-Fatihah* [The Opening] 1:1–7)

This first chapter of the Qur'an opens with four of the All-Beautiful Divine Names and through them provides an entry into a brief exploration of Gülen's thinking on the Names and the Divine Attributes as relevant to his vision for the worlds' beginning and endings. Gülen's Sufi-based descriptions of the Divine Attributes make several distinctions that are not directly applicable to the present study but may be found elsewhere in his writings.[129] For our purposes, I cite the Divine Attributes of Will and Action, and the Divine Attribute of Speech. Closely linked to and developing from the Attributes is the All-Beautiful Names of God. Again, Sufis distinguish at least six different ways to speak of the Names: Names Indicating the Divine Essence, Names Originating in Divine Attributes of Glory, Names Indicating Divine Acts, Foundational Names, Names of Majesty, and Names of Grace.[130] For Gülen:

> God has many Names that define Him. Each Name defines an "aspect" of the Divine Being and is manifested in the universe to give existence to beings and events. Some of the Names are the All-Merciful, All-Compassionate, All-Creating, All-Seeing, All-Hearing, All-Powerful, All-Willing, All-Providing, All-Knowing, and the Giver of Life.[131]
>
> All of God's Names are great. But, with respect to comprehending manifestation and inclusiveness, some may be greater than others. For example, Allah (God), the Proper Name of the Divine Being, is the most comprehensive of all and includes all other Names. This is also true of the name the All-Merciful, which is considered as almost synonymous with God.[132]

---

[129] Ibid, Vol. 4, pp. 168–174. Among the Divine Attributes considered are Attributes of Glory, Essential Attributes, Positive or Affirmative Attributes, Attributes of Action, and God's Figurative Attributes.

[130] See also Gülen, *Sufism*, Vol. 4, pp. 154–174.

[131] Ibid, Vol. 1, pp. 173–174.

[132] Ibid, Vol. 1, p. 86, note 101.

Gülen uses the term *tajalli* —manifestation, in relationship to the Divine Attributes and Divine Names:

> *Tajalli* has several meanings, such as being uncovered, coming forth, appearance and development within a certain framework and, to a certain extent, Divine Attributes and Names revealing themselves through their works individually or collectively, Divine mysteries and lights making themselves felt in hearts with certain signs, numerous unknown states and particularities that pertain to the Unseen coming to be known through the conscience and seen with the eye of the heart, and spiritual enlightenment through a continuous, sound relationship of servanthood with God Almighty. This term, which has the same meaning as the terms "dawning," "enlightening," and "illuminating" when used for people as objects, is also used for God with some modifiers, such as "the manifestation of the Divine Being or the Divine Essence," "the manifestation of Divine Essential Qualities," "the manifestation of Divine Attributes," "the manifestation of Divine Names," "the manifestation of Divine Works," and "the manifestation of Divine Acts." There are a few who mention the manifestation of Divine Essential Qualities, and some include the manifestation of Divine Works in the manifestation of Divine Acts.[133]

## CONSIDERATIONS OF THE DIVINE NAMES AND CREATION

As pointed above, God's purpose in creating the universe is first of all to know and worship Him properly, and thus attain proximity to the Almighty God. If God had not introduced Himself to us through His countless Beautiful Names, we would neither have an accurate and thorough knowledge of the Ultimate Truth, nor supplicate Him for His blessings through those proper Divine Name(s), or be able to establish a proper relationship with the All-Transcendent God. In a sense, God is transcendent in His Essence and yet immanent in the manifestations of His Names that are revealed in the "created books" of both the universe and the human as well as the "revealed Books." It is through these Beautiful Names that we, human beings, get to know our Cre-

---

[133] Ibid, Vol. 3, p. 65.

ator better and attain the goal of proximity with the All-Transcendent God, Who is, indeed, closer to each of ourselves than our own selves.[134]

Surah al-Fatihah opens the Qur'an with four of these Divine Names through which God seeks to be known throughout the cosmos and especially by humans. The initial Names are in the *Basmala*: the All-Merciful (*ar-Rahman*) and the All-Compassionate (*ar-Rahim*). Both originate in the Divine Attributes of Glory. Gülen, as did Sufis with whom he agrees, wrote that *ar-Rahman* means the One Who is All-Merciful to the whole of existence and Who provides for all that exists. *Ar-Rahim*, the All-Compassionate, signifies the identity of the One-Only God "Who has particular compassion for each of His creatures in their maintenance, and for His believing servants in the other world."[135] The entire cosmos, from Beginning to End, is suffused with God's Mercy and Compassion. The other two Names that are embedded in the phrases of *Rabbi'l-'alamiyn* (The Lord of the worlds) and *Malik-i Yawmi'd-Din* (The Master of the Day of Judgment) indicate the Divine Essence.[136] The Name *ar-Rabb* carries the sense of Lord, Provider, Trainer, and Director. All worlds are embraced in terms that lend themselves to guidance, nurture, and growth in the context of being safeguarded. *Al-Malik* connotes Master of all, the All-Sovereign One. The Name "Master" is understood specifically in the context of the Day of Judgment, hereby giving *al-Fatihah* an eschatological orientation that is borne out in the petition that the merciful and compassionate God, Who is the Creator, will lead the worshiper on the Straight Path. Compassion and Mercy disclose the foundational disposition of God to all in His worlds, yet there will be a Day when His creatures will be held accountable for their faithfulness in worship, thought, and action. When asked why God created the universe, Gülen gave the two-fold answer of transcendent purposeful power and love:

---

[134] See, for instance, the verse, "*Assuredly, it is We Who have created human, and We know what suggestions his soul makes to him. We are nearer to him than his jugular vein*" (Surah Qaf 50:16).

[135] Gülen, *Sufism*, Vol. 4, p. 170.

[136] Ibid, p. 168.

All artistry in the universe informs us of God's Names. Each Name, displayed by what has been created, illuminates our way and guides us to knowledge of the Creator's Attributes. They stimulate and awaken our hearts by His signs and messages addressing our senses.

The Creator wills to introduce Himself to us clearly and thoroughly. He wills to show His Splendor through the variety and beauty of creation; His Will and Might through the universe's magnificent order and harmony; His Mercy, Compassion, and Grace through His bestowal of everything upon us, including our most secret wishes and desires. And He has many more Names and Attributes through which He wills to make Himself known.

In other words, He creates and places things in this world to manifest His Might and Will. By passing all things through the prism of the intellect and understanding of conscious beings, He arouses their wonder, admiration, and appreciation. Great artists manifest their talents through works of art; the Owner of the universe created it simply to manifest the Might and Omnipotence of His Creativity.[137]

He continues by emphasizing that "God created the universe as a manifestation of His love for His creatures, in particular humanity, and Islam became the fabric woven out of this love."[138] God's love is designed to unite Him and His human creatures. God is faithful and true – and just.

The love of God is the essence of everything and is the purest and cleanest source of all love. Compassion and love flow to our hearts from Him. Any kind of human relation will develop in accordance with our relation to Him. Love of God is our faith, our belief, and our spirits in the physical body. He made us live when we did. If we are to live today, it is only through Him. The essence of all existence is His love, and the end is an expansion of that divine love in the form of Paradise. Everything He created depends on love and He has bound His relationship with humankind to the holy pleasure of being loved.[139]

---

[137] Gülen, *Questions and Answers*, Vol. 1, pp. 18–19.
[138] Ibid, *Love and Tolerance*, p. 60.
[139] Ibid, p. 11.

## THE THREE BOOKS

> The Qur'an, humanity and the universe are the three "books" that
> make the Creator known to us, and are three expressions of the
> same truth. Therefore, the One Who created humanity and the uni-
> verse also revealed the Qur'an. You cannot find people who do exact-
> ly what they ask others to do, or whose deeds reflect them exactly.
> However, the Qur'an is identical with Prophet Muhammad, and is
> the embodiment of him in words just as he is the embodiment of
> the Qur'an in belief and conduct. They are two expressions of the
> same truth.[140]

Everything goes through five stages or degrees of existence applicable
particularly to this world:

1.  Existence in the Creator's eternal Knowledge;
2.  Existence in the Creator's will as part of the Divine Plan;
3.  Existence as a material object in this transient world (*dunya*);
4.  Existence as a memory and/or in its offspring after its death; and
5.  Existence eternally in the Hereafter.[141]

Gülen continued:

> The universe, which science studies, manifests God's Names and
> therefore has some sort of sanctity. Everything in it is a letter from
> God Almighty inviting us to study it and acquire knowledge of
> Him. The universe is a collection of those letters or, as Muslim
> sages call it, the Divine Book of Creation issuing primarily from
> the Divine Attributes of Will and Power. The Qur'an, which issues
> from the Divine Will of Speech, is the universe's counterpart in
> written form....Similarly, humanity is a Divine book correspond-
> ing to the universe and the Qur'an. This is why the term used to
> signify a Qur'anic verse [*ayah*] also means events occurring within
> human souls and phenomena occurring in nature.[142]

The three books proclaim that the One-Only God exists and that
God is to be worshiped and willingly served by all existence. From its
coming into existence, every creature has covenanted the willingness
to obey God. In that sense, Islam is the religion of the universe even

---

[140] Gülen, *Essentials*, p. 225.

[141] Ibid, pp. 249–250.

[142] Ibid, p. 250. I supplied the bracketed term "*ayah*" for clarity.

before the Revelation to Muhammad. All that exists is part of the network of signs (*ayah*s) that point to and testify about the One-Only
God. As creatures emerge in their respective worlds, they are surrounded by the evidences, Names, and reflections of God. Those with
free will are summoned to worship and willing service' and are
accountable for their thoughts, intentions, and actions. The three
books are arranged so that every creature bears within itself the elements or seeds of the message that nothing is worthy of worship but
God and that Muhammad is God's servant and Messenger.[143] In addition, every creature is part of the cosmic mirror that reflects the Oneness and absolute Unity of God and His Names:

> The universe is a book which is displayed by the Creator before
> the eyes of man to be referred to frequently. Man is a lens open to
> observe the depths of existence, and a transparent index of all worlds.
> Life is a manifestation, the assumption of forms, the meanings of
> which are filtered from that book and index, and is the reflection
> of that which reverberates from the Divine discourse. If man, life
> and the universe are considered to be different on account of their
> outward forms and colors when these are but various faces of the
> same truth—and that is the reality—then their separation from
> one another ruins the harmony of the truth, which is a wrong, an
> injustice and disrespect toward man and existence.
>
> As it is an obligation to read, understand, obey and submit to
> the Word of God, which comes from His divine attribute of Speech,
> so it is an indispensable essential to know and understand God in
> the entirety of things and events, which He planned by his
> Knowledge and created by His Divine Will and Power, and then
> to seek for and confirm conformity and congruity in all things and
> events. The Qur'an came also from God's attribute of Speech; it is
> the soul of all existence and the sole source of happiness. The book
> of the universe is the body of this truth and a very important
> dynamic of this world directly and of the other world indirectly
> with respect to the various branches of science it includes and rep-
> resents. That is why understanding of and transferring these two
> books into practice and organizing the whole of life in accordance

---

[143] See Gülen, *Sufism*, Vol. 2, pp. 292–97. Muhammad is called the highest representation
of humanity and is "the universal man" who serves as the model for all humanity.

with them merits reward; and neglecting, ignoring, and even being unable to interpret and apply them to life merits punishment.[144]

## A. THE WORLDS' BEGINNING:
## THE BOOK OF THE UNIVERSE

> All praise and gratitude are for God, the Lord of the worlds,
> The All-Merciful, the All-Compassionate,
> The Master of the Day of Judgment.
> (Surah *al-Fatihah* [The Opener] 1:2–4)

The use of the plural "worlds" in the verse above is deliberate. *Al-Fatihah* (The Opener) shows that God created *al-'Alamin*, the term regularly translated as "worlds." Within and beyond the translation is an Islamic cosmology grounded on the principle that God is the Originator (*al-Badi'*) of all existence and is not part of or enmeshed in what has been made. Nevertheless, God is profoundly involved in what He has made in that He knows everything that happens throughout all the worlds, for God is the All-Knowing (*al-'Alim*) One. The root *'a-l-m* of the word *'alam* (sing. of *'Alamin*) and its associated terms indicate that all that exists is known to God, able to know God, and be known to creatures as God reveals such knowledge. The entire *'Alamin* is living, conscious, responsive to, and responsible to God. At other times, the worlds, that is, all that exists, especially *Dunya*, is termed the Book of the Universe and is in harmony with the Qur'an.[145] Gülen stated, "Like a mirror's two sides, existence has two aspects or dimensions: one visible and material, the realm of opposites and (in most cases) imperfections; and a spiritual realm that is transparent, pure and perfect."[146] We find the image of a mirror again in conjunction with the Book of the Universe, this time directing our gaze to the Hereafter:

---

[144] Ibid, *The Statue of Our Souls*, p. 37.

[145] See Ünal, *The Qur'an with Annotated Interpretation*, p. 5, note 8 for a basic discussion of the terms and worlds.

[146] Gülen, *Essentials*, p. 28.

Everything in this universe is a mirror pointing to God Almighty, like an articulate language telling of Him, and a tune singing His Name. Human beings, things, and the whole of existence always reflects Him and bears witness to Him in their sounds and silences, acts and positions, in their beings and the fruits they yield. In their manners and stances, they allude and point to Him. They are like shadows emanating from His existence in their weave, pattern, and accents. Let those who cannot see fail to see; those who can see with their insight read His signs in everything, and listen to such sounds and words from His different manifestations. If hearts are open to Him and eyes can see beyond corporeality—this may not be to the same degree in everyone—whenever we look at existence as if we were reading it like a book, whenever we visit the exhibition of this earth and set ourselves to gazing at it, we find everything in it as mesmerizing as in dreams.[147]

For such people, this universe and its contents seem like a comprehensive book. This magical palace called the world becomes an exhibition of divine art. The life they lead turns into an enjoyable journey to the Hereafter and what they see and sense makes them realize that they are alive. And then they feel as if they were soaring past the horizons of the heart and spirit for a lifetime. As existence and what is beyond open to their consciousness, the knowledge and love of God within them transforms into a deeper love and attachment. Now these people feel Him in everything and relate every event and every object to Him. Life becomes more beautiful to them than ever before; everything changes its manner and language and assumes a more magical identity. Then their spirit, which ascends beyond all obvious considerations, awakens to deep secrets never unlocked before.[148]

I suggest taking seven steps to sketch the scope of Gülen's cosmology.

## COSMOLOGICAL STEPS

First, all of the worlds can be spoken of as "dimensions," "aspects," and "realms" without necessarily ascribing to any of these physicality or visibility to humans. Each, except for our visible world (*dunya*), is a pure-

---

[147] Ibid, *Speech and the Power of Expression*, p. 107. The whole chapter (pp. 107–112) is titled "The Cosmos Is a Mirror to the Divine."

[148] Ibid, pp. 108–109.

ly spiritual world-dimension. Dunya, too, has spiritual aspects along with its visibility and materiality. Therefore, in broad terms, the worlds are of two types or categories: the physical-material dimension that we know as the Visible World (Dunya) and the normally Invisible-Unseen Worlds. God may make these known to some extent to human beings whom only He enables to perceive them. Beings in the purely spiritual worlds may communicate with one another and with creatures in this world.

Yet, on the basis of Qur'anic passages such as Surah ar-Rahman (55:29), Gülen holds that God is always creating and sustaining whatever exists individually in every world so that everything, from angels to sub-atomic particles, is a world in itself, created repeatedly.[149] Gülen wrote:

> From the perspective of Islamic epistemology, whether visible or invisible, transparent or opaque, observable or unobservable, animated or unanimated, from this world or other world, everything is an *'ālam* (realm or world). Derived from the same root as *'alam*, meaning a sign or mark, everything and what lies beyond it is a sign for the existence of the Divine Being, a document of His acts, a mirror to His Perfection, a register of Destiny, a site where the relevant Divine determination is manifested, and a location for the manifestation of Divine Attributes and Names. For this reason, whether visible or invisible, everything bears traces belonging to or is a sign for the Divine Being; therefore, it is regarded as an *'ālam* (realm, world).[150]

The second step recognizes that while God is the Absolute One, God has provided energy and accountability through what may be termed complementarities or balances that result in tensions or polarities. These are presented to humans and jinn as choices so that these beings may use their free will to choose which path they will follow. In turn, they will be held accountable for their choices and consequences on the Day of Judgment and often sooner:

---

[149] Surah ar-Rahman (55:29): *"All that are in the heavens and on the earth entreat Him (in their needs). Every (moment of every day) He is in a new manifestation (with all His Attributes and Names) as the Divine Being."*

[150] Gülen, *Sufism*, Vol. 3, pp. 86–87.

A close analysis of the universe's functioning shows that two opposed elements are prevalent and firmly rooted everywhere. Those elements result in good and evil, benefit and harm, perfection and deficit, light and darkness, guidance and misguidance, belief and unbelief, obedience and rebellion, and fear and love. The resulting continual conflict causes enough alteration and transformation to produce the elements of a new world. These opposite elements eventually will lead to eternity and materialize as Paradise and Hell. The eternal world will be made up of this world's essential elements, which will then be given eternal permanence.[151]

The third step moves from worlds as dimensions and the categories of the visible world (Dunya) and the Unseen Worlds to distinguishing six worlds. Indeed, above the corporeal/physical world are many other worlds or realms, all of which are spiritual and transcendental to varying degrees, and in each of which the measure of time is completely different. All of these worlds are infinitely contained by the Divine "Realm," where any aspect of corporeality is out of question.[152] Accordingly, there is no above and below relationship between the "realm" of Divinity and the realm of creation. There is the insurmountable boundary between the infinite "realm" of the Creator and all of the created worlds. This infinite "realm" is the all-encompassing "realm" of God in His ineffable Essence, or Self. Some Sufis have termed it *Alam al-Hahut,* the Realm of He-ness, the Divine Ipseity, or the One-Only God in total Oneness.

The six created worlds-realms-dimensions may be visualized as concentric circles or a hierarchical pattern that ranges from the highest dimension to the world (*dunya*).[153] As far as humans are concerned, that which is beyond Dunya is usually invisible and beyond human approach and unaided comprehension. "Usually" means that there will be some persons who have ascended into and even have gone

---

[151] Ibid, *Essentials*, p. 141. The theme of complementarity-tension may also be noted in the Names of God. For example, among the Names are *al-Mumit* (the One Who Causes Death) and *al-Muhyi* (the Giver of Life); *ar-Rafi* (the Exalter) and *al-Khafid* (the Abaser).

[152] See also Ünal, *Qur'an*, p. 63.

[153] See Gülen, *Sufism*, Vol. 3 pp. 86–96, and Ünal, *The Qur'an with Annotated Interpretation*, p. 5, note 8.

through the Unseen World (*'Alam al-Ghayb*). It is through God-willed and God-activated revelation/inspiration that the creatures in this world will learn anything about the worlds beyond them. The following presents the dimensions:

1. *Lahut:* the highest realm, that is, the High Empyrean. This is the world, or realm, of pure Divine Realities and closest to the Divine Essence-Presence of God. The Attributes and Names are disclosed in this realm;

2. *Rahamut:* the transcendent manifestation of Divine mercy and compassion;

3. *Jabarut*: another of the immaterial worlds where Divine realities are manifested in their pure, immaterial forms;

4. *Malakut:* the world of the pure inner dimension of existence; realm of the Divine Commands;

5. *Mithal:* the world of the symbols, ideals, archetypes, immaterial forms of things;

6. *Shahadah*: the present corporeal world, including the visible world and firmaments. The realm includes Dunya.

From another angle, the worlds may be referred to as the world of spirits, this world, the intermediate world of the grave (*al-Barzakh*), and the eternal world of the Hereafter (*al-Akhira*).[154] Gülen uses both patterns.

The fourth step connects the Above with the Below by placing this world (*dunya*) in relation to the spiritual realms just mentioned, that is, to dimensions related to God's Plan for the universe. One dimension of Shahadah-Dunya is *al-Alam al-Barzakh*, the realm humans enter after death. It is the "Between World" in that the deceased is in the grave between death and the resurrection on the Day of Judgment.[155] The culmination of the Divine Plan is the world-dimension of *Akhira*—the Hereafter, that is, the Gardens of Paradise

---

[154] Ünal, ibid.
[155] See Surah al-Anfal (7:46–49).

and the punishments of Hell.[156] Muslims debate as to whether Paradise and Hell exist already, are developing from seeds planted by present human actions, or will come into existence after the Day of Resurrection. In any event, they agree that the theme and dynamic of the Hereafter runs throughout and empowers Islam (and Gülen's thought) because all worlds and beings, except for the All-Living God, will die and be raised on that final Day.

The fifth step in understanding the worlds or dimensions concerns Dunya. Surah al-Baqarah (2:29) describes God creating and arranging seven heavens.[157] Surah at-Tahrim (66:12) implies that Dunya may have seven dimensions as well. Muhammad's Night Journey and Ascent (*Isra'* and *Mi'raj*) provides a description of the unseen spiritual dimensions of Dunya and a two-fold eschatological promise.[158]

Muhammad, guided by Archangel Gabriel (Jibril), traveled in spiritual time to the Furthest Mosque (Masjid al-Aqsa, traditionally the Temple Mount in Jerusalem). With his revealer-angel guide, the Messenger ascended through six heavens. Muhammad went further; he entered into the very presence of God. As he and Gabriel passed through the various heavens, the Messenger was unencumbered by the earthly limitations and witnessed spiritual worlds. When he met Adam in the first heaven, Muhammad saw the blessedness and glories of the Gardens of Paradise (*Jannah*) and the miseries and punishments of Hell (*Jahannam*). He continued and encountered previous Prophets and Messengers in the several Heavens and welcomed by the guardian

---

[156] See Surahs al-Hijr (15:43–44); al-Fatir (35:71); and az-Zumar (39:72). Traditionally the seven levels reflect the intensity of the fires: *Jaheem*; *Jahannam*; *Ladthaa*; *Sa'eer*; *Saqar*; *Hatamah*; and *Haawiyah*. It is usual for Muslims to use "Jahannam" as the generic name for Hell.

[157] Surah al-Baqarah (2:29): "*It is He Who (prepared the earth for your life before He gave you life, and) created all that is in the world for you (in order to create you – the human species – and make the earth suitable for your life); then He directed (His Knowledge, Will, Power and Favor) to the heaven, and formed it into seven heavens. He has full knowledge of everything.*"

[158] See Surah al-Isra' (17:1); *Wagner*, "Journeying to God"; *Sahih al-Bukhari*, Vol. 5, Book 58, Item 226; and *Sahih Muslim*, Vol. 1, Book 1, Item 309f.

angels that opened the gates of each Heaven.[159] The Prophets in the second heaven above the visible portion of Dunya were John the Baptist (Yahya) and Jesus ('Isa). Jesus, then, is in a heavenly spiritual dimension close to the earthly realm. The spiritual messianic aspect of the mission represented by Jesus will again have a general influence at the end of time and this spiritual/messianic aspect will be given prominence in conveying the Truth to the entire world.

The Night Journey and Ascent provide the opportunity to consider the eschatological promises. One is the nature of spiritual places and persons. Traditionally, the journey began at the Ka'ba with al-Quds (the Muslim title for the Temple Mount and the greater area of Jerusalem) as the earthly destination. Both places were sites for pre-Islamic religious shrines.[160] In addition, the Ka'ba was associated with Abraham and Ishmael, while al-Quds was the site where Jews believed Abraham bound Isaac for sacrifice (2 Chronicles 3:1). Muhammad's ascent gathered together all of the previous religious expressions and revelations, fulfilling them in his Ascent, Descent, and Prophethood. Islamically understood, the way was now opened for Jews, Christians, polytheists and all others to join in walking and living according to the Straight Way as revealed in the Qur'an and to the final Messenger-Prophet. The complete revelation, given through the Qur'an and Muhammad, would be the basis for the judgment that will be rendered on the Last Day.

The other aspect of the Journey-Ascent and Return involves what Muhammad saw and did. He was given the five daily Prayers and the assurance that God hears the pious prayers and petitions of individu-

---

[159] Gabriel asked the guardian angels to open the gates of heavens as they reached a different level of the seven heavens. The Prophets Muhammad met in order from the closest to this earth to the highest are cited as: Adam; 'Isa-Jesus and Yahya-John (the Baptist); Yusuf-Joseph; Idris-Enoch; Harun-Aaron; Musa-Moses, Ibrahim-Abraham. Some traditions reverse Musa and Ibrahim's positions.

[160] The Ka'ba had turned out to be the site in which representations of the gods of the pre-Islamic pagan Arabs were placed and was still the destination for an annual pilgrimage before the time of Muhammad. The Temple Mount had been a pre-Israelite Canaanite worship center, was linked to Jesus, and was the site of Greco-Roman altars during the rule of the pagan Roman Empire.

als and the community of believers. Gülen agrees with Nursi that during the Ascent, Muhammad saw Paradise and understood that life in it was eternal joy in an everlasting realm. He also saw the dreadful punishments the damned will suffer in Hell Fire. He went still further. The Ascent took him above the worlds-dimensions of angels, past Prophets and earlier Messengers, to God's close proximity—the nearness not even Gabriel or any other creature ever had. In that nearness and vision, Muhammad also realized that the destiny of the pious who serve the One-Only God is to be closer to God than the highest angels. When he returned to the world's space-time, Muhammad gave the good news of eternal joy to humans and jinn that God is truly All-Merciful and All-Compassionate, and those who journey on the Straight Path can have the assurance of eternal happiness in an everlasting dimension-world.[161] Muhammad's journey-ascent-descent-return provides analogous access to God's presence through the Prayers, devotion, and actions even while in the world.[162]

The sixth step grows out of Surah *al-Kahf* (the Cave), a Qur'anic chapter cherished by those steeped in Muslim spirituality. Surah al-Kahf (18:60–82) describes Prophet Moses' encounter with a figure named Khidir.[163] He is a spiritual personality whose mission relates to the spiritual domain of existence. He is a man of wisdom who is blessed with knowledge of God and raised to a spiritual dimension of reality. Although the text is not clear, it appears that he is in *Mithal*—the realm of symbols, archetypes, and ideals. Gülen uses Nursi's exposition of five degrees of life that began with the account involving Khidir. The degrees of life are:

---

[161] Ünal, *The Qur'an with Annotated Interpretation*, pp. 1294–1295 summarized from Nursi's *Risale-i Nur Collection*, *The Words*, "The Thirty-first Word."

[162] The Prayer (*Salah*) is, for instance, said to be one of the supreme means for the goal of being near to God; it is the Ascension of the believer to the proximity of his or her Lord. It is reported that Muhammad said, "The closest a person comes to his Lord is when he prostrates in Prayer, so increase your supplication when you prostrate (and thus submit yourself wholly to God)." (See Muslim, Salah, 215; Abu Dawud, Salah, 152; Muslim, Iman, 33).

[163] See Ünal on Surah al-Kahf, notes 23–28 (pp. 617–620) and Surah al-Baqarah (2:154), note 102. (p. 165). Sometimes the name is rendered as Khadr.

1. Life now in this world (*dunya*) where we are limited by physical conditions;

2. Life in the realm-degree or station in which Khidir and Elijah exist. In that dimension they can be in different places at the same time and are free of regular human necessities such as needing food.

3. Life in the degree or station in which Jesus and Enoch abide. They are in the heavenly dimension in their human bodies, but they are not bound by human necessities. They have gained a refinement and luminosity like that of the stars and enjoy an angelic type of life.

4. Life of the martyrs. Passages such as Surah Al Imran (3:168–170) indicate that the martyrs exist in an intermediate dimension of a painless world-like joy and satisfaction. They are unaware that they are dead.

5. Life in the grave. The persons know they are dead and are waiting for the trumpet call of Resurrection.[164]

Note the presence of Jesus in a spiritual realm, most probably in *Mithal*, his luminosity and angelic way of life. His proximity to this earthly realm will be of eschatological importance. In the Qur'an, Jesus is the Messenger who received the Injil (Gospel) from God, taught the Wisdom of God to the Children of Israel, gathered the helpers (apostles) for God's cause and, by the leave of God, healed the blind and lepers, raised the dead, fed his followers with Divine providence (Surah Al Imran 3:45–51). Like others in the spiritual dimensions, Jesus is able to communicate with humans in the physical world and even appear to them.[165]

The seventh step leads to a further consideration of *Mithal*, the intermediate spiritual dimension between this visible world and the Unseen.[166] Mithal, just like other immaterial dimensions of existence, is essential to grasp the true nature of events, physical things, all beings,

---

[164] Nursi, *Risale-i Nur Collection*, *The Letters*, "First Letter," pp. 3–4.

[165] *Sahih Muslim*, Vol. 1, Book 1, Chapter 76, Item 325.

[166] See Gülen, *Essentials*, pp. 41–49. For Gülen's further exposition of Mithal from a Sufi perspective, see *Sufism*, Vol. 3, pp. 79–85. See also his brief discussion of

expressions of religion, and the spirit and souls and every human being. Indeed, Mithal is the realm of anologies, symbols, representations, archetypes, and forms of what will appear in our world within objects and faculties of specific things and particular persons. It is possible that archetypes and forms that are seen in Mithal may appear in this world not only as material bodies but also as analogous representations, ideologies or systems.[167] More specifically for the present, the immaterial world of Divine Laws and Commands (*'Alam al-Amr*), which is beyond the *'Alam al-Mithal*, is the dimension in which God has lodged the two forms of Divine Laws. One set is the Attribute of Divine Speech. It is manifested in this world as Divine Revelation (*Din*) and expressed through Law (*Shari'a*). The other Law is that of the Attributes of Will and Power. This law is expressed in what Gülen terms laws of nature and laws of life. He connected both Divine laws to the Judgment, the Hereafter, and existence in the present:

> God Almighty has two kinds of laws. One is the Shari'a, which comprises His laws issuing from His Attribute of Speech, governs humanity's religious life, and serves as the basis for reward or punishment, which are usually given in the Afterlife. The second is the Divine laws governing creation and life as a whole, which issue from His Attributes of Will and Power and are generally (but mistakenly) called the "laws of nature and life." Their reward or punishment for them is usually given in this world. For example, patience and perseverance are rewarded with success, while indolence brings privation. Industry brings wealth, and steadfastness victory.[168]

## THE THREE FACE-FACETS OF THIS WORLD

Turn now to this world, that is, Dunya. Gülen, in broad agreement with Nursi, wrote of Dunya having three faces, or facets. In summary, the three faces can be expressed as:

> The first face is turned toward the transient, materialistic world, in which people seek the satisfaction of their bodily (animalistic) desires.

---

*'Alam Malakut*, in "Realm of Transcendental Manifestation of Divine Commands," *Sufism*, Vol. 3, pp. 93–96.

[167] Gülen, *Essentials*, pp. 61–63.

[168] Ibid, pp. 250–251.

The second face is turned to the "arable field" of the Hereafter, in which a person's seeds of action are sown and, at the proper time, harvested in the Hereafter. The third "face" is the area in which the Beautiful Names of God are manifested.[169]

Throughout the discussion, Gülen emphasizes the purposefulness of God in creating the existence so that all events, structures, dimensions, things and persons are aimed toward consummation in *al-Akhira*—the Hereafter. In other words, the beginning forecasts the final end, which in turn becomes the ultimate new beginning of the everlasting Hereafter of Paradise and Hell. The three faces or facets of the world are reflected in the faces and orientation of human beings in terms of body, soul, and spirit.

The first face-facet for consideration is the physical, material, and visible world. It is the facet that deals with human bodily desires and emotions. God has so arranged humanity so that we are to satisfy our physical and emotional needs in lawful ways. How we seek and gain that satisfaction is a matter of our free will. God has created a good world that has all the capacities to feed, clothe, and shelter individuals and communities within the framework of compassion, mercy, and justice. To be sure, Gülen advocates bringing carnal soul under control and seeking the middle way between the extremes of denial and surfeit. Since such creaturely needs are natural and good, humans are to help one another in meeting those needs. Implicit is the ability and responsibility of persons to create those social and educational structures that will meet those needs. Individuals who engage in sharing with others discipline themselves in how they live while others are in want so that they are modest in what they take for themselves.

The second facet-face of the world is directed toward the Hereafter. The operative themes are seeds-growth—Dunya as the arable field in which the seeds are planted, and human free will—all comprehended in the Divine Plan that culminates in the harvest of those seeds in

---

[169] Ibid, *Sufism*, Vol. 1, p. xiii, footnote 3. The footnote was added by the translator, Ali Ünal. In *Reflections on the Qur'an*, Gülen made this world the third face, p. 241. Ünal abridged Nursi's passage in *Resurrection and the Afterlife*, p. 40. It is based on Said Nursi's *Risale-i Nur Collection*, *The Words*, Twenty-fourth Word, p. 311.

the Hereafter. The following part of a verse in Surah al-Baqarah concerns God's foreshadowing the joyful surprise of those who will be granted eternal life in Paradise. When they enter the Garden and eat of the delicious fruits therein, they will exclaim:

> "This is what we were provided before." They [the fruits] are given to them [the persons admitted to the Garden] in resemblance (to what was given to them in the world). (2:25)

Gülen commented on the verse under discussion as follows:

> We cannot grasp the relationship between our actions in the world and the results that they will give in the Hereafter. In the world, we approach and consider everything within the framework of cause and effect; hence we cannot always be saved from the influence of cause-and-effect relation in our thoughts and analyses.... The reality of the matter will be manifested and understood with all aspects of the Hereafter. As a result, the believers who performed good deeds in this world will announce, "These are what we were provided with in the world or some time ago while in Paradise" whenever the bounties of Paradise are bestowed on them. Each bounty given in Paradise is either the otherworldly reward of a good deed done in the world or its otherworldly form, or it is the harvest of the deeds sowed as deeds here. Therefore, there is an internal or essential similarity between the worldly bounties and their counterparts in the Hereafter....For the worldly bounties are the seeds of Divine Wisdom while eternal bounties are the fruits of Divine Power. Also, the former are temporary and blurred while the latter are permanently purified and limpid.[170]

Gülen's depiction of Dunya as a field and farm that is to be cultivated, planted, and cared for occasioned some of his reflections on angels and rewards that fed directly into his eschatology. Humans are an index and third book of existence. That entails each human having within herself and himself the entire range of what God has created, and therefore, externally and internally humans contain the linkages to the heavenly and material dimensions. Through our mental and spiritual faculties, we share in the angelic and spiritual worlds, and through

---

[170] Ibid, *Reflections on the Qur'an*, portions from pp. 12–14.

our physical-bodily faculties, we share in the realm of animals and plants. The latter is manifested in our need for nurture, food, shelter, guidance, and so on. Through the former, we have a yearning for eternity, an intuitive longing to return to the Creator who fashioned us and with Whom we are in a covenantal relationship. We are distinguished, however, by the Divine gift of free will and the ability to rise from our current stations to positions even above the angels. The great proviso is that we keep the covenant that enjoins belief and good works. The warning-alternative to keeping the covenant is that evil deeds are the seeds that will be harvested in terms of condemnation and punishments in the Hereafter. The second facet-face orients the depictions of the Names and reflections so that they beam toward the Hereafter and illuminate the present world with the eschatological importance of human devotion and actions in Dunya.

The third face-facet builds on the understanding that everything in all the worlds, and specifically in our world, is a polished mirror of the All-Beautiful Names of God. As such, every part of it reflects and shines forth the Names and Divine Attributes to every other creature and feature in Dunya, including to humans – and humans are the most highly polished mirror in the world. The expression "mirror" has a double aspect. On the one hand, the Light from God shines into all the worlds and onto the faces-facets of Dunya so that everything in the worlds reflects the Light of the One-Only God. On the other hand, the creatures are projectors from which the Light shines into, through, and among the beings and physical entities of the worlds. As Gülen observed, God has planted the Divine Names into the worlds, and especially within humans. For God manifests all of His Names through humanity.[171] Further, Gülen holds:

> *Each person is a miniature universe, a fruit of the tree of creation or the universe, and a seed of this world, for each of us contains samples of most living species.* It is as if each person were a drop distilled from the universe, having the most subtle and sensitive balance. To create such a living being and to be its Lord requires having total control of the universe.

---

[171] Ibid, *Essentials,* p. 75.

Given this, we understand that the following things represent stamps unique to the Creator of all things, the All-Majestic Lord of the universe making a honeybee a small index of most things; inscribing most of the universe's features in humans; including the program for a fig tree's life cycle in a tiny fig seed; exhibiting the works of all Divine Names manifested throughout the universe in the human heart; and recording in our memory, located in a lentil-sized place, enough information to fill a library, as well as a detailed index of all events in the universe.[172]

All three faces-facets point from the Beginning to the End of the worlds, the Judgment, and the opening of the Hereafter. And all that exists has been made to fulfill God's Plan for humanity. Gülen rejoices in the beauty and harmony in God's Book of the Universe:

Everything that exists, whether an individual or a species, has a collective identity and performs a unique, universal function. Each flower displays a superlative design and symmetry and recites, in the tongue of its being, the Names of the Creator manifested on it. The entire Earth performs a universal glorification as though it were a single flower. The vast "ocean" of the heavens praises and glorifies the Majestic Maker of the universe through its suns, moons, and stars. Even inert material bodies, although outwardly inanimate and unconscious, perform a vital function in praising God.[173]

From the Book of the Universe that has issued from God's Divine Attribute of Will and Power, we listen to that which proceeds from God's Divine Will of Speech, the Qur'an.

## B. THE WORLDS' BEGINNING: THE BOOK OF DIVINE SPEECH

*Iqra'* is a command to *read* the signs the Creator placed in creation so that we can understand something of His Mercy, Wisdom, and Power. It is a command to learn, through experience and understanding, the meaning of His creation. Moreover, it is an infallible assurance that the creation can be read, that it is *intelligible*. The better we learn to read it, the better we grasp that the created

---

[172] Ibid, p. 11. See also *Sufism*, Vol. 3, p. 289.
[173] Ibid, p. 64.

world is a single universe whose beauty and harmony reflect the Supreme Preserved Tablet (85:21) upon which, by the Divine decree, all things are inscribed.

> Every created thing resembles a pen that records its actions. But only humanity can read what is written. That is why the Qur'an tells us to "read" instead of to "behold." We are to know the creation, not just to experience it, as is the case with all other creations.[174]

The Qur'an and the Book of the Universe belong together for the Qur'an interprets the Book of the Universe. Gülen extols the matchless quality and inimitability of the Qur'an in agreement with other Muslim thinkers. In accord with them, he holds that the Qur'an has a special place in the Supreme Preserved Tablet (*al-Lawhu'l-Mahfuz*). It was in the Preserved Tablet until God sent it down to the heaven above the earth on the Night of Power. From there, Gabriel brought it to begin the Revelation to Muhammad.[175] Gülen enumerated four major themes in the Qur'an:

1. God's existence and His absolute Unity and One-ness,
2. Resurrection and the eternal life of the Hereafter,
3. The mission, or office, of Prophethood,
4. Justice.

These themes are woven throughout the revealed book of the Qur'an and the created Book of the Universe.[176] The two Books are in total agreement, for they have the same Author, and both Books are directed to the Resurrection and the Hereafter. Gülen extended the affirmation of the Books' harmony and Divine authorship to insist that the sciences originate in the Beautiful Names:

> The Qur'an is not a science textbook that has to expound upon cosmological or scientific matters; rather, it is the eternal interpretation of the Book of the Universe and the interpreter of all natural and other sciences. It comments upon the visible and invisible worlds and discloses the spiritual treasures of the Divine Beautiful Names in the heavens and the Earth. The Qur'an is the key lead-

---

[174] Ibid, *Questions and Answers*, Vol. 1, p. 95.
[175] Ibid, *Reflections on the Qur'an*, p. 293. Note also Surah al-Qadr (97).
[176] Ibid, *Essentials*, p. 158.

ing to an understanding of the hidden realities behind events taking place in nature and human life and is the tongue of the hidden
worlds in the manifest world.[177]

Gülen is convinced that the Qur'an is the Book of Divine Truth
containing neither errors nor contradictions. Although he does not
use the expression, Gülen rejects the principle of the "Double Truth."
The basic position proposed by Ahmad ibn Rushd (known in the West
as Averroes, 1126–1198) occasioned significant controversies and con-
demnations among Muslims and Christians in the 13th century. Nevertheless, it developed into a major position in the Western Enlight-
enment and consequent secularism.[178] The Western post–Enlighten-
ment embraced the core views of the Double Truth and emphasized
only as true what could be ascertained based on observations made by
"objective" witnesses and which was quantifiable and duplicable. Religion–Revelation is relegated thereby to subjective, emotional, psycho-
logical, and individualistic experiences. Gülen maintains that among
the pernicious effects of the Western approach and its influences on
Muslims has been to split science and religion into separate and hos-
tile camps so that universal ethics and spiritual values are inadequately
considered or virtually eliminated from serious public discourse and
education. As a result, Western societies have lapsed into materialism,
exploitation of the vulnerable and the environment, and pragmatic
atheism. Clearly, such results are diametrically opposed to the Qur'an
and Islamic principles, and those who operate on those principles will
be held accountable on the Last Day.[179]

Gülen's positive evaluation of the truths and the Divine One Who is
Truth is clear and consistent. God is (the Ultimate) Truth (*al-Haqq*), so:

---

[177] Ibid, p. 238.

[178] Averroes held that there was one truth that could be known separately by philosophy–human reason and religion–revelation. A number of his alleged and actual
propositions were condemned by the Bishop of Paris in 1277. Siger of Brabant
(died ca. 1280) expanded the view into holding that there are two separate truths.
The truths of philosophy–reason dealt with factual or hard truths. That left religion
with improvable claims based on unscientific supernatural assertions.

[179] See, for example, *Essentials*, p. 23; *Questions and Answers*, Vol. 2, pp. 117–123;
*Toward a Global Civilization of Love and Tolerance*, pp. 193–196.

All truths...that are either exoteric or esoteric, material or spiritual, peripheral or central, are each a theophany of the divine name the Truth revealing itself in various wavelengths. Each is a shade or reflection from the disclosure, permanence, and existence of this name in the realms in which it operates (*af'al*) and produces works (*asar*). The Truth may sometimes relate to the imagination and at other times to what is apparent; but what we behold and comprehend beyond this noble name is the reconciliation between the mind and the eyes, the subjective and the objective, and between knowledge and the known. Yes, the Truth is a title of the agreement between these phenomena, and it ultimately alludes to the "self existent One."[180]

Based on the unity and union of all truths in the One Who is the Ultimate Truth, Gülen sees the Qur'an as the guide to understanding science and its results:

The Qur'an considers creation only for the sake of knowing its Creator; science considers creation only for its own sake. The Qur'an addresses humanity; science addresses only those who specialize in it. Since the Qur'an uses creation as evidence and proof to guide us, its evidence must be easily understandable to all of us non-specialists. Guidance requires that relatively unimportant things should be touched on briefly, while subtle points should be discussed as completely as possible through parables and comparisons.

Guidance should not change what is obvious, so that people are not confused. If it did, how could we derive any benefit?

Like everything else, science has its source in one of God Almighty's Beautiful Names. The Name All-Healing shines on medicine; geometry and engineering depend on the Names All-Just, All-Shaping, and All-Harmonizing; and philosophy reflects the Name All-Wise....[T]he Creator refers in the Qur'an to everything that He has allowed us to learn and use for our material and spiritual progress.[181]

The acceptance of science and other disciplines as affirmed by God in the Qur'an is the basis for Hizmet's emphasis on education,

---

[180] "Truth and Rights and More," in *Fountain Magazine*, issue 82, July–August, 2011.
[181] Gülen, *Essentials*, p. 239.

social services, and health care.[182] Gülen holds that "[t]he Qur'an's primary aims are to make God Almighty known, to open the way to faith and worship, and to organize our individual and social life so that we may obtain perfect happiness in both worlds."[183] The truths from al-Haqq also include those that are the foundation for all human rights and relationships. He wrote that those who seek to know, to be guided by, and to do God's will consider all rights as manifestations of the Beautiful Divine Name of the Truth.[184] The Qur'an is that speech and document that contains the knowledge and guidance for the Umma and all humanity.

## INTERPRETATIVE MATTERS

> It is He Who has sent down on you this (glorious) Book, wherein are verses absolutely explicit and firm: they are the core of the Book, others being allegorical. Those in whose hearts is swerving pursue what is allegorical in it, seeking (to cause) dissension, and seeking to make it open to arbitrary interpretation, although none knows its interpretation save God. And those firmly rooted in knowledge say: "We believe in it (in the entirety of its verses, both explicit and allegorical); all is from our Lord"; yet none derives admonition except the people of discernment. (Surah *Al Imran* [Family of Imran] 3:7)

The Qur'an invites interpretation. Ali Ünal noted regarding the verse above that there are two types of *ayat*, or verses. While all Qur'anic words and verses are spoken by God and therefore are "firm and perfect," *Muhkam* verses are the verses that are "not open to any ambiguity or equivocation." These verses are the core of the Qur'an. They include the essentials of the faith, warnings, instructions about worship, ethics, duties, and prohibitions. The *Mutashabih* verses have

---

[182] As a result, Gülen joins others who reject Darwinian-style evolutionary positions in which species evolve from one another through natural selection and chance. He draws ethical and theological implications from the differences between Darwinian-style evolution and the Qur'anic position of God's intelligent design and Plan for the whole of existence. In other areas of scientific endeavors, Gülen encourages research and education. See, for example, *Essentials*, pp. 16–17.

[183] Gülen, *Essentials*, p. 239.

[184] "Truth and Rights and More," in *Fountain Magazine*, issue 82, July–August, 2011.

more than one meaning because "time progresses, conditions change, human information increases, and there are as many levels of understanding as the number of human beings, thus addressing all humanity from the time of its revelation to the Day of Resurrection." These passages seek to explain to humanity God's will through "metaphors, similes, personifications, and parables." There are more *Mutashabih* than *Muhkam* verses. Ünal continued, "Since the allegorical verses have multiple meanings, the interpreters of the Qur'an may be able to discover one or more of those meanings. Each of their discoveries can be regarded as being true, provided it is in conformity with the *Muhkam* verses and the essentials of Islam, and the rules of the science of interpretation." Clearly, only God knows their full meanings.[185]

The distinction between the *Muhkam* and *Mutashabih* passages is vitally important in understanding the Qur'an. Gülen stands solidly within the mainstream of Islamic understandings of the Qur'an as the direct speech of God. For him, the Qur'an is a universal book in two senses. First, it is intended for and applicable to all creation, especially for humans and jinn. In another sense, it is universal in terms of time: its truths and purposes are not bound to any one society or era. Even those passages that cite particular historical events such as the battle of Badr or Moses' confrontations with Pharaoh contain within them messages for the umma and for all persons in every time until the Final Day. Gülen, therefore, rejects attempts to reduce the Qur'an to a network of symbols as well as limiting any passage to its historical revelatory occasion. The Qur'an's God-willed purposes are clear, and those purposes involve ever-deepening understandings of the profound wisdom it contains.

Gülen's interpretational procedures include al-Ghazzali's treatises on the *Ninety-Nine Beautiful Names of God* and *Niche of Lights* as well as Nursi's *Words*.[186] Al-Ghazzali went beyond the literal meanings and comparisons of the reports contained in several Hadiths in order to understand the many meanings and numbers of the Divine Names.

---

[185] Ünal, *The Qur'an with Annotated Interpretation*, p. 124, note 2.
[186] See especially Nursi, *Risale-i Nur*, *The Words*, "The Twenty-fifth Word," pp. 390–478. The whole extensive portion his thinking and applications to some Qur'anic passages.

His Sufi-based probing of the "Light Ayah" (Surah *an-Nur* [The Light]
24:35) disclosed layers of meanings and distinctions beneath the surface of the expressions of the light, niche, and lamp. Nursi also argued
against restricting the Qur'anic passages and Hadith statements to literalistic applications for all times as well as to limiting their applications to the Messenger's times. He argued that the Messenger and his
community recognized that the Revelation applied to all times through
adaptation to subsequent situations and contexts but that later believers comprehended the passages and statements in a fixed and literal
manner. That development, Nursi felt, led to misunderstandings and
dissension, especially about life in this world, the destruction of the
world, and the existence in the Hereafter. Consequently, Nursi advocated, on the one hand, understanding the Qur'an as God's Speech
expressed in parables and stories that uneducated persons could grasp
readily for guidance in their daily lives. On the other hand, he proposed
that persons who were more advanced intellectually and spiritually
could be open, under God's guidance, to deeper meanings. Gülen, as
we will see in Chapter Four, adapted these points in his writing.

The following passage may be taken as the core of Gülen's interpretative perspective:

> *According to its nature and significance, worth and place in existence,*
> *everything has its own place in the Qur'an.* The Qur'an contains
> everything, but not to the same degree. It pursues four purposes:
> to prove the existence and Unity of God, Prophethood, bodily res-
> urrection, and worship of God and justice.
>
> To realize its purposes, the Qur'an draws our attention to God's
> acts in the universe, His matchless art displayed through creation,
> the manifestations of His Names and Attributes, and the perfect
> order and harmony seen in existence. It mentions certain historical
> events, and establishes the rules of personal and social good conduct
> and morality, as well as the principles of a happy, harmonious social
> life. In addition, it explains how to worship and please our Creator,
> gives us some information about the next life, and tells us how to
> gain eternal happiness and be saved from eternal punishment.
>
> Everything is contained in the Qur'an, but at different levels.
> Therefore, not everything is readily apparent. The Qur'an's main
> duty is to teach about God's perfection, essential qualities, and

acts, as well as our duties, status, and how to serve Him. Thus, it contains them as seeds or nuclei, summaries, principles, or signs that are explicit or implicit, allusive or vague, or suggestive. Each occasion has its own form, and is presented in the best way for making each Qur'anic purpose known according to the existing requirements and context.

Human progress in science and industry has brought about such scientific and technological wonders as airplanes, electricity, motorized transport, and radio and telecommunication, all of which have become basic and essential for our modern, materialistic civilization. The Qur'an has not ignored them and points to them in two ways: The first is ...by way of the Prophets' miracles. The second concerns certain historical events. In other words, the wonders of human civilization only merit a passing reference, an implicit reference, or an allusion in the Qur'an.[187]

In the context of the foregoing statements, the passage offers five affirmations and positions that recur in Gülen's Qur'an–based views of the worlds' beginnings, endings, and new beginning:

1. The Qur'an contains everything that is required for everything and every being in their present worlds and the world to come;

2. The Qur'an's four purposes offer an agenda for human belief and action. The absolutely foundational principle is to state, show, and inculcate faith in and obedience to the One-Only God. That principle leads to God's revelations through the Prophets directly and through the Scriptures revealed through them implicitly in order to call and challenge humans to be open to God's will. The principle of the Oneness and absolute Unity of God (*Tawhid*) and the gracious revelations through the Prophets disclose to humans the certainty of their bodily resurrections at the termination of the present world and the opening of the new dimension of the Hereafter. Having established the existence and sovereignty of God, the revelations of God's will through the Prophets, and the God–ordained Day of Judgment, the Qur'an prescribes the proper forms and heartfelt intentions of worship and the ways in which humans are to establish and carry out their caliphate, or vicegerency, in this world with justice.

---

[187] Gülen, *Essentials*, p. 230.

3. In order to disclose its message to humans, the Qur'an address-es individuals and communities in ways that are understandable and at different levels of human development, in a variety of cultural con-texts, and in all times. Those disclosures may be likened to seeds plant-ed into Qur'an which will germinate and grow in human understand-ing over time. They are the nuclei around which other passages and the Prophet Muhammad's Sunnah, or Practice, will gather to make the messages clearer or summarize points mentioned in more diffuse pas-sages. They are the principles that will inform later specific interpreta-tions and understandings and offer signs pointing to future realizations. All or any of these may be explicit or implicit in the Qur'anic texts.

4. The entire creation testifies to what God makes known through His numerous Names as well as His Attributes of Will and Power.

5. Through its selective use of historical events, instructions, and exhortations, the Qur'an provides a sound basis for personal morality and just, compassionate societies, thereby informing humans about the Hereafter and how they may gain eternal joy and avoid everlasting dam-nation. The Qur'an's main duty is to teach about God's perfection, qual-ities, and actions as well as to show humans their duties and ways to serve God. The Qur'an invites interpretation within the parameters of Islam's teachings and main articles of faith, Muhammad's practice, and those factors which are contained in Gülen's four purposes. He pro-vides a summarizing statement on the primary purposes of the Qur'an that contains an important metaphor, the rosebud.

> The Qur'an's primary aims are to make God Almighty known, to
> open the way to faith and worship, and to organize our individual
> and social life so that we may attain perfect happiness in both worlds.
> To achieve this aim, it refers to things and events, as well as scien-
> tific facts, in proportion to their importance. Thus the Qur'an pro-
> vides detailed explanations of the articles of faith, the fundamentals
> of religion, the foundations of human life, and essentials of wor-
> ship, but only hints at other relatively less significant things. The
> meaning of a verse may be compared to a rosebud: it is hidden by
> successive layers of petals. A new meaning is perceived as each petal

unfolds, and people discover one of those meanings according to their capacity and are satisfied with it.[188]

The image of the unfolding rosebud is an apt illustration that provides a perspective for Gülen's views on the worlds' endings. As a preview of Chapter Four, Gülen ventured that the Qur'an contains hints about technological advances that have unfolded across the centuries such air travel, the healing of illnesses, transmission of pictures and objects instantly through the universe, discoveries of black holes in galaxies, and so on. These and other developments will, he suggests, become realities in a coming age of knowledge and information that will be characterized by faith and belief.[189] The Qur'an gives both guidance for life in the present and is guidance to the Hereafter:

> The Qur'an is like the sun shining in the spiritual and intellectual sky of Islam. It is the sacred map of the next world; the expounder of the Divine Attributes, Names, and acts; and the educator of humanity that guides us to truth and virtue. It is a book of law and wisdom, worship and prayer, Divine commands and prohibitions. Fully satisfying our spiritual and intellectual needs, it leaves no theological, social, economic, political, or even scientific issue unaddressed, whether in brief or in detail, directly or through allusion or symbols.[190]

The Qur'an, then, covers all aspects of life, giving guidance, encouragement, and warnings. It makes clear that life in this transient world is a rehearsal for the other world, thereby underscoring the point that after the teaching and acceptance of the Oneness of God, the next most important step is for humans to know, accept, and live in anticipation of the Resurrection and Hereafter.[191] The message attested to by the Prophets and Messengers follows from faith in the Oneness and Unity of God to belief in bodily Resurrection and the following Judgment before the Divine Court. Since the Day (of Judgment) is certain, all humans are responsible for their actions in the present, thereby making

---

[188] Ibid, p. 239.
[189] Ibid, pp. 239–240.
[190] Ibid, p. 238.
[191] Ibid, *Toward a Civilization of Love and Tolerance*, p. 63.

justice a key Qur'anic theme. The Qur'an directs humans to look to the future while gaining insights, instructions, and incentives to live now according to God's will. And that injunction moves us to hear our guide again as we turn to the Book of Humanity:

## C. THE WORLDS' BEGINNING: THE BOOK OF HUMANITY

> Humanity, with all of its attributes, is a creation that is difficult to understand. As with all the realms, the essence of all created things is present in humans, and in a way, with their characteristics, in one respect it is possible to understand existence by knowing humanity, while, in another respect, knowing humanity is possible by understanding existence. In truth, understanding humanity is the principle mission of humanity, since humanity is also the window that opens on understanding the Creator. For this reason, the first and foremost duty of human beings is to discover and know themselves and then to turn their gaze toward their Lord with the lens of their enlightened nature.[192]

Gülen's statement that the chief mission for humans is to understand humanity fits well into his understanding of humanity as a book that is to be read in light of the Books of the Universe and the Qur'an. Such a reading is an invitation and command to worship God and get on the Straight Path that leads to the Hereafter:

> As it is an obligation to read, understand, obey and submit to the Word of God, which comes from His divine attribute of Speech, so it is an indispensable essential to know and understand God in the entirety of things and events, which He planned by His Knowledge and created by His Divine Will and Power, and then to seek for and confirm conformity and congruity in all things and events. The Qur'an came also from God's attribute of Speech; it is the soul of all existence and the sole source of happiness. The book of the universe is the body of this truth and a very important dynamic of this world directly and of the other world indirectly with respect to the various branches of science it includes and represents. That is why understanding of and transferring these two books into practice and organizing the whole of life in accordance with them

---

[192] Ibid, p. 234.

merits reward; and neglecting, ignoring, and even being unable to interpret and apply them to life merits punishment.[193]

Indeed, "[e]ach person is a miniature universe, a fruit of the tree of creation or the universe, and a seed of this world, for each of us contains samples of most living species." We are drops distilled from the universe. The works of all the Divine Names are in the human heart.[194] Continuing the metaphor of a book, humans are the index to the Book of the Universe, for we are part of that universe, and the universe was created for the sake of humanity. As the universe is a mirror of the Names of God, humans are made to be the most highly polished mirror shining in creation, returning the light of love to the Creator and reflecting that love to fellow humans and the rest of the world.[195] As humans look into and examine themselves, they ought to discern that they are part of the creation's system of mirrors and are responsible for their roles to return the love-light to God and to manifest it in this world through enacting the Beautiful Names of God that God has planted within each person.

Gülen already established that God created the worlds out of love and has structured love within all aspects of the worlds. One of God's Names is the Sultan, the Sovereign ruler. He returned to the idea of the Sultan, now calling it love and the human heart its rightful throne. Gülen looks forward to the time when the sultan will ascend to its throne, that is, when all rancor, ignorance, and cruelty will end so that love can reign among humans and through humans in all creation.[196] He anticipates that time will come before the final ending of the present worlds.

The cosmological arrangement described earlier is an important component for humans in order to understand their place in God's Plan and to respond so that they realize that Above and Below are bound to

---

[193] Ibid, *Statue of Our Souls*, p. 37.
[194] Ibid, *Essentials*, p. 11.
[195] Ibid, *Toward a Civilization of Love and Tolerance*, p. 116.
[196] Ibid, p. 13.

each other as they move from beginning to ending. For our purposes, I begin with the dimension called *'Alam al-Mithal*—the world of the symbols or ideal, immaterial forms, or analogies, of things.[197]

*Mithal*, one of the immaterial worlds beyond our time and space-bound visible world, is essential for spiritual life. It is the intermediate realm in between this visible realm and the realm of the Unseen (*'Alam al-Ghayb*) in which is the World of Spirits (*'Alam al-Arwah*). It is this World of Spirits that human spirits originate and reside before descending into bodies in our world. The spirit (*ar-Ruh*) is breathed into humans by God out of God's own Spirit (Surah al-Hijr 15:29). It is the "essence of human existence and nature" that makes possible the perfection of humanity in the person's journey to God.[198] Gülen holds that the body is a "mechanism for the spirit to exercise its control

---

[197] The *'Alam al-Mithal*—the World of Analogies, Representations or Ideal Forms, is one of the spiritual worlds. These worlds, or realms, (called *al-'Alamiyn* in Arabic), ought to be thought of as dimensions rather than distinct locations: the Divine truths or realities manifested in material forms in this world are manifested in other worlds, or realms, in the forms peculiar to each. Gülen defines the *'Alam al-Mithal*—the World of Representations or Ideal Forms, as "the world where the immaterial forms or models belonging to the archetypes [*al-A'yanu'th-Thabita*] are reflected. The forms or reflections in this realm are termed 'the ideal or reflected forms'." Gülen further states that "[s]ome saints can at times observe the [future] states of the archetypes [that will be brought into the time and space-bound world of existence] plainly or in the form of symbols as in dreams…The information and observations concerning the archetypes are usually presented to God's specially chosen, purified servants in the forms of 'ideal' tablets. These tablets are manifested either identically with their future, corporeal existential forms, or in symbols according to their meaning and contents. [Such] symbolic representations require interpretation, like dreams…. [For instance, in dreams] knowledge appears in the form of or is represented by milk, and Islam is symbolized by a splendid container; the Qur'an, as honey or an orange; and the feeling of enmity, as snakes or vermin."
Some Sufis see this realm as "the intermediate realm between this world and the Hereafter, and between matter and spirit, and the realm of immaterial sacred spirits…It is a mysterious corridor between the physical and metaphysical worlds, a veil between two different dimensions,…a realm where meanings or abstract truths begin to be clothed in worldly existence." Some define this intermediate realm "as the point where the world of spirits and abstract meanings meets with the corporeal world…. It is like a waiting lodge that resembles both the Unseen and the corporeal realms at the point where the world and the Hereafter meet." See *Sufism*, Vol. 3, pp. 82–85.
[198] Gülen, *Sufism*, Vol. 3, p. 172.

over, or an instrument with which it voices its feelings" while not being a part of, attached to, or contained by the body.[199] He continued,

> But if it is made subservient to the body, then whatever a person does, says, and thinks becomes like a growl or a snarl.... The spirit is a subtle, refined being that resembles the angels. It commands all the physical and immaterial senses and faculties of a person.... It is the most subtle, purest, and refined of creatures. It is a mirror for the reflection of the Divine Attributes and Names, one that is able to penetrate the densest of things. It reminds us of the Divine Being.[200]

*An-Nafs*, the soul, is between the body and the spirit:

> [It] is a substance that is essentially free of matter but which is in close connection with it in its acts and functions; it is the origin or essence of something or its "self."... [The] soul is the origin or center of certain states or faculties such as lust, anger, ill will, grudge, hatred, and irritation, and it is a transformable, re-formable, and refineable mechanism connected to human corporeality. It is through this connection that humans receive, recognize, and distinguish their outer and inner sense perceptions and go beyond the corporeal realm into metaphysical worlds. It is again through this connection that any state, experience, or gift that occurs in the spirit leaves its imprint on the body and provokes it to move in a certain direction.[201]

The soul is capable of being refined toward becoming what Sufis term, based on Surah al-Fajr 89:27–28, *"the soul at rest"* from the negative drives and attachments it experiences in its relationships with the body and the world. The soul covenants to be obedient to the One-Only God in the World of Spirits. To be sure, when in this world the soul longs to be free from its forbidden carnal desires and will be judged in the Hereafter on its deeds and faithfulness to that covenant. Yet this material world (*dunya*) is not evil. It is a testing ground, a veil over the worlds that are eternal and the worlds that are to come according

---

[199] Ibid, p. 174.
[200] Ibid, p. 174.
[201] Ibid, p. 216.

to the Plan that is focused on humanity and directed toward the Day of Judgment and the Hereafter.

Gülen emphasizes Islam's conviction that God's Plan for all the worlds will culminate on the Last Day and extend into the eternal Hereafter. The spiritual beings in the heavenly realms are aware of the Divine Plan as much as God informs them of the Plan and about God's ways to fulfill it. His will is carried out immediately and directly in those spiritual dimensions, for God is the Source of all that exists; whatever happens in any world happens because God wills it to occur. While in the spiritual realms God commands directly and the responses are immediate, the situation in this visible world is different as God's acts in our visible world are veiled through networks of causes and effects. Humans perceive events such as earthquakes, floods, diseases, and death as effects caused by "natural laws" when actually both causes and effects manifest God's purposeful will in action. Gülen provides at least six explanations for God's use of the veils of causes and effects in this world:

1. to prevent persons from verging into blasphemy lest they blame God for suffering and loss;

2. to test humans as to the ways in which they will use their free will toward either good or evil so that based on humans' choices, God will render just judgments on the Last Day;

3. to aid humans to "observe and study the patterns in phenomena" so as to discern the goodness in creation;

4. to enable humans to endure some of the glory of God's Names and Attributes gradually without being "lost in those manifestations" or being overcome by the Divine transcendence; and

5. to drive humans to repentance so that "their sins might be forgiven or so that we will be promoted to higher spiritual ranks."[202]

The sixth reason for the veils derives from an altruistic incentive to action based on human free will and contributes directly to Gülen's eschatological vision for the present world:

---

[202] Based on Gülen's *Essentials*, pp. 28, 55, 101 and 115–116, and Ünal, *The Qur'an with Annotated Interpretation*, Surah18:26, note 13, pp. 607–608.

[Hardship, illness, and calamity] help us appreciate God's blessings, express our gratitude, and encourage the rich and healthy to help the poor and the sick. Those who never experience hunger cannot fully appreciate the conditions of the hungry. Nor can anyone who has not been sick be aware of what sick people live through. So, hardship, illness and calamity may establish closer relations between different groups or classes of people.

Calamity and suffering increase our resistance to hardships of life and train us to persevere and endure. They also separate the strong and sincere supporters of a cause from those who are supporters out of convenience or some other personal (and therefore inappropriate) reason.[203]

Although this world may be described as an "arena of trial" and a "realm of trouble," it also is the place "where we seek to acquire the state appropriate for the other life" for "in this world we sow the seeds that will be harvested in the Hereafter."[204] This world is always God's creation, and God "never wills evil for His creatures."[205] Indeed, "in absolute terms, every event and phenomenon is good and beautiful in itself and in its consequences. Whatever God does or decrees is good, beautiful, and just."[206] Those who give themselves to faith, worship, and the quest to know and serve God will be enabled to see through the veils to visionary awareness of God's wisdom and mercy.

One result of Gülen's use of the image of the veils is to aver that since both science and religion deal with causes and effects, they are not antithetical but have the same source (God) and the same goal (to fulfill God's will). In the Hereafter, there will be no need for veils because God's will shall be done directly, immediately, and completely. The Hereafter will be the realm of Divine Power exercised justly toward the unrighteous and compassionately toward the righteous.

Gülen, as might be expected on the basis of the Qur'anic designation of humans as God's *caliph*s, or representatives on earth, holds that humans are the highest of all creatures, including the angels, as

---

[203] Gülen, *Essentials*, p. 116.

[204] Ibid, p. 112–113.

[205] Ibid, p. 101.

[206] Ibid, p. 28.

the last and highest link on the chain of existence, the "final and most comprehensive fruit" on the tree of creation.[207] Even further, since the angels do not have free will and since God bade all spiritual beings to prostrate themselves before him, Adam, the representative of all subsequent humans, is destined by God to have a higher rank or station than the angels and the obedient jinn. Adam had been instructed by God to know the names of the angels, all creatures, his own descendants throughout time, and the Beautiful Names of God. Such wisdom-knowledge is transmitted to Adam's posterity so that they will grow and be educated in those names from their ancient father to the Last Day. In between those times, God will send Prophets and Messengers culminating in the Qur'an and Muhammad to be the sources and leaders of that wisdom, revealing it in the changing circumstances of life in this world. Only humans are given by God the ability either to change their rank up toward fuller knowledge of, devotion to, and obedience to God culminating in Paradise or to descend into disobedience, deceptions, destruction, and Hell. God offers humans the prospect of being higher than the angels, of being closer to God than anything or anyone else.[208] Indeed, Muhammad's Ascension into the presence of God was a preview of the destination for those humans admitted into the Hereafter's everlasting blessedness. Humans, as individuals and in concert, are called on by the structures of creation, Prophets and Messengers, Holy Scriptures, and most fully by the Qur'an and Muhammad to see, obey, and carry out God's will in this world. Moreover, they will be held accountable in the Judgment for their intentions, faithfulness, and efforts.

Humans, unlike many other animals, require time to grow physically and spiritually. Beyond the care necessary for a person to develop biologically and physically, the person needs education, guidance, discipline, and encouragement to develop intellectually, morally, and spiritually. We have already noted the spiritual-educational-enlightening roles of the creation, Prophets, Messengers, and Scriptures. Quite

---

[207] Ibid, p. 5.
[208] Ibid, pp. 67–68, 75.

Islamically, Gülen also cites the roles of angels. Part of Gülen's thinking about angels includes his description of some ranks of angels in the form of shepherds and farmers who are appointed to oversee the animals and plants, translating their praises of their Creator into the great chorus of worship of the One-Only God.[209] Gülen transitioned from the roles of such angels to the image of the world as a great palace with four classes of laborers. In the present world, the first group consists of the angels and spiritual beings whose reward is the joy of serving and worshiping God. Inanimate things and plants receive no reward or wages, and animals serving God unconsciously and receiving food as their compensation are the second and third type of laborers. Human beings, the fourth classification of workers, receive their wages in this world and in the Hereafter.[210]

As noted earlier in the explication of the three faces-facets of this world, the first facet-face considered is this world and human life in the present. Dunya is the realm of impermanence even before the Last Day. While it is marked by change, risk, decay, and the temporary dissolution of the bonds between the human spirit-soul and body at death, it is also God's creation. This world (*dunya*) is the dimension of testing by God and the challenge of being deceived by Satan. Nevertheless, Dunya is also the dimension in which its animate and inanimate creatures reflect the Divine Names and testify to the existence, Will, and Plan of the One-Only God:

> (This is) the Book being sent down in parts from God, the All-Glorious with irresistible might, the All-Wise. In the heavens and on the earth, there are indeed (clear) signs for the believers (pointing to God's Existence, Oneness, and Lordship); and in your creation and His scattering (innumerable kinds of) living creatures (through the earth), there are (clear) signs for a people who seek certainty of faith (in His existence, Oneness, and Lordship); and in the alternation of night and day (with their periods shortening and lengthening), and in the provision (rain) God sends down from the sky and reviving thereby the earth after its death, and in His turning about of the winds — (in all this) there are (clear) signs for

---

[209] Ibid, pp. 64–67.
[210] Ibid, p. 66–67.

a people who are able to reason and understand. Those are the
Revelations of God that We recite to you (through Gabriel) with
truth. In what other statement, if not in God and His Revelations,
will they, then, believe? Woe to everyone addicted to inventing false-
hoods, addicted to sinning! He hears God's Revelations recited to
him, and yet he persists in unbelief haughtily, as if he had not heard
them. So give him the glad tidings of a painful punishment. When
he has come to some knowledge of Our signs (whether in the universe or in the Qur'an), he takes them in mockery. For such there
is a humiliating punishment. In front of them there is Hell; and all
that they have earned (of this world) will be of no avail whatever
to them, and nor will those whom (apart from God, and in defiance
of Him) they have taken as guardians (to entrust their affairs to).
For them there is a mighty punishment. This (Qur'an) is the guidance, and for those who disbelieve in the signs and Revelations of
their Lord, there is a painful punishment of a loathsome kind
(brought on by their loathsome deeds). (Surah *al-Jathiyah* [The
Kneeling Down] 45:2–11)

God's beautiful, harmonious arrangement makes possible human
community, commerce and prosperity, justice, mercy, and peace – if people obey the Lord and keep to His Straight Path. The passage in Surah
al-Jathiyah continues, pointing to a future time of reckoning as every
human and all of creation will return to their Maker for judgment:

God it is Who has made the sea to be of service to you by making
it subservient (to His command), so that the ships may run
through it by His command, and that you may seek of His bounty, and that (in return) you may give thanks. He has also made of
service to you whatever is in the heavens and whatever is on the
earth; all is from Him (a gift of His Grace). Surely in this there
are (clear) signs for a people who reflect. Tell those who believe
that they should pardon those who do not hope for the coming of
the Days of God (when He will make them understand what their
unbelief means), seeing that He will recompense people for what
they have earned. Whoever does a good, righteous deed, it is for
(the good of) his own soul; and whoever does evil, it is against it.
Thereafter (in all events), it is to your Lord that you will be
brought back. (45:12–15)

Built into the structures of nature and human beings is the awareness of, witness to, and longing for eternity. The path to the Hereaf-

ter passes through the end of this world to the Resurrection of the dead and the Judgment before the final goal is reached. As a committed Muslim, Gülen insists on the importance of believing that the Resurrection influences life in our world now:

> After belief in God, belief in the Resurrection has the primary place in securing a peaceful social order.... Everyone, regardless of age, gender, and any other artificial human-devised difference, needs belief in the Resurrection as much as they need air, water, and bread.... Belief in the Resurrection is the most important and compelling factor urging us to use our free will properly and not to wrong or harm others....The Resurrection provides for the completion and actualization of Divine justice. The resurrection and belief in the afterlife of absolute justice consoles the wronged and oppressed, and dissuades them from seeking vengeance.[211]

## SUMMARY AND TRANSITION

Beginnings and Endings are tied to each other, just as our world and transcendental dimensions of existence are bound together. Chapter Three presented Fethullah Gülen's positions on God's structuring of the worlds from their beginnings to the edge of their endings while providing a cosmology that illustrated the relationships of the worlds beyond our time and space-bound world in which humans live. The Beautiful Names and Attributes of God linked to the three Books testified to the Truth of the One-Only God's sovereignty. That sovereignty unites justice, love, and accountability in the lives of individuals, the Muslim community, and the whole human community. The interpretation of the Qur'an offered ways in which the Book will be the source for understanding Gülen's vision for the Endings of the worlds and the Beginning of the Hereafter. It is to that vision we turn next.

> In the flow of time and existence, the difference between a beginning and an end is almost impossible to tell. Every thing that exists can be likened to a drop of water which, absorbed by the earth, becomes invisible. Or it may be likened to a stream which flows down to a sea and becomes extinct when it mixes with it. This is

---

[211] The quotes are taken from *Gülen, Essentials,* pp. 131–134.

the destiny of all beings. They all come into life and pass away according to this destiny.

All beginnings imply their ends; all comings-in are the first point of all goings-out. He that has no beginning has no end, and that One is God, Who is Eternal. It is God Who governs all beings that come into existence within time and He it is Who decrees each individual destiny. [212]

---

[212] Gülen, *Questions and Answers,* Vol. 2, p. 9.

## Gülen's Vision of the Worlds' Endings and New Beginning

> Without belief in the resurrection and the afterlife, how can we survive? But if there is a resurrection and a judgment, we have to look at the world in a totally different way. We must prepare ourselves for that day by doing what the Qur'an and the Prophet tell us to do; good deeds, help and care about others, fight injustice and oppression, bring the carnal self under control and seek to fulfill our obligations to God Almighty. People will control themselves and help others, which results in social peace and cooperation.[213]

The Endings are coming. This world and the worlds above will vanish in cataclysms that are preludes to the Day of Judgment when the balances will be set up to weigh how well or poorly every creature fulfilled its covenant with the One-Only God. Then humans and jinn will take the final steps in their life-journey across the narrow bridge into the unending realm of the New Beginning. The eternal world will have no veils, for God's will and the desires of those reckoned to be righteous companions shall be fulfilled immediately and completely. As expected, the fate of the unrighteous will be painfully grim. Yet before the scroll of the present worlds is rolled up, God's Plan calls for another Ending. That Ending shall surely come, and God will raise up a new generation of women and men to bring this world to its completion.

Chapter Four is intensely eschatological, that is, it addresses the Terminal End Time while expanding on the challenges people have in

---

[213] Ünal, *Resurrection and the Afterlife*, p. viii.

the present and immediate future to establish the Fulfillment-Con-summation End Time of justice, equality, harmony, peace, and love. Chapter Two set the background of a basic general Sunni view of the worlds' beginning and ending with references to analogous positions in Judaism and Christianity. Chapter Three focused on Gülen's views of the worlds' beginnings. Building on Chapters Two and Three, the present Chapter opens with another way to meet and understand Gülen. That introduction yields to presenting his understanding of human beings as composed of body, spirit, and soul. The exposition under-girds the balance of the Chapter. The main body of the Chapter is structured around God's Plan in three eschatological acts leading from within the present and the first ending, through the final ending, and into the New Beginning of the Hereafter. The Chapter concludes with a Summary and Transition to Chapter Five.

## MEETING FETHULLAH GÜLEN AS A MAN OF HOPE

> For a Sufi, *Raja* [hope] means waiting for that which he or she wholeheartedly desires to come into existence, acceptance of good deeds, and forgiveness of sins. Hope or expectation, both based on the fact that the individual is solely responsible for his or her errors and sins and that all good originates from and is of God's Mercy, is seen in this way: To avoid being caught in vices and faults and brought down by self-conceit over good deeds and vir-tues, an initiate must advance toward God through the constant seeking of forgiveness, prayer, avoidance of evil, and pious acts.
>
> One's life must be lived in constant awareness of God's super-vision, and one must knock tirelessly on His door with supplica-tion and contrition. If an initiate successfully establishes such a balance between fear and hope, he or she will neither despair (of being a perfect, beloved servant of God) nor become conceited about any personal virtues and thereby neglect his or her responsi-bilities.[214]

Gülen is neither naïve about the difficulties faced by millions nor is he a stranger to opposition. He knows and feels intensely the events and tensions in the world. Moreover, he possesses an exile's longing for

---

[214] Gülen, *Sufism*, Vol. 1, p. 38.

his homeland. Nevertheless, his faith and confidence in God's compassion, mercy, justice, and truth keep him from descending into pessimism. He speaks sternly and critically about human evil, institutional corruption, and distortions in religious matters. Still, he is firm in the Islamic conviction that God's Plan for individuals and the cosmos will be accomplished. As a result, he lives *Raja*, that is, a hope-filled expectation centered on the All-Merciful God Who is the Best of All Planners.[215] Gülen practices what he teaches through asking for and extending forgiveness, praying and encouraging others to pray, avoiding evil, and engaging in pious acts. While he strives actively and patiently for God's cause, he teaches, writes, advises, and serves as a model for being a man of hope and expectation.

## GÜLEN'S UNDERSTANDING OF HUMAN BEINGS

To begin considering Gülen's vision for the worlds' Endings and the New Beginning of the Hereafter, we step back to review and deepen what has already been offered as his understanding of humanity. His positions are grounded in the Qur'an and the Prophet's Sunna, particularly in the light of Sufism and the insights of thinkers such as Muhammad Lüfti Efendi and Bediüzzaman Said Nursi. We return to the Beginning, that is, the "Above," the "Then," at the origin of the worlds. An initial essential point is God's imprinting into the structures of all existence His Beautiful Names and a knowledge of His One-ness as well as making every created thing a mirror to His glory and will. Love, justice, concord, and interdependence of all that exists were already present throughout the worlds when the first humans were created, and these will continue throughout the worlds' existence. Of these qualities, love stands out for Gülen:

> When we enter this world, we find everything prepared to meet
> all the needs of our senses, and intellectual and spiritual faculties.
> This clearly shows that one who is infinitely merciful and knowl-

---

[215] Surahs Al Imran 3:54 and al-Anfal 8:30. Translation by Abdullah Yusuf Ali.

edgeable provides for all created beings in the most extraordinary way, and causes all things to collaborate to that end.[216]

\* \* \*

Love is the most essential element of every being, and it is the most radiant light, and it is the greatest power, able to resist and overcome all else. Love elevates every soul that absorbs it, and prepares these souls for the journey to eternity. Souls that have been able to make contact with eternity through love exert themselves to inspire in all other souls what they have derived from eternity. They dedicate their lives to this sacred duty; a duty for the sake of which they endure every kind of hardship to the very end, and just as they pronounce "love" with their last breath, they will also breathe "love" while being raised on the Day of Judgment.

Each being takes part in the grand orchestra of love in the universe with its own particular symphony and tries to demonstrate, by free will or through its disposition, an aspect of the deep love that is found in existence....Love is ingrained in the soul of a human being.[217]

God's Plan for existence involves the Creator's disclosing to the angels and other spiritual beings His will to make humans. The extension of that intention and God's carrying out the action involve God's purposes. One of those purposes was God's further statement that all of existence is for the sake of humanity and that humans' faithfulness to obey God were to be tested. Another purpose was God's declaring the primal man (and presumably woman and their offspring), to be God's caliphs, that is, God's deputies or representatives in this world so they were to act with His authority to lead all creatures and care for the world's inanimate entities. The third purpose is that at least some of the Divine Beautiful Names are to be manifested in human beings so that every person is to be the most highly polished of all the mirrors in the creation.

The "Above" setting includes God's making humans a composite of three factors: body, spirit, and soul. The body-component literally grounds humans into this world (*dunya*) so that humans are connect-

[216] Gülen, *Essentials*, p. 6.
[217] Ibid, *Toward a Civilization of Love and Tolerance*, pp. 1–2.

ed to the creatures and inanimate entities for which men and women are to care and lead in proper worship of and obedience to God. The body-component also in entails human needs, such as nourishment, emotions, shelter, and companionship. The body is subject to change, corruption, and almost total dissolution through death and decay in the grave. Further, the body requires training, discipline, and order if it is to fulfill its God-intended roles. If physical and emotional bodies are left untrained, Satan will deceive it by luring the person into greed, lust, and sin. Nevertheless, the body is part of God's good creation, and it will be raised in the resurrection and continue to be with the individual into the eternal life of the Hereafter. The Prophet himself ascended to the highest heaven in his full humanity. Jesus, Khidir, Enoch, and Elijah have not died yet; they live in heavenly dimensions while in their bodies.

The second component is spirit (*ruh*). While the term has several applications, the present focus is on the spirit God breathed into Adam and thence into all humanity. The spiritual dimension of *Mithal* is the "world" that contains the symbols, ideals, archetypes, and immaterial forms of what may take material forms in Dunya. In addition, the World of the Transcendental Manifestation of Divine Commands (*'Alam al-Malakut*) is the dimension in which the two types of Divine Law are issued; that is, the Attribute of Divine Speech and the Attributes of Will and Power. These are manifested as spiritual forms in the *'Alam al-Mithal* and become apparent in our world (*'Alam al-Mulk*) as Divine Revelation (*Din*) expressed through the laws of life (*Shari'a*) and laws of nature respectively. *'Alam al-Malakut* is also the dimension in which the spirit that is given to each person abides before they are sent to this world for trial. Ünal provides a helpful summary of Gülen's description of spirit:

> [The spirit is] a conscious, powerful thing which is able to learn and which thinks, senses, and reasons, continually developing, usually in parallel with the physical development of the body, both mentally and spiritually, through learning, reflection, belief, and worship. It is also the spirit that determines the character, nature, or identity of an individual, i.e. what makes one person different or distinguishable from others. Although human beings, from the

first to the last, are essentially made up of the same elements, they
all differ from one another in character, nature, and features. Thus,
the only thing that can determine this difference is the spirit....[I]t
is the spirit which directs or commands the human conscience, as
well as the other faculties. The spirit seeks the world from which it
has come and yearns for its Creator.[218]

Through its origin in the World of Spirits within the '*Alam al-
Malakut*, the spirit of each person becomes aware of the God's existence, unity, and will; the two forms of Divine Law; and the existence
of the spiritual worlds. The spirit is capable of growth; it is educable.
But it is also subject to degeneration and sin. The spirit-component is
that component that gives a person the desire for eternity. Indeed, each
person's spirit is capable of being eternal in that it provides each person
with her and his individuality in the Hereafter. In any case, the spirit
cannot act in this world unless and until it is embodied. Gülen wrote:

> The spirit is breathed into every embryo directly, making it a
> direct manifestation of the Divine Name the All-Living, and there-
> fore the basis of human life. Like natural laws, which issue from the
> same realm as the spirit, the spirit is invisible and known through
> its manifestations.[219]

During its time in the body, the spirit experiences suffering, joy,
pain, and pleasure as does the body. Although the spirit is present in
every part of the body, it is separable from the body. That separation
occurs at the death of the body. The body may decay almost completely, but the spirit remains conscious in the intermediate stage following death as noted in Chapter Two. The body will be reconstituted at
the Resurrection and rejoined with its spirit for the Judgment and in
the Hereafter. Gülen, as do Sufis generally, holds that the spirit is seated in the individual's spiritual heart.[220]

Gülen's understanding of the origin and capacities of each person's
spirit is vitally important for his vision of how and through whom

---

[218] Ünal, *The Qur'an with Annotated Interpretation*, Appendix 12, p. 1308. He noted
that he has summarized Gülen's views in *Essentials*, pp. 41–49.

[219] Gülen, *Essentials*, p. 48.

[220] Ibid, *Sufism*, Vol. 1, pp. 22–28.

the Fulfillment-End will be achieved. As Ünal wrote, "The spirit is only at ease when there is belief in God, and worship and remembrance of Him."[221]

The third component of human beings is the soul (*nafs*). Again, the term admits a number of meanings. Sometimes Gülen and others use it to refer to human beings in general. An inclusive definition of the term in wide usage, the Qur'an, philosophy, and Sufism is:

> [*Nafs* is] a general designation for the self or true self, interpreted as the spiritual reality of all living creatures. In philosophy, the specifically human *nafs* is often described as the potential to actualize the fullness of self-awareness, often equated with the intellect (*aql*). In Sufism, often described as the "lower self," associated with physical rather than spiritual impulses, by contrast to *ruh*, understood to be ...the "higher self."[222]

For present purposes, Gülen usually takes *nafs* as that divinely bestowed part of a human being which is the source or mechanism of the worldly life (possessed not only by human beings but also by the jinn). In the following quotation, he regards the soul as the "self":

> God's good pleasure is the ultimate goal. The soul is before and ahead of the body. The self is an essential dynamism that will ignite the consciousness of duty under the heart's rule. The love of humanity and country is an indispensable passion, and the duty to be moral is a vital provision for the journey. We must adhere to the Qur'an, and recognize humanity's character and real human values as significant sources of power. Goals and objectives must be just, fair, and sacred, and the ways leading to them must be indicated by the Qur'an and the Sunna.[223]

Following a Sufi line, he refers to soul as the self that is involved in seven stages, or steps in training the "self," which is prone to evil:

> [T]he seven steps of the human self or soul: the Evil-Commanding, the Self-Condemning, the Inspired, the Serene and Peaceful or the

---

[221] Ünal, *The Qur'an with Annotated Interpretation*, Appendix 12, p. 1309.

[222] Esposito, *Oxford Dictionary*, pp. 226–227.

[223] Gülen, "What We Expect from the Righteous Generation," The Fountain, July-September 2003, Issue 43.

Soul at Rest, the Content (with however God treats it), the (Soul) Pleasing (to God), and the Purified or Innocent Self or Soul.[224]

In the well-ordered person, the soul is subject to the spirit and leads the body to the proper worship and service of God. To fulfill its roles, however, the soul needs to be trained and disciplined by making use of the free will. Yet the human free will makes choices for good or evil. The risk is that the soul will become enamored with the pleasures and fears of the body so that the self will become carnal, giving itself to those pleasures, desires, anxieties, and fears. In turn, the soul can then cause the spirit to lose its purity and devotion to God. Satan targets the soul with deceptive whisperings about corrupt pleasures, vice, greed, and idolatry. Souls then can become brutal, undisciplined, and rebellious.[225] He developed the view further:

> [It] is a substance that is essentially free of matter but which is in close connection with it in its acts and functions; it is the origin or essence of something or its self....[The] soul is the origin or center of certain states or faculties such as lusts, anger, ill will, grudge, hatred and irritation, and is a transformable, reformable, and refineable mechanism connected to human corporeality. It is through this connection that humans receive, recognize, and distinguish their outer and inner sense perceptions and go beyond the corporeal realm into metaphysical worlds. It is again through this connection that any state, experience or gift that occurs in the spirit leaves its imprint on the body and provokes it to move in a certain direction.[226]

The soul can be turned to a perfected or "pure" soul (*nafs as-safiyah*). The spirit is able to shed its heavenly light into the soul, recalling it to the One Who is its origin and judge. Since such a soul has a share of the breath of God, it longs for eternity beyond this transient world and can be brought to remember from Whom it came and to Whom it will return. The soul can repent, and through austerity and discipline pull away from the illicit pleasures of the body and return to the Straight Path. Gülen holds that God floods the soul with love,

---

[224] Ibid, *Sufism,* Vol. 1, p. 155.

[225] Ibid, *Toward a Civilization of Love and Tolerance*, p. 5.

[226] Ibid, *Sufism,* Vol. 3, p. 216.

and the soul may respond with faith and obedient service. The soul's return will result in the spirit and soul acting through the body to carry out the role of God's vicegerency in this world. The return of the lapsed soul with the cleansing of the spirit that may have been misled by the soul as well as the obedience of those who did not sin so greatly requires, undoubtedly, significant exertion. That exertion is the Greater Jihad, the struggle within one's own soul.[227]

> Improvement of the inherent potential and the attainment of a second nature that is open to a relationship with the Almighty depend on success in this struggle, a struggle that takes place deep in the soul, on whether or not those undergoing the struggle appreciate this victory, and on whether or not they bend their heads to the level of their feet forming a circle in modesty and humility.
>
> The weak-willed, who are unable to pass beyond superficiality to look into their inner depths, to see the gaps and defects within their nature as well as the merits of their souls, and while unable to restore themselves every new day, can never progress in their inner worlds....To love and care for those who preserve and improve their humanity is to give them what they deserve. As for the rest, they should be shown love and sympathy so that they can be saved from the grasp of the evil feelings and passions. Such an attitude is an expression of caring for human beings, whom God created is worthy of respect....And the human being is an entity created to be loved.[228]

Gülen's understanding of the human being as a composite of body, spirit, and soul provides the basis for his understanding of the dire plights of humanity and the capacities for the First Ending of the worlds, while it points toward the Final Ending.

## GOD'S ESCHATOLOGICAL PLAN: ACT ONE, THE END AS FULFILLMENT

> Human beings can sometimes become so heavenly that they reach the height of the skies; yet sometimes they are so mean that they become worse than snakes or venomous insects. Human beings are

---

[227] Ibid, *Toward a Civilization of Love and Tolerance*, p. 120; see also his *Muhammad*, p. 205.
[228] Ibid, pp. 120–121.

creatures who can demonstrate such a wide range of behavior that they can possess corrupt qualities alongside the merits; and they can be readily tempted to evil, in spite of possessing lofty virtues. Faith, wisdom, love, and spiritual pleasures are as much a part of them as their own hearts are; loving others, embracing everyone, living with feelings of kindness and making others live with the same is the ultimate goal of their lives. Eliminating evil through goodness, loving "love," and being in constant struggle against the feelings of enmity are as sweet to them as the whisper of their own souls.[229]

Human beings are a mixture of God-given capabilities and their own freely willed contrasts intended to be lived out in this world, the corridor that leads to the Hereafter. Fethullah Gülen, a man of hope-filled expectation, also has a realistic awareness of human intentions and deeds.

## GÜLEN'S NEGATIVE ANALYSIS OF THE WORLD'S PRESENT STATE

The present state of the world makes Gülen cry from his heart and yet hope with faith:

> Certainly, those who live in this world as if blind, deaf, and dead will not even get a glimpse of the above. Those who act unwarily, even taking lightly these grave conditions today will be likely to continually wail in penitence in future. Then, let us be vigilant today so that we will not be troubled for rest and sleep tomorrow. Let us weep abundantly today so that we will not cry from regret tomorrow. Let us concentrate at all times on the horizon to which we are heading, so as not to be distracted by the attractive things on the side of the road. If we fail to regard this world as a marketplace where trade is carried out for gains to be taken onto the Hereafter and do not manage our life accordingly, if we lead our life in line with the whims of carnal desires, then we should not be surprised when one day somebody puts a packsaddle on us and mounts us. This is indeed the kind of treatment that the narrow-minded, the feckless, and conceited people will receive. The value of humankind is directly proportional to the degree of their connection with God and the continuation of their sincere relations with Him. A human-shaped body contaminated with carnal desires

---

[229] Ibid, p. 120.

and alienated from Him will have less value than mud, even if decorated with gold, silver, and satin.[230]

He sees intellectual and cultural bankruptcy and the misdirection of science and malaise pervading individuals:

> Humankind has never been so wretched as they are today. They have lost all their values: the "table of art and literature" is "vandalized" by drunks; thought is capital wasted in the hands of people suffering from intellectual poverty; science is a plaything of materialism; and the products of science are tools used in the name of unbelief. Amid such disorder and bewilderment, the people neither know their destination in the world nor the direction to follow to reach that destination.[231]

He does not soften his analysis of bitter sort that points to the *fitna*s, or seditions, looming out in front of us:

> Society reaches every morning and evening in the shadow of the signs of the apocalypse, almost in expectation of the trumpet blast announcing its arrival. Our peace and tranquillity have become naught but a dream. Our collective spirit and thought, which were our main shelter until today, have become twisted and deformed. Our hopes have become more tattered than they have ever been. Our willpower is crazed with a network of cracks. Our determination is totally paralyzed. And as a society we continually pass through delirious states. We have become so detached from our essence that if we were to meet our own spirit round the corner, we might not even recognize it. We have never been so alienated from our own values in any period of history. We have never left our spirit so hungry, thirsty, and deprived of air. Nowadays, different noises keep coming at us from all sides, but we are unable to hear among them the voice of our spirit that makes us ourselves. We are in such a state of bewilderment, terror, or rather confusion that we are unable to see what we are supposed to be. I think it will not be possible for us to be saved from this deadly chaos until we wash away our mental and spiritual dirt with the clear flow of our own belief and thought. Surrounded by strange, shrill noises, by shows tempting people to self-alienation, and by nightmarish troubles that stab our

---

[230] Ibid, *Speech and the Power of Expression*, p. 76.
[231] Ibid, *Towards the Lost Paradise*, p. 86.

hearts, take strength from our helplessness and make our souls lament, we go through shock after shock, writhe in pain, keep swallowing helplessly, and feel our spirit grow more and more corroded every day.[232]

Nevertheless, his being literally moved to tears at the plights of so many persons and the violence in the world is balanced by his faith in the God who is All-Merciful, All-Compassionate, and also the Lord of the Worlds and Master of the Day of Judgment. While his heart-spirit cries out, he avoids apocalyptic predictions but envisions eschatological fulfillment in the near future.

## GÜLEN'S BIFOCAL VISION FOR TODAY'S WORLD

Gülen wrote about his perspective on life in the present, its meaning, and its goal:

> For some this life consists of a few days passed in this earthly guest-house in pursuit of the ego's desires. Other people have different views, and so give life a different meaning. For me, this life consists of a few breaths on the journey that begins in the World of Spirits and continues eternally either in Heaven or, God forbid, Hell.
>
> This life is very important, for it shapes our afterlife. Given this, we should spend it in ways designed to earn the eternal life in Paradise and gain the approval of the Giver of Life. This path passes through the inescapable dimension of servanthood to God by means of serving, first of all, our families, relatives, and neighbors, and then our country and nation, with finally humanity and creation being the object of our efforts. This service is our right; conveying it to others is our responsibility.[233]

Therefore, everything a creature does in this life is a "rehearsal for the afterlife."[234] All persons are expected to worship rightly, do good, righteous deeds and serve with good intention regardless of the conditions of the societies in which they live, but Gülen understands God's Plan for the world to include a time of fulfillment-consummation led

---

[232] Ibid, *Speech and the Power of Expression*, pp. 6–7.
[233] Ibid, *Toward a Civilization of Love and Tolerance*, pp. 200–201.
[234] Ibid, *Muhammad*, p. 283.

by men and women of intellect, integrity, reverence and, above all, love and *hoşgörü* before the Final End of the worlds. In spite of the atrocities, failures, and perversions by men and women over the centuries, from their creation to the present, many humans have been growing morally and spiritually as well as in their capability to invent, organize, and apply their abilities to their communities. Especially the revealed religions of Judaism, Christianity, and Islam have provided Prophets, Messengers, and Scriptures that have witnessed to the Creator's will and wisdom while they pointed to the certainty and reality of the Resurrection and Judgment. Gülen is convinced that the time is fast approaching when God's Plan for the world's consummation is at hand and that God is preparing leaders as well as providing heavenly influences to bring that consummation to fruition:

> Our old world will experience an excellent "springtime" before its demise. This springtime will see the gap between rich and poor narrow; the world's riches distributed most justly according to one's work, capital and needs; the absence of discrimination based on race, color, language, and world-view; and basic human rights and freedoms protected. Individuals will come to the fore and, learning how to realize their potential, will ascend on the way to becoming "the most elevated human" with wings of love, knowledge and belief.[235]

Gülen's unified vision for the Fulfillment-End of the world (*dunya*) and the Final End for the worlds (*'alamin*) may be seen through a bifocal lens. The upper portion of the lens is for seeing distant objects and vistas while the lower portion enables the viewer to examine what is close at hand. Our brains are able to resolve the two sights into a whole. In like manner, Gülen's vision for the world today and into the future before the eschaton-end is bifocal yet unified. Both lines of sight converge to form one picture that is moving toward the Hereafter. The lens used for distant viewing gives celestial fullness and cosmic depth to the vision. It is directed toward the Divine Plan and the worlds beyond this world. Negating or neglect-

---

[235] Ibid, "At the Threshold of a New Millennium," in *Essays, Perspectives, Opinions*, pp. 30–31.

ing that lens' orientation toward the heavens and that to which it calls the viewer to see, even if obscurely, risks making Gülen's vision just another utopian proposal. The lower lens brings into view the quite human Dunya-dwellers. How are they to be raised up to the spiritual stature that the vision anticipates and requires? What are the agendas that they are to set for themselves? How will they begin to relate to the societies around them and to potential partners in achieving the vision? Moreover, how will the spiritual influences and Divine will impact their efforts and results? Gülen provided an exhortation and guiding statement that keeps the vision from becoming an abstraction or hallucination:

> The purpose of our creation is obvious: to reach our utmost goals of belief, knowledge, and spirituality; to reflect on the universe, humanity, and the Divine Attributes, and thus prove our value as human beings. Fulfilling this ideal is possible only through systematic thinking and systematic behavior. Thought will provoke action, and thereby start a "prosperous cycle." This cycle will produce more complex cycles, which are generated from between the spirituality of the heart and the knowledge of the brain, thereby developing ever-more complex ideas and producing more ambitious projects.[236]

Those who dare to participate in the vision's realization need to be prepared to commit themselves intellectually, ethically, and spiritually to the task and to be eager to use their creativity responsibly for the universe, fellow humans, and God.

## THE VISION VIEWED FROM THE ABOVE

Aspects of the view from the Above, that is, from the spiritual worlds, are familiar. God's unthwartable strategy is to have this world as the testing ground or arena for those beings who have free will, that is, human beings and the jinn. The Above view looks through and beyond the events that take place in the world in order to see what lies beyond the present worlds and into the Hereafter. While the angels and spiritual beings in the spiritual dimensions are aware that

---

[236] Ibid, *Toward a Global Civilization of Love and Tolerance*, p. 133.

there is a Plan, they do not know it completely. Satan and his supporters have key and punishable roles in tempting and seeking to deceive humans. Operating from behind the veils of cause and effect, God educates, disciplines, and tests humans. In order to alert humans to the Divine Plan, God arranged all that exists to mirror God's existence, the Divine will for the present, and the inevitability of the Resurrection, Judgment and Hereafter. The Messengers and the Scriptures revealed to them as well as the Prophets, renewers, and other religious figures explicitly warn, advise, and proclaim to humans the different stages of the Plan while other figures in league with Satan seek to deceive humans so that they will be condemned to Hell. The Qur'an and Muhammad's disclosures of the Plan require interpretation in order to be understood and acted upon. As noted earlier, the Qur'an and Muhammad recognized that there were levels of meaning within the Qur'anic text and among the words and actions of the Messenger. Some of those meanings will be manifested more clearly in a future time than they appeared to be during the occasions of their revelation. Therefore, some Qur'anic passages are explicit and decisive yet others are allegorical and oriented toward future circumstances. The Qur'an also makes clear that it contains allegorical verses whose profound meanings are known to God alone in their fullest extent, thus inviting the believers who are firmly rooted in knowledge to discover their meanings until the End of Time.

We are now able to bring together several factors mentioned in Chapters Two and Three as they bear on Gülen's vision of the world's Fulfillment Ending. In presenting a Sunni version of the Final End, I surfaced the roles of Jesus the Messiah, the Mahdi, the Centennial Renewers, the Great Dajjal, and the Great Sufyan. A section in Chapter Three discussed issues involved in the interpretation of the Qur'an and Hadith. The Qur'an and Hadith may be regarded as providing everdeepening and extending inspiration along with application and meanings for humans as they grow in their knowledge, spiritual development, and abilities in God's world. I noted especially the interpretative contributions of Bediüzzman Said Nursi. These elements coalesce in Gül-

en's vision for the present and lead into his understanding of the Fulfillment Ending.

Gülen agreed with Nursi that Qur'anic statements and Hadith
sayings may have their fullest meanings in the dimensions we considered as spiritual realms and/or in the Hereafter. In our world, the terms
may be expressed in material entities such as Mahdi or the Dajjals. Gog
and Magog, for example, may refer to any of numerous groups that
arose from time to time to wreck destruction instead of to a specific
people. The progress of a number of Dajjals toward the End of Time
may not only be the progress of particular evil persons but also the
spread of their irreligious, materialist ideologies or the evil committees working for recurrent turmoil and crises. In other words, the figures may be representatives of ideologies and/or communities. He
advised spiritually attuned believers and interpreters to use their reason and discernment so that when extraordinary figures do appear,
they may be recognized and responded to appropriately.[237] On the
basis of this understanding, figures such as the Dajjal, Sufyan, Messiah, and Mahdi act as representatives of ideologies, committees, communities, or movements at least during the present stage of the
world's existence. That approach provides a means of avoiding apocalyptic speculations and identifications.[238] In doing so, Gülen keeps the
theological bases of the vision intact, relevant to changing times, and
consonant with Islam's tenets.

Specifically and with regard to the age of the telos-eschaton, Gülen
indicates that the collective spiritual personality of Jesus the Messiah,
who is alive in a heavenly dimension above our world, will exercise spiritual influence on the world and be engaged in raising up the new generation of leaders who will form what Gülen calls the "Golden Generation." In addition, he feels that the descent of the spirit of the Messiahood as a collective spiritual personality will be realized soon, but
not in the apocalyptic sense. Gülen wrote:

---

[237] Nursi, *Risale-i Nur Collection, The Words*, p. 364.

[238] Such an approach may avoid literalistic identities such as that which led to the seizure of the Grand Mosque (1979) by a group that claimed one of its members was
the awaited Mahdi.

Some Islamic scholars consider the descent of Jesus as a person would be contrary to the divine wisdom of God Almighty. They rather think that it will take place as a descent of a "collective spiritual personality." Some other scholars have interpreted Qur'anic verses and Traditions in a different way. Bediüzzaman, on the other hand, while not discarding the possibility of Jesus' descent as a person, stresses the spiritual personality more, and interprets this descent as the conformity of the Christian world to Islam. He also argues that the descent of Jesus as a person might not be a distant possibility: "The Glorious Sovereign, Who sends angels from heavens to the Earth at all times, Who sometimes transforms them into human form as did Gabriel into Dihya (a Companion of the Prophet), Who make the spiritual beings from the realm of spirits come to this world in the form of a man, or late saints in an imaginary body, would certainly dress Jesus in a human form who is alive and resides in the worldly sky, even if he had gone to the farthest end of the afterlife and was really dead, and would send him for such a substantial result." Bediüzzaman never went further into these details which exist in certain reports....

I believe the descent of Messiah as a spiritual personality is not too distant a future. It may indeed take place that this spirit, or meaning, may descend, and nobody should oppose this possibility. The coming of the Messiah as a spiritual personality simply means that a spirit of compassion or a phenomenon of mercy will come to the foreground, a breeze of clemency will waft over humanity, and human beings will compromise and agree with each other. The signs of such a phenomenon are already present: Muslims are sometimes invited to churches to read the Qur'an, it is now an accepted fact that Prophet Muhammad is a Messenger of God, and that the Qur'an is a divine revelation. Some people as well may come to declare themselves as "Muslim-Christians." It does not seem improper to me to regard these as an introduction to the spirit of Messiahhood.[239]

Viewed from Above, God has provided all that is needed for humans. We have the means, guidance, and incentives to remain faithful to God no matter how stringent the tests may be, to undertake the task of transforming the world and human relationships so that justice, compassion, and peace will be realized before the Final End-

---

[239] Gülen, *Questions and Answers*, Vol. 2, pp. 148–149.

ing of the worlds takes place. We look now through the Dunya-side of the bifocal lens.

## THE VISION VIEWED FROM BELOW

> In this world sometimes evil resides next to beauty, bad deeds among good ones, and darkness behind light and so on. However, for those who always see the good and think of the good, the positive aspects are always stronger, longer lasting, more desirable, and more attractive. On the other hand, the unattractive aspects that displease us are beneficial in their results and other more subtle aspects. In fact these types of things and events are the sources of good deeds through inspiring our feelings in unusual ways, sharpening our intentions and ambitions, and promising surprises to our free will. This can be illustrated through the elements that are destructive or combustive by themselves, but which in different combinations are sources of life. Hence, through patience, submission and obedience negatives can be turned into positives.
>
> Compared to the heavenly bodies and the universe, and for our limitless ambitions, the world that we live on is small; however, it is the heart of everything. It is just a dot compared to the universe but it is more valuable than the galaxies. It is like a droplet compared to everything that exists and drifts in ether, but such a droplet that it is more valuable than everything combined in this universe. The world is the unique host of the human being who has been created as a complete and transparent mirror of the Divine Names and Attributes, and in addition to being a host, it acts like a ramp that enables the human being leap toward the Hereafter.[240]

Gülen's vision for today's world is framed by the Beginnings and Endings of the worlds (*'alamin*) as the worlds are being led to their consummation in the Hereafter. The entire vision looks toward the opening of that endless realm, the Hereafter. And all is comprehended in and energized by God's Plan for humanity: "It can also be said that God created not only this world, but also the next, in the name of the realization of human perfection."[241]

---

[240] Ibid, "*The World and Its Contents from the Perspective of a Believer,*" *The Fountain*, October-December 2004, Issue 48.

[241] Ibid, *Towards a Global Civilization of Love and Tolerance*, p. 113.

As was the case with familiar characteristics of the worlds Above, there are familiar factors concerning the present world and the intermediate world of the grave. Above and Below are bound to each other so that what is in the heavenly dimensions will be manifested to some degree in the structures of and events in this world. The most important pair of factors is that this world is a creation willed into existence by God and not an accumulation of random forces, and that whatever happens in this world occurs through the Plan of God. Supplementary factors include:

1. The three "Books" that disclose the Attributes of God's Will and Power through the Book of the Universe, the Book of Divine Speech, and the Book of Humanity converge to show humankind that it is the index and subject matter of those books and the index through which all knowledge, abilities, and skills may be employed in this life;

2. All humans are accountable to God for their relationships to God, other humans, and the world;

3. The world is a network of mirrors in which humans are the most highly polished of the reflectors;

4. The world and humans have within themselves the Names of God and that humans are to bring those Names from latent potentiality to full actualization;

5. The world may be compared to an arable field in which human deeds are planted as seeds that may germinate here, yet they will be harvested in the Hereafter;

6. Humans are to be God's caliphs-deputies in building societies marked by the proper worship of God, justice, compassion, understanding, peace, and love; and

7. God provides guidance on the Straight Way that leads through this world and into the Hereafter, yet it is up to each person to use her/his free will to take her/his journey on that road. That guidance includes pointers, persons, and spiritual guides to show the right ways to worship and serve God.

With these factors in mind, we turn to the vision below. Sights in that vision will include a synopsis of Gülen's vision for the Fulfillment-

End, the major issues to be addressed in relation to the humanity's common problems such as ignorance, the split of scientific studies and spirituality, disunity, and poverty and his proposals to meet those issues, the rise of what he terms as the Golden Generation, and the status and role of the Muslim community in the envisioned End Time.

## SYNOPSIS OF GÜLEN'S VISION

With strong conviction and high hope, poised to move forward; with firm resolve, our will ready as a taut bow-string is ready; in sweet imagination of paradise-like scenes of tomorrow, whose beauty we experience in spirit – we speak of the future once more, alert to its being near. It is as if the dark clouds – clouds that have been covering our foundations built of a deep spirituality, and our shining past built of ivory and pearl, crystal and coral, and our culture woven with threads of satin and silk, and gold and silver – the dark clouds are moving away and an attractive, enchanting world is gliding across the horizon. The scenes appearing to us, as yet afar, produce such thrills of pleasure in our souls that we feel as if the happy, promised time had all but arrived. Realities mixed with imagining, we feel we are half-way to the peaceful union of the modern with the traditional, the scientific with the religious and spiritual, the reason with the heart, the experienced with the revealed, and the military power with sense, justice and right. We are travelling toward this goal and feel as if we heard lyrical melodies that harmonized the past and the future. With the hope that the day will certainly come when souls conceive of nothing but goodness and fairness, when feelings overflow with love and compassion and eyes become more generous than clouds in pouring tears of mercy, when the soil fully awakens to life and the earth becomes as safe and comfortable as a nest, when human beings compete with spiritual beings in goodness and virtue – we try to meet in cheerful faith all the requirements of travelling to those horizons where we shall taste life once again as it should be.[242]

---

[242] Ibid, *Towards the Lost Paradise*, p. 67. Originally the chapter was an article published in a Turkish journal and rendered for the English speaking audience in *The Fountain Magazine* with the title, "The Horizon of Hope." See *The Fountain*, Volume 17, Number 3, 1995.

The synopsis' exhilarant tone exudes hope-filled expectation about the future of this world and expresses the confidence that the hope is based on realities projected from the future hereafter on to the screen of this world. It is an eschatological statement about the future's influence on sharing the present. Within the preacher-teacher's rhetoric are points related to changes that he fully expects to be realized before the Final End. Those points include among humans the union of the traditional and the modern, the reconciliation of scientific and the religious-spiritual dimensions, the harmonization of reason and revelation, and the proper balance of coercive power with justice. Gülen anticipates that love, compassion, and generosity among peoples will awaken the forces within nature to produce abundant food and resources for all persons. Then looking toward the Above, he adds that humans will compete with each other and with the righteous jinn in goodness and virtue. Although he admits that this may happen in the distant future, he nonetheless feels persons need to be alert and ready – and resolute to work for achieving that future as much as possible now.

Specifically, Gülen cites three critical areas that must be addressed in the process that leads to the Fulfilment of God's will for the world: the problematic triad of Ignorance, Poverty, and Division. The interrelated solutions are Education, Justice, and Dialogue. Not coincidentally, the problems and the solutions are mirrored in the efforts and activities of Hizmet. Gülen wrote:

> [O]ur three greatest enemies are ignorance, poverty and internal schism. Knowledge, work capital and unification can struggle against these. As ignorance is the most serious problem, we must oppose it with education, which always has been the most important way of serving our country. Now that we live in a global village, it is the best way to serve humanity and to establish dialogue with other civilizations....I encouraged people to serve the country in particular, and humanity in general, through education. I called them to help the state educate and raise people by opening schools. Ignorance is defeated through education; poverty through work

and the possession of capital; and internal schism and separatism through unity, dialogue, and tolerance [hoşgörü].[243]

For Gülen, the world will become increasingly the God-willed fulfilled world as these three problems are resolved.

## A - IGNORANCE RESOLVED THROUGH EDUCATION

Gülen directly connects the heavenly dimensions, education, and the Hereafter:

> The main duty and purpose of human life is to seek understanding. The effort of doing so, known as education, is a perfecting process through which we earn in spiritual, intellectual, and physical dimensions of our beings, the rank appointed for us as the perfect pattern of creation. At birth, the outset of the earthly phase of our journey from the World of the Spirits to eternity, we are totally impotent and extremely needy.... [I]t will take us our whole lives to acquire intellectual and spiritual perfection. Our principle duty in life is to acquire perfection and purity in our thinking, perception and belief. By fulfilling our duty of servanthood to the Creator, Nourisher, and Protector, and by penetrating the mystery of creation through our potential and abilities, we seek to attain the rank of true humanity and become worthy of a blissful, eternal life in another, exalted world.[244]

Gülen makes clear that the type of education needed is one in which science and reason are not set as polar opposites to ethics and spiritual values. Indeed, education is the essential first step persons must take toward developing the Fulfilled Society. The educational principles he advocates fit neatly into the synopsis. He urges reuniting science and religion, reason and revelation, tradition and modernity throughout all curricula, arguing that the Western Post-Enlightenment emphasis on science and reason to the virtual exclusion of religious values

---

[243] *Essays, Perspectives, Opinions: Fethullah Gülen*, excerpted from pp. 84–85. Nursi had surfaced the three problems along with others in the *Damascus Sermon* of 1911. The sermon was expanded several times and is now published in the *Risale-i Nur* collection. Nursi expressed the third problem as disunity, (p. 78), strife (p. 81) and conflict (p. 85).

[244] Gülen, *Toward a Global Civilization of Love and Tolerance*, p. 202.

has led to materialism, a degradation of humanity, and an impoverishment of moral values regardless of the particular religious or lack of religious commitments on the part of the majority of persons. His comments on education are passionate exhortations for a holistic understanding of human nature, societies, and the environment.[245]

Education has a cosmic and eschatological purpose that, when consummated, leads to the completion of human nature: "But above all else, education is a humane service; we were sent here to learn and be perfected through education.[246] For all his emphasis on reuniting of science and religion, Gülen carefully and constructively factors the uniqueness of various human cultures, traditions, and history into his proposed educational endeavors. While he looks to the future, he does so without jettisoning the past. As the Qur'an indicates, God made the varieties among humans so that we might learn from one another (Surah al-Hujurat 49:13). Education, therefore, protects the national-cultural traditions and histories of those being educated while at the same time encourages learners to realize that we live in a globalized world that brings us into ever-closer relations with others:

> Due to rapid developments in transportation and communication, the world has become a global village. Nations have become like next-door neighbors. However, we must remember that in a world like this, national existence can be ensured only by protecting the specific characteristics of each nation. In a unified mosaic of nations and countries, those that cannot protect their unique characteristics, "patterns," or "designs" will disappear.[247]

His approach to and exhortations concerning education consider the educational process as the key to more than human survival; it is the way to prevent one socio-political system from dominating over and oppressing others. Gülen sees the unity of all forms of learning in religious terms without imposing one religious system on all:

---

[245] Ibid, pp. 193–214; also *Ünal and Williams,* pp. 305–350.
[246] Ibid, p. 198.
[247] Ibid, pp. 197–198.

Education through learning and leading a commendable way of life is a sublime duty that is the manifestation of the Divine Name *Rabb* (Educator and Sustainer). By fulfilling this, we are able to attain the rank of true humanity and to become a beneficial element of society.

Education is vital for both societies and individuals. First, our humanity is directly proportional to the purity of our emotions. Although those who are full of evil feelings and whose souls are influenced by egoism appear to be human beings, whether they really are so is questionable. Almost anyone can train themselves physically, but few can educate their minds and feelings. Second, improving a community is possible by elevating the coming generations to the rank of humanity, not by obliterating the bad ones. Unless the seeds of religion, traditional values, and historical consciousness are germinated throughout the country, new negative elements will inevitably grow up in the place of every negative element that has been eradicated.[248]

## B - POVERTY RESOLVED THROUGH JUSTICE

The Names of God, imprinted into the structures of the worlds and into humans provide a basis for understanding Gülen's approach to alleviating and eliminating poverty:

> Consider our claims of ownership and control over what we regard as our property. What share do we have in producing the food we consume? Each morsel of food requires the existence of the entire universe. Given this, and if we can claim ownership and control over our private property in which we have so little share, why should God, the Creator and unique Owner of the universe and all of its contents, not have complete control of His property?
>
> The Name All-Providing supplies beings with what they need to live, the Name All-Healing enables patients to recover, and the Name All-Answering comes to the aid of the needy. He warns the heedless with His Name All-Distressing, and relieves the distressed with His Name All-Relieving. If we study the manifestations of God's Names, we can see the beauty in the variety they bring to the universe, and understand the wisdom underlying the differences in creation. God makes Himself known by manifesting His Names. For example, flowers smile at us as the result of the mani-

---

[248] Ibid, p. 205.

festation of His Names originating in His Grace, while natural catastrophes remind us of His Wrath as the manifestation of His Names originating in His Majesty.[249]

Underlying all assertions about human relationships, institutional purposes, and economic policies is the Islamic conviction that God is the Source and Judge of justice and human rights. The corollary is that justice and human rights are for all persons equally. As noted in Chapter Three, Gülen sees four major themes in the Qur'an: the Oneness and absolute Unity of God, the Resurrection and afterlife, the mission of Prophethood, and Justice (or Worship).[250] Poverty is a matter of justice (*'adl*). It is God's prerogative to render absolute justice on the Day of Judgment while it is a human responsibility to strive for and to achieve social justice in this world. Islamically understood, the Book of the Universe points to the wholeness and unity of God's creation that is open and available to all persons; the Qur'an provides the principles and some specific rules applicable to all human communities and to the umma, and each person is an index of those two books as well as bound in a covenant relationship with the Creator.

The whole creation, including human beings, is to be a network of signs and mirrors pointing to God and in mutual relationships of helping one another to reach their God-appointed goals. Gülen knows that poverty in the world is the result of the misuse and misappropri-

---

[249] Ibid, *Essentials*, p. 111–112.

[250] It is the very purpose of our creation, and therefore "full justice," to submit to and worship God and to devote ourselves to doing good, righteous deeds for God's sake. In his explanation of a verse in Surah an-Nahl (16:90), Gülen interprets the term "justice" (*'adl*) as a vitally important Islamic discipline. Citing *"justice"* (*'adl*) among the four fundamentals of religion, he expounds the concept of *justice* as the very basis of *"excellence in worship and devotion to doing good"* as follows: "Used in the Qur'an and Sunnah sometimes in the meaning of worship and sometimes in the meaning of justice, the word *'adl* has, in fact, a very broad range of meanings. For example, although it is used in the verse under discussion to mean "justice, right conduct, and balance," *"devotion to doing good and excellence in the worship"* can also be encompassed by the concept of *'adl*. In any case, if *"justice"* in the meaning of worship of and servanthood to God is not established in an individual or a society, then, to expect the other virtues from such an individual or society is in vain." For further details, see Gülen, *Reflections on the Qur'an*, pp. 161–163.

ation of the resources and wealth that God has built into Dunya's structures. He is blunt about the exploitation of the poor by Western nations in the pursuit of and in attempt to maintain their power as well as the failures and corruptions of so-called Muslim nations that have adapted to materialism. Yet, while he denounces the causes and results of that exploitation, he rejects revolutionary, radical, and violent reactions. Instead, he advocates using the means of universal education for all persons and dedicated, conscientious leadership to halt the spread, depth, and persistence of poverty. Naturally, his principles are based on Islamic perspectives.

Those perspectives include treating all persons as individuals who have God-given abilities and purposes. He calls on social institutions, governments, and individuals to provide opportunities for children and adults to use their abilities, to grow in knowledge and skills, and to participate mutually in developing moral societies. Within the Muslim community, for example, the obligatory alms to aid the poor and the needy (*zakat*) is not intended as condescending relief but as a means to eradicate poverty.[251] Two other essential Islamic contributions to the elimination of poverty is the end of corporate, national, and individual greed and the elimination of usury (*riba*).[252]

Gülen knows poverty from his personal experience of growing up in straightened circumstances in a poor village in rural eastern Anatolia. He also is convinced that persons, including the poor, are able to use their free will, abilities, energy, and opportunities to transcend social class structures and discouragement to gain the knowledge and skills needed to earn by ethical means the resources that provide for their necessities of food, shelter, and clothing – and to show God gratitude and praise. All persons have the responsibility to use their talents, positions, and possessions to encourage and help others move toward their God-appointed goals. In that manner, he looks forward to defeating poverty through the empowerment of the poor in partnership with those

---

[251] Büyükçelebi, *Living in the Shade of Islam*, p. 242.
[252] See Büyükçelebi, pp. 242–257. He reflects Gülen's views.

who are economically more advantaged in order to develop a just, compassionate, and equitable society.[253]

## C - DIVISION RESOLVED THROUGH DIALOGUE

The third of the pressing issues is Disunity-Separatism-Conflict within and between religious communities, ethnic and racial groups, nations, families, and individuals. Ignorance and fear of the "Other" certainly account for many of the clashes between cultures, faiths, and ideologies. The Qur'an recognizes human diversity as a God-given condition not to be eliminated but to be used to develop human knowledge, justice, and compassion among peoples with gratitude toward God. One key passage is in Surah *al-Hujurat* (The Private Apartments):

> O humankind! Surely We have created you from a single (pair of) male and female, and made you into tribes and families so that you may know one another (and so build mutuality and co-operative relationships, not so that you may take pride in your differences of race or social rank, or breed enmities). Surely the noblest, most honorable of you in God's sight is the one best in piety, righteousness, and reverence for God. Surely God is All-Knowing, All-Aware. (49:13)

Gülen's response to Division is deep, persistent, open dialogue:

> Dialogue means the coming together of two or more people to discuss certain issues, and thus the forming of a bond between these people. In that respect, we can call dialogue an activity that has human beings at its axis.[254]

The two sentences just quoted deserve careful study. Dialogue goes beyond two or more persons getting together to talk. That is a conversation or, when matters go awry, an argument. A dialogue focuses on agreed upon topics and involves forming positive relationships among the participants. Religions do not dialogue; people dialogue. In the process of mutual searching, sharing, and openness, the

---

[253] *Essays, Perspectives, Opinions: Fethullah Gülen*, p. 84; Gülen, *Toward a Global Civilization of Love and Tolerance*, p. 199.

[254] Gülen, *Toward a Global Civilization of Love and Tolerance*, p. 50.

dialoguers develop respect, trust, and understanding. Dialogue is itself an educational venturing in self-searching and self-understanding as much as it is listening to and learning from the partners. The partners gradually realize that they are not strangers or "others" but fellow humans who have much in common as well as differences. Gülen's style of dialogue is non-confrontational for it faces the future through not letting past actual and perceived traumas and distortions determine present perceptions and relationships: "[W]e must forget the past, ignore polemics, and focus on common points."[255]

Dialogue, he insists, cannot exclude the religious dimension nor must it be restricted to religion. I have replaced "tolerance" with the proper and difficult to translate *hoşgörü*, a term described in the Prologue as regarding someone else in the best and most accepting manner even though there may be differences and disagreements. Perhaps we may understand it as openhearted and open-minded empathy.

> People are talking about peace, contentment, ecology, justice, tolerance [*hoşgörü*], and dialogue. Unfortunately, the prevailing materialistic worldview disturbs the balance between humanity and nature and within individuals. This harmony and peace only occurs when the material and spiritual realms are reconciled.
>
> Religion reconciles opposites: religion-science, this world-the next world, Nature-Divine Books, material-spiritual, and spirit-body. It can contain scientific materialism, put science in its proper place, and end long-standing conflicts. The natural sciences, which should lead people to God, instead cause widespread unbelief. As this trend is strongest in the West, and because Christianity is the most influenced, Muslim-Christian dialogue is indispensable.
>
> Interfaith dialogue seeks to realize religion's basic oneness and unity, and the universality of belief. Religion embraces all beliefs and races in brotherhood, and exalts love, respect, tolerance [*hoşgörü*], forgiveness, mercy, human rights, peace, brotherhood and freedom via its Prophets.[256]

Although he calls for Muslims to dialogue with Hindus and Buddhists, he is particularly concerned with developing dialogue with

---

[255] *Essays, Perspectives, Opinions: Fethullah Gülen*, p. 34.
[256] Ibid, pp. 32–33.

Christians and Jews. The Qur'anic passage in Surah Al Imran is cited as the invitation to dialogue because the People of the Book and Muslims share a "*common word*" (3:64). The word for Gülen is "Let us not worship anything but God."[257] That is the starting point for dialogue among Muslims, Christians, and Jews. He lists five pillars of dialogue:[258]

1. Love
2. Altruism
3. Compassion
4. Forgiveness
5. Hoşgörü

Altruism as defined by Gülen is essential in dialogue and life:

> Altruism is an exalted human feeling, and its source is love. Whoever has the greatest share in this love is the greatest hero of humanity; these people have been able to uproot any feelings of hatred and rancor in themselves. Such heroes of love continue to live even after their death. These lofty souls who, by each day kindling a new torch of love in their inner world and by making their hearts a source of love and altruism, are welcomed and loved by people, have received the right to an eternal life from the Supreme Judge. Death, not even Doomsday, will be able to remove their traces.[259]

That list of Dialogue Pillars is bracketed by two absolutely essential factors: Love and Hoşgörü. The pillars of Love and Hoşgörü have eschatological connotations:

> Love is a person's most essential element. It is a most radiant light, a great power that can resist and overcome every force. Love elevates every soul that absorbs it and prepares it for eternity. Those who make contact with eternity through love seek to implant in others what they receive. They dedicate their lives to this, and endure any hardship for its sake.... Hoşgörü is the most essential element of moral systems, and a very important source of spiritual discipline and virtue. It causes merits to attain new depths and extend to infinity, and mistakes and faults to shrink into insignifi-

---

[257] Gülen, *Toward a Global Civilization*, p. 73.

[258] *Essays, Perspectives, Opinions: Fethullah Gülen*, pp. 41–43.

[259] Gülen, *Toward a Global Civilization of Love and Tolerance*, p. 2.

cance. God's treatment passes through the prism of hoşgörü, and
we wait for it to embrace us and all of creation.[260]

Education, Justice, and Dialogue are the necessary actions that
must be employed by humans to participate in consummating God's
Plan for the Fulfillment End of this world. The issue now becomes
who will take the lead and guide in enacting those steps, what and
who will oppose those efforts, and how will God be involved with
the leaders and their opponents.

## THE NEW MILLENNIUM-NEW SPRINGTIME: ITS SHAPE

In the opening months of the year 2000, Gülen reflected on the progress toward the Fulfillment-End:

> As every dawn, every sunrise, and every upcoming spring signifies
> a new beginning and hope, so does every new century and every
> new millennium. In this respect, within the wheels of time over
> which we have no control, humanity has always sought a new
> spark of life, of breath as fresh as the wind of dawn, and has hoped
> and desired to step into light from darkness as easily as crossing a
> threshold....[261]
>
> People live in perpetual hope, and thus are children of hope.
> As to the instant they lose their hope they also lose their "fire" of
> life, no matter if their physical existence continues. Hope is direct-
> ly proportional to having faith.[262]

He perceived that a dialogue of civilizations and religions was making progress and that such efforts, linked to education, were offering
genuine hope and expectations, such that people in general were awak-
ening to their capacities to end poverty and division. Indeed, in 2000
the then president of the Islamic Republic of Iran, Mohammad Khata-
mi, proposed that the United Nations dedicate the year 2001 as the
beginning of the "Dialogue of Civilizations" as an antidote to the Clash

---

[260] *Essays, Perspectives, Opinions: Fethullah Gülen*, pp. 41–43.
[261] Ibid, p. 21.
[262] Ibid, p. 22.

of Civilizations.[263] The United Nations did so designate 2001 and set up the steps to inaugurate programs among scholars, economic experts, and political leaders. The events of September 11, 2001 and the aftermath of the conflicts in Afghanistan and Iraq have cast dark shadows on the United Nations' sponsored effort, but annual conferences are still held to promote the concept. Gülen has not lost hope that interfaith dialogue will lead the way toward other dialogues that will advance peace:

> I believe and hope that the world of the new millennium will be a happier, more just, and more compassionate place, contrary to the fears of some people. Islam, Christianity, and Judaism all come from the same root, have almost the same essentials, and are nourished from the same source. Although they have lived as rival religions for centuries, the common points between them and their shared responsibility to build a happy world for all of the creatures of God make interfaith dialogue among them necessary. This dialogue has now expanded to include the religions of Asia and other areas.[264]

He holds that behind the conflicts and animosities lurks the split between science-reason and religion-spirituality as the basis for materialism, imperialistic socio-political drives, and the degradation of ethical values. He is convinced that through education and dialogue, leaders and average persons will call for and implement new and unifying patterns of education that will lead to the "springtime" of the Fulfillment End:

> The end of this conflict [between religion and science] and a new style of education fusing religious and scientific knowledge with morality and spirituality will produce genuinely enlightened people with hearts illumined by religious sciences and spirituality and with minds illuminated with positive sciences characterized by all kinds of humane merits and moral values, and cognizant of the socioeconomic and political conditions of their time. Our old world will experience an excellent "springtime" before its demise. This springtime will see the gap between rich and poor narrow; the world's

---

[263] See *Huntington*. Note the work of B. *Jill Carroll* who related Gülen's positions to various philosophical traditions.

[264] *Essays, Perspectives, Opinions: Fethullah Gülen*, pp. 29–30.

riches distributed most justly according to one's work, capital, and needs; the absence of discrimination based on race, color, language, and worldview; and basic human rights and freedoms protected. Individuals will come to the fore and, learning how to realize their potential will ascend on the way to becoming "the most elevated human" with the wings of love, knowledge, and belief.

Gülen, feeling that the Qur'an forecasts great technological advances that we will understand in the future, looks forward to inter-planetary travel and advances in medicine and agriculture that will end poverty and renew the environment. All within God's Plan and built on the foundations God has called upon humans to actualize:

> In this new springtime, when scientific and technological progress is taken into consideration, people will understand that the current level of science and technology resembles the stage when an infant is learning how to crawl. Humanity will organize trips into space as if traveling to another country. Travelers on the way to God—those self-immolators of love who have no time for hostility, will carry the inspirations in their spirits to other worlds.
>
> Yes, this springtime will rise on the foundations of love, compassion, mercy, dialogue, acceptance of others, mutual respect, justice, and rights. It will be a time in which humanity will discover its real essence. Goodness and kindness, righteousness and virtue will form the basic essence of the world. No matter what happens, the world will come to this track, sooner or later. Nobody can prevent this.
>
> We pray and beg the Infinitely Compassionate One not to let our hopes and expectations come to nothing.[265]

## THE NEW MILLENNIUM-NEW SPRINGTIME: ITS SHAPERS AND MIS-SHAPERS

The New Millennium-New Springtime, or the Fulfillment-End of Dunya, will come neither rapidly nor without Divine influence nor without struggles and tests. In that way, the establishment of the Fulfillment-End is a preview of the Final-End, which will come with intensified signs, Divine action, struggles, and tests. As indicated in Chapter Two and above, Muslims, including Gülen, anticipated the return

---

[265] Ibid, pp. 30–31.

of the spirit of the Messiahood as a collective spiritual personality in the End Times. Gülen agreed with those scholars who interpreted the Qur'an and recognized in the Hadith that there would be two returns of the collective spiritual personality of Jesus the Messiah and the Mahdi, one for each of the Endings. In a similar manner, they understood the Hadith reports to forecast two types of the Dajjal and the Sufyan, again for the two eschatological Endings. Reflecting Sufi understandings and Nursi's insights, Gülen advanced his understandings of the Shapers and the attempted Mis-Shapers of the New Millennium-New Springtime. We turn again to his view of the descent of Jesus as a spiritual personality, influencing inspired persons in the world.

> Islam has a Prophetic Tradition that Jesus will return during the last days. For Muslims this means that such values as love, peace, brotherhood, forgiveness, altruism, mercy, and spiritual purification will have precedence. As Jesus was sent to the Jews and all Jewish Prophets exalted these values, dialogue with the Jews must be established, as well as a closer relationship and cooperation among Islam, Christianity and Judaism.[266]

Gülen noted and agreed with Nursi's idea:

> If there is a need for Islam, the manifest religion, to express itself in various places in the world again, the Messiah will come back right away, even from the remotest corner of the other world. However, in order to shed light upon his general outlook, he [Nursi] interpreted the descent of Jesus as a spiritual personality. He further stated that the Messiah would be represented by a group or a section of the society.[267]

Gülen does not expect Jesus to be manifested at this point as an apocalyptic demon-slaying warrior. He was the Messenger of spirituality to what the Qur'an and Hadith characterize as an almost totally materialistic society. He will be the source of influence from the heav-

---

[266] Ibid, p. 33.

[267] Ibid, *Questions and Answers*, Vol. 2, p. 154. Both Nursi and Gülen warn against identifying any particular person as the returned Messiah or as the Mahdi. Those who make such a claim are by that very claim abusers of the concepts of Messiahhood and Mahdi-hood and heretics. (See also footnote 95).

enly dimension to raise up persons who, in turn, will carry forward God's message and purpose in the telos-age. As cited earlier, Jesus the Messiah's "coming simply means that a spirit of compassion or a phenomenon of mercy will come to the foreground, a breeze of clemency will waft over humanity, and human beings will compromise and agree with each other."[268]

Gülen understands Jesus in his earthly mission as preaching faith, justice, mercy, humility, peace, love, repentance, and helping others while urging his followers to be pure in intention and action. That set of actions is incumbent on Muslims and Christians in the present world.[269] We will return shortly to the persons who will be raised up through the influence of the the the spirit of the Messiahood of Jesus.

As the "return" of Jesus in the Fulfillment–End is not a physical but spiritual guidance, so too the function of the Dajjal in that time is through ideologies, organizations, and persons who seek to oppress, distort, and injure others and the environment through deception, violence, and destructive power. In other words, the Dajjal in the present is not a single individual but a set of dajjals.[270] Therefore, those who are raised up to be the women and men that will move the world to its Fulfillment-End will struggle with the ideological and personal dajjals at least until their efforts at education, justice, and dialogue succeed. Sometimes Gülen suggests that the major role of the spirituality of Jesus in this time is to influence the non-Muslims, especially the Christians, to join believing Muslims on the Straight Path.

Two other "End Time" figures, the Sufyan and Mahdi, and the once-a-century Renewers mentioned in Chapter Two have analogues in the struggle toward the realization of the Fulfillment-End. As was the case with the Dajjal(s), the Sufyan in the present circumstances can be an individual as well as ideologies, misrepresentations, distortions, and distorters of the religion who aim to mislead Muslims. Likewise the Mahdi and Renewers now are not single identifiable individuals but leaders who will guide and lead the believers away

[268] Ibid, pp. 148–149.
[269] Ünal, *Resurrection and Afterlife*, pp. 177–179.
[270] Ibid, pp. 169–170.

from error so that there will be a genuine revival of Islam as a religion of peace, justice, compassion, and mercy.

In discussing the Messiah, Mahdi, Dajjal, Sufyan, and Renewers, Gülen is careful and firm. His caution is that it is risky for anyone to point to one or another individual, claiming that the person is a messiah, mahdi, renewer, dajjal, or sufyan. He is firm in stating that for someone to present himself (and presumably herself as well) as one of these figures is an unacceptable deviation.[271]

In the course of his reflections on these figures, Gülen notes that claims about them has led to abuse within the Muslim community and distorting criticisms from outside the community. On numerous other occasions, Gülen has been strongly and consistently adamant to the point of denunciation of the use of violence and terror in the name of Islam or any religion. He "hates" Osama bin Laden for tainting the pure image of religion and states unequivocally that no matter what persons may say their motivations are, no Muslim can ever be a terrorist.[272]

> One of the people whom I hate most in the world is [Osama] Bin Laden, because he has sullied the bright face of Islam. He has created a contaminated image. Even if we were to try our best to fix the terrible damage that has been done, it would take years to repair.
>
> We speak about this perversion everywhere on many different platforms. We write books about it. We say, "this is not Islam." Bin Laden replaced Islamic logic with his own feelings and desires. He is a monster, as are the people around him. If there are other people similar to them anywhere, then they too, are nothing more than monsters.
>
> We condemn this attitude of Laden. However, the only way to prevent this kind of deeds is that Muslims living in the countries seeming to be Islamic—and I stated earlier that I do not perceive an Islamic world, there are only countries in which Muslims live—will solve their own problems.
>
> Should they think in a totally different way when electing their leaders? Or should they carry out fundamental reforms? For the

---

[271] Gülen, *Questions and Answers*, Vol. 2, pp. 143–156.

[272] Ibid, *Toward a Global Civilization of Love and Tolerance*, p. 187. See also *Essays, Perspectives, Opinions: Fethullah Gülen*, pp. 95–100.

growth of a well-developed younger generation, Muslims must work to solve their problems. Not only their problems in the issue of terror, an instrument that is certainly not approved of by God, but also those concerning drugs and the use of cigarettes, two more unlawful habits. Dissension, civil turmoil, never-ending poverty, the disgrace of being governed by others, and being insulted after having put up with government by foreign powers are all problems that could be added to the list.

## THE NEW MILLENNIUM-NEW SPRINGTIME: THE GOLDEN GENERATION

Sometimes he calls them the "Golden Generation (*Altin Nesil*), the New Man and Woman, People of Heart, persons of integrity, discoverers of the unknown, lovers of God, and Heroes of Love. Whatever the titles may be, his hope is a confident expectation that the men and women of the "Awaited Generation" are already active in the world:

> We have long been awaiting a generation, with hearts as pure and kind as angels, with will-power strong enough to overcome the most formidable obstacles, and minds keen enough to solve all the problems of the age. Had it not been for the persistence of our hope for the coming of such a blessed generation, we would long ago have been a thing of the past.
>
> We live in the darkest of nights until they appear on our horizon with radiant faces promising the breaking of dawn. Once they have appeared on our horizon, this land of the wretched and the miserable, resembling a gloomy graveyard, will begin to be cheered by flowers of every kind. If our hopes are not blighted by a poisonous wind, this land, changing into a flower-garden through the reviving water that that generation brings, will be a place of happiness and "spiritual recreation" for all the world's people, a place of peace, harmony and serenity. The world of the future will be so enlightened by their light that the moon and the sun will be dim in comparison. In their enlightened ethos, the universe will be studied as a meaningful book and the music of brotherhood will be played everywhere. Art and literature will be refined of coarseness and vulgarities of all kinds and find noble-minded practitioners.
>
> This world will indeed be built anew when they sound the note of revival, and those who fell into a kind of winter sleep will wake up. The music of despair composed by Satan and played by

some indolent persons will stop; people will be exhilarated with melodies of hope and activity which they compose and play.

The awaited generation are successors to the mission of the master of the Prophets, and therefore have inherited the loyalty and faithfulness of Adam, the resolve and steadfastness of Noah, the devotion and gentleness of Abraham, the valour and dynamism of Moses, the forbearance and compassion of Jesus. When found together in a group, these qualities are such a great source of power that those who have them will inevitably seize the "reins" of the world, provided they remain loyal to the covenant God has made with them.

The world is to be saved by that "golden" generation who represent the Divine Mercy, from all the disasters, intellectual, spiritual, social and political, with which it has long been afflicted. The world will come back, through their efforts, to its "primordial" pattern, on which God created it, and be purified of all kinds of deviation and ignorance, so that people may rise to "the highest of the high" on the ladder of belief, knowledge and love, supported against the heavens by the Divine Message.[273]

Put in terms of the telos-eschaton, now is the time for the rise of a new generation. That generation will be composed of women and men who are mirrors of the Divine manifestations, conscious bearers and manifesters of the Beautiful Names that accord with the abilities of the individuals. They will be persons who are becoming fully human as God intended, and in the growth process, they will serve humanity as members of the Golden Generation seeking to achieve the New Millennium-Springtime.[274] He realizes that the unfolding and rise of the new generation will be difficult, even painful:

> The coming-to-be of such people will not be easy. All births are painful, but these blessed births will take place and provide the world with a new, brilliant generation. Just as rain pours out of slowly gathering clouds and water wells up from underground, so too will the "flowers" of this new generation appear amongst us.... These

---

[273] Ibid, *Toward a Lost Paradise*, p. 5.

[274] See Gülen, *Toward a Global Civilization*, pp. 81–94. These individuals bear some resemblances to the fully fulfilled humans in Sufism called the "Universal Man." See *Sufism*, Vol. 2, especially pp. 286–299. "Universal Man" may also be rendered "Perfect Human."

new people will unite profound spirituality, diverse knowledge, sound thinking, a scientific temperament, and wise activism. Never content with what they know, they will continuously increase in knowledge: knowledge of self, of nature, and of God.... Equipped with the good morals and virtues that make them truly human, these new men and women will be altruists who embrace humanity with love and are ready to sacrifice themselves for the good of others when necessary. As they shape themselves in the mould of universal virtue, they will simultaneously strive to illuminate the way of others. They will defend and support what is good and recommend it to others, while seeking to challenge, combat, and eradicate all evils.... As they remove through faith and knowledge, the veils covering the face of reality, they will become even more eager to advance further. With messages from the Heavens, the earth and the seas, they will continue to journey until they return to their Creator. [275]

Granted that Gülen's expectations for such a generation are expressed in the ornate rhetoric of a visionary preacher-scholar and granted that the statement contains numerous elements of his theological positions, that generation is, nevertheless, being actualized. Hizmet is one of the forms that it is carrying out this vision in the world today. Obviously, the name of the Pennsylvania retreat center where Gülen resides, "Golden Generation," is a statement about the goals of the programs, activities, incentives, and influences that are associated with the persons who look to Gülen and seek to be part of the wide-ranging efforts his thinking and person engender. Yet the activities are best understood in light of the journey of all creation and creatures to the Hereafter, the return to the Creator. Gülen realizes that the telos-eschaton has not blossomed forth – yet. He sees the dawning of the New Age, and all persons are invited, even urged, to be part of its light. Hizmet may be understood as the nascent Golden Generation expressed in community (*camia*) form, that is, as the groupings of individuals and entities that seek to spread that dawn's light.

---

[275] Gülen, *Toward a Global Civilization of Love and Tolerance*, excerpted from pages 81, 82 and 83.

While a more complete exposition of Gülen's proposals for the Golden Generation and what those who link themselves to it need to do is beyond the scope of this study, some comment is fitting about what Gülen advises those affiliated with him and Hizmet to do in society.[276] He understands these to be part of the Divine Plan that aims toward the Day of Judgement and the Hereafter. At the same time, the scope of his thinking embraces all persons, especially the People of the Book, to join in those influences and efforts. Hizmet's activities match the three pressing issues and their resolutions.

Gülen made clear that the type of education needed was one in which science and reason were not set as polar opposites to ethics and spiritual values. Typically, in Gülen-inspired schools, religion is not one of the subjects. Parenthetically, Gülen himself has no connections with the schools and does not know where or how many have been established.[277] Educational institutions from day care centers to universities have been opened in many countries throughout the world.

Poverty is addressed through education and also through relief agencies such as Kimse Yok Mu, a Turkish organization that provides emergency assistance in times of natural disasters (for example after recent earthquakes and flood in Turkey, Haiti, Pakistan, and Japan) and immediate and on-going humanitarian crises (for example refugee camps in Darfur and Somalia as well as construction aid in Bosnia). Advocacy efforts with governmental and non-governmental organizations are undertaken by numerous Turkish Cultural Centers. These often sponsor programs and forums on social issues that include political, financial, and societal organizational leaders. Most recently, those Centers have taken one of Gülen's ideas to form what he called Peace Islands Institutes. Gülen regards every family, school, community service organization, and dialogue as a locus for peace building. The vision

---

[276] I suggest that interested readers may refer to *Ebaugh; Esposito and Yilmaz*; and *Ahsan Khan*.

[277] In *Essays, Perspectives, Opinions* (p. 5), Gülen states concerning the Gülen-inspired schools: "It is impossible for me to know about all of the schools that have been opened here and abroad. Since I only recommended and encouraged this, I do not even know the names of many of the companies that opened them or where the schools are located."

is that as these "islands" expand, they will touch other areas of their communities with concerns to establish harmony and understanding and to effect appropriate changes.[278]

Gülen regards Disunity-Separatism as perhaps the greatest challenge for Muslims, and it is certainly a serious problem within religions and societies as well as between societies. The prescription he advocates is deep, persistent, open dialogue. In response to Gülen's call for interfaith dialogue, affiliates of Hizmet have established scores of interfaith and intercultural dialogue centers in dozens of countries. Through the centers, Hizmet sponsors and subsidizes tours to Turkey. Gülen and Hizmet affiliates understand Turkey to be the bridge between East and West; Judaism, Christianity and Islam; Europe and Central-East Asia; and even among Muslim groups. Both informally and formally, these centers are gathered under the umbrella of, for instance, the Peace Islands Institute in the US.

Viewed from Below, Gülen's vision of the Fulfillment-End of this world is eschatological in that it calls on persons to examine the recent and then to act to prepare the world and themselves for the coming Terminal-End. For Gülen and Hizmet that preparation entails justice, peace, and unity among all peoples. Linked to the view from Above Together, the bifocal approach addresses the present and looks to the future.

> We expect love and respect, *hoşgörü* and forgiveness, and liberality and affection, especially from God. But can we expect these if we do not first offer them to others?....Those who want to reform the world must first reform themselves; purify their inner worlds of hatred, rancor and jealousy; and adorn their outer worlds with virtue. Those who lack self-control, self-discipline, and refined feelings may seem attractive and insightful at first. However, what they inspire in others disappears quickly.
>
> Goodness, beauty, truthfulness, and being virtuous are the essence of the world and humanity. Whatever happens, the world will one day find this essence. No one can prevent this.[279]

---

[278] See *Esposito and Yilmaz* for a development of Gülen and Hizmet in regard to "Peace Building."

[279] *Essays, Perspectives, Opinions: Fethullah Gülen*, p. 43.

## BETWEEN THE ACTS: DEATH AND THE GRAVE

Death is an essential part of God's Plan for all the worlds and is the transition for humans no matter when on the span of time a person dies. Gülen is in full agreement with the Islamic and Sufi traditions that believers should not fear but welcome death and the grave:

> Believers and those who do righteous deeds do not need to fear death. Although death seems to bring decomposition, extinguish life, and destroy pleasure, in fact it represents a Divine discharge from the heavy duties of worldly life. It is a change of residence, a transferal of the body, an invitation to and the beginning of everlasting life....
>
> Death releases us from the hardships of worldly life—a turbulent, suffocating, narrow dungeon of space that gradually becomes more unbearable through old age and affliction—and admits us to the infinitely wide circle of the Eternal, Beloved One's mercy. There, we may enjoy the everlasting company of our beloved ones and the consolation of a happy, eternal life.[280]

Chapter Two covered the basic view of the departure of the souls of believers and those who were righteous in life together with their ascent into the presence of God and return to the grave to await the Day of Resurrection. In the same context, we noted the dire plight of the wicked and rejecters whose departure from their bodies and their treatment on their ascent and return to the grave was a painful disclosure of their eternal fate. Gülen is in full agreement with those views concerning the blessed righteous and the hell-bound damned:

> Mankind exists to experience death, dies to experience the resurrection, and is resurrected in order to experience the eternal life. One by one, each individual is born into this world...one by one, each individual travels along this extremely long path of life...and regardless of the various aspects humans may have in common, each lives in accordance with their own fate...experiences their own fate, and then according to the scope of the program of life, many continue onto the eternal realm to experience a totally different life without glancing back even for a moment.

---

[280] Gülen, *Essentials,* pp. 51–52.

As for those whose souls are adorned with faith, whose hearts are adjusted according to life in the Hereafter, and who are in a state of complete metaphysical intensity amidst the emotion and perception "Faith is both a form of light and strength, a human who attains true faith is capable of challenging the universe"; experience their childhood as a ballad of pleasure and always exclaim their existence with immense enthusiasm and spirit...their youth passes with great discipline, as a character of willpower and dignity like the Prophet Joseph...and their years of maturity are adorned with actions and behavior that is to be an example for others in the future, and like reflectors which light up the roads of darkness, they constantly emphasize the necessity of remaining on the straight path...they spend their days of old age in a state of hope and steadfastness, a belief of such that it is virtually as if they are travelling along the corridors towards Paradise, a determination and devoutness of the great Prophets, a reassurance associated with the Prophets.

To be more precise, unlike the others whose souls bear the seed from the tree of hell that constantly casts a shadow of darkness and gloom on their worlds, these individuals who bear the seeds of faith in their hearts encounter the world beyond and the scenes adorning it with pleasure. They imagine themselves on a trip to Paradise and its slopes from which God can be observed, and in a sense they feel and experience the physics-metaphysics, the universe-hereafter and the spirit-body as a single integration.

When the time arrives and the world beyond begins to unveil, the seed of hell in the imagination makes itself apparent in the entire environment like a nightmare of gloom...it froths like magma, and releases fear into the souls...encompasses the entire horizon like a cloud of fog or smoke...transforms into a form of torment causing affliction to the souls...turns into tribulation showering pain and anguish...and naturally the seed of the tree of Paradise in the souls begins to release its roots and branches...showering a radiance of bliss into the souls in which it develops, and is then encompassed by the sweet fragrance of basil...and like mystical escalators, those who grasp onto its leaves are carried towards tranquility, security, bliss and eternity...ensuring they reach Paradise, reach the horizon from which the beauty of God is observed. In brief, with the seeds carried in the hearts of both groups and the development of these seeds, what they experience in their consciences briefly, what they interpret and actually see and experience appears in a much different dimension and they begin to see everything more clearly:

*"Then when the horn is sounded, that Day will be a day of hardship, for the unbelievers—not easy."* (al-Muddathir 74:8–10) *"And when the heaven is torn away, and when the Blazing Flame is kindled, and when Paradise is brought near, every person will come to know what he has prepared (for himself)."* (at-Takwir 81:11–14).[281]

Except for Prophets, Messengers, and some other extraordinarily righteous persons, most believers and those who sought to live justly will die with some unforgiven sins on their records. Gülen, in agreement with many Muslims, understands that God is All-Merciful, All-Compassionate, and All-Forgiving. For those persons, the time in the grave will be a period of cleansing and repentance to prepare the individuals for the Judgment and their journey to the Gardens.

> The intermediate world [of the grave]is the realm where the spirit feels the "breath" of the bliss of Paradise or the punishment of Hell. If we led a virtuous life in the world, our good deeds (e.g., prayers, recitations, acts of charity) will appear as amiable fellows. Also, windows onto heavenly scenes will be opened for us and, as stated in a hadith, our grave will become like a garden of Paradise. However, if some of our sins still remain unpardoned, regardless of how virtuous we were, we may suffer some punishment in the intermediate world until we become deserving of Paradise. Unbelievers who indulged in sin will be met by their deeds, which will assume the forms of bad fellows and vermin. They will see scenes of Hell, and their graves will become like a pit of Hell.[282]

Gülen, ever-imparting encouragement to persons in the present, observed:

> Our account is not closed after we die. If we leave behind good, virtuous children, books, or institutions from which people continue to benefit, or if we have raised or contributed to raising those who benefit others, our reward increases. If we leave evil behind, our sins increase as long as our evil harms others. Therefore, if we want to help our beloved ones who have died, we should do good,

---

[281] Ibid, "What Death Brings to Mind, and the World Beyond," "Ölümün Hatırlattıkları ve Ötesi" in *Işığın Göründüğü Ufuk* (The Horizon Where the Light Appeared). Istanbul: Nil Yayınları, 2011, excerpted from pp. 199–206.

[282] Ibid, *Essentials*, p. 54.

righteous deeds. If we help the poor, take part in Islamic services, lead a good and virtuous life, and especially spend to promote Islam and the good of Muslims and humanity at large, we will cause the reward to increase.[283]

Act One of God's eschatological Plan leads to Act Two: the Final End.

## GOD'S ESCHATOLOGICAL PLAN: ACT TWO, THE FINAL END

In addition to agreeing with the general Islamic understanding of the Terminal End, with the various signs and now personages who will be part of the End Time, Gülen is cautious about speculations that cannot be rooted in the Qur'an and Sunna:

> The unprecedented developments in science and technology will cause humanity to believe that it has so much knowledge and power that an authority above itself is no longer required or necessary. This will lead people to rebel against Heaven and indulge in debauchery to the extent that a worldwide apostasy will take place. Few believers will be left, and the unbelieving, rebellious forces will destroy the Ka'ba. This will mark the end of the world. God Almighty will gently take the souls of the believers. According to Said Nursi, as the result of a probable collision of a heavenly body with the Earth, the Earth will begin to rotate in the opposite direction and the sun will rise in the west. This is the final sign of the world's destruction.[284]

The Fulfillment of Dunya is part of God's Plan but is not the consummation of the Plan. Although life in Dunya's First Ending is just and peaceful, it is only temporary. The New Springtime will fade into a dark and destructive winter. Gülen himself does not engage at great length or in detail about the duration of the New Millennium-Springtime nor the conditions that lead up to its conclusion.

---

[283] Ibid, p. 55. A Hadith recorded in *Sahih al-Bukhari* (Vol. 9, Book 92, Item 601) states that even the believers who have committed major sins and will thus be sentenced to Fire will be saved in the end. Muhammad will be permitted by God to intercede for those of his followers who will be sentenced to Hell, and they will be brought out of the fire and will enter the Gardens.

[284] Ünal, *Resurrection and Afterlife*, p. 180.

[A] reason the Qur'an does not concentrate on future events explicitly is that the whole point of religion is to examine and test the individual so that elevated and base spirits may be distinguished.... Since the Qur'an was sent to perfect humanity through trial in this abode of testing and competition, it can only allude to future events that everyone will witness one day, and only opens the door to reason to a degree that proves its argument.[285]

Ünal includes selections from Nursi's chain of reports from different Hadith collections on the signs and their meanings. While he and Gülen hold out the possibility that the Prophetic reports of the antichrist figures such as the Great Dajjal and Great Sufyan may not be exclusively about their persons but also about "their ideologies and committees, and the [false] systems they will establish in all aspects of life," they leave the prospects open to the knowledge of God.[286]

In any event, Gülen recognizes that as the Final End approaches, the hearts and minds of many persons will be satiated with peace, justice, and prosperity. Most will lose their zeal for worship, spirituality, and mutual love. They will focus on entertainment, dissipation, immoral behavior, and pride in what they suppose are their own accomplishments. The Dajjal and/or dajjals will mislead persons into false worship throughout the world while the Sufyan and/or sufyans will do similar things within the Muslim world. In those dismal circumstances, the Last Signs detailed in Chapter Two will begin to unfold. Gülen cites Hadith traditions to the effect that practicing Muslims and other righteous persons will not be subjected to the horrors and anguish of the Final End of Dunya. According to some Hadiths, a gentle wind from Yemen will waft over the world, and believers and righteous persons will die quietly and without trauma.[287] Gülen cites Hadith material that quote Muhammad speaking about the signs of the End such as the drying up of the Euphrates, the mountain of gold, and so on. Again, these

---

[285] Ibid, pp. 168–169.
[286] Ibid, pp. 170–173.
[287] *Sahih Muslim*, Vol. 1, 43 and 898.

may be taken literally or symbolically. He suggests that it might point to the discovery of oil in Iraq and Iran that trigger wide conflicts.[288]

Gülen also anticipates the return-descent of Jesus and his partnership with the Mahdi in overcoming the forces of evil. As mentioned in Chapter Two, the Muslim expectation is that the returning Jesus will follow the Law of Muhammad and will correct the errors that crept into Christianity, leading Christians into Islam.

The balance of the Day of Judgment, including the death of all the worlds, the sounding of the trumpets, resurrection of the dead, setting up of the balance scales, and the marshaling of the resurrected to the Gathering Place for the Judgment follow the traditional Qur'anic and Hadith descriptions. For example, on that Day, the heat will be so great that people will sweat profusely:

> God will shade seven (groups) of people under His shade on the Day when there will be no shade except His: the just ruler; young people who have grown up in worship of God, may He be glorified; those people who are greatly attached to mosques; two persons who love each other for God's sake, meet and then leave each other because of this love; men who refuse the invitations of beautiful women of rank, saying: "I fear God"; those who spend in the way of God so secretly that when they give charity to the one on his left, the one on the right does not see it; and those whose eyes fill with tears when they mention God in seclusion.[289]

He holds the Hadith traditions concerning the Resurrection, the Place of Gathering, the Final Reckoning, the Bridge, Paradise, and Hell.[290] Throughout those considerations, Gülen advises and warns that deeds done in this world will bear good or bitter fruit on the Day of Judgment and into the Hereafter. The great Sufi master, al-Ghazzali wrote of that Day:

> [B]eware of denying any of the wonders of the Day of Resurrection because they [the wonders] are not to be measured in accordance with the measure of mundane things. Had a unit seen the wonders

---

[288] Gülen, *Muhammad*, p. 58.

[289] Ibid, p. 118.

[290] Ibid, pp. 66 and 358.

of this present world, and they were intimated to you before you witnessed them you would deny them most vehemently. Bring to mind, then, an image of yourself, as you stand naked, uncovered, outcast and ashamed, bewildered and dazed, awaiting the Judgment which will decide your rapture or misery. Make much of this state, for it shall be momentous.[291]

## GOD'S ESCHATOLOGICAL PLAN:
## THE NEW BEGINNING OF THE HEREAFTER

Allah's Messenger (peace and blessings be upon him) said that Allah would say to the inmates of Paradise: "O, Dwellers of Paradise," and they would say in response: "At Thy service and pleasure, our Lord, the good is in Thy Hand." He (the Lord) would say: "Are you well pleased now?" They would say: "Why should we not be pleased, O Lord, when Thou hast given us what Thou has not given to any of Thy creatures?" He would, however, say: "May I not give you (something) even more excellent than that?" And they would say: "O Lord, what thing can be more excellent than this?" And He would say: "I shall cause My pleasure to alight upon you, and I shall never be afterwards annoyed with you."[292]

The Endings are almost over. The New Beginning without end is coming. The Plan reaches its consummation as humans cross the final steps of the Straight Way, which has narrowed so that they have to go single file. According to tradition, the unrighteous will fall from the Path, plunging thereby into their places in Hell. The righteous will be welcomed by the angels into the eternal Gardens. Gülen expends little time describing the torments of those who have condemned themselves to damnation through their unbelief and sins. The Qur'an and Hadith cover their fate sufficiently. He accepts gladly the descriptions of Paradise, allowing for expressions of metaphor and symbolism in language on the Dunya-side of life.

As the newly arrived inhabitants of Paradise arrive, they are surprised not by what is different from earthly existence but what is so familiar. The veils that prevented them from seeing through the gauze

---

[291] *Al-Ghazzali*, p. 179.
[292] *Sahih Muslim*, Vol. 4, Book 38, Chapter 1172, Hadith number 6787.

of causes and effects are removed. Now they can see the actual archetypes and the realities that were mirrored in this world. The pool of Zamzam near the Ka'ba is the reflection of the heavenly pool of Kawthar.[293] The fruits and trees they knew in their previous lives are revealed as eternally beautiful – and available to them. In Dunya, they had to think about what they wanted, move to get it, or even work to earn it. Now simply desiring something will make it materialize for them. Of course, what they desire and how they use it will be for love and peace. Gülen wrote:

> [Death] is a door opening to light, a corridor delivering people to luminous realms and a launch pad of the soul to take flight towards the beyond. Those who completed their parade duty before the Infinite Witness or got completely prepared for the eternal bliss by adding profundity to their faith with worship and adding profound *ihsan* (perfect goodness) into their worship through an expansive integrity of service in this world where they had been as soldiers march through this corridor towards the transcendent sets of bliss which no eyes had seen and no ears had heard.
>
> In proportion to their belief, capitals of faith and horizons of the *marifah* (knowledge of God) in their realms of heart, they are already "seated on lined thrones encrusted with precious stones, reclining upon them facing one another at the most select locations of the Gardens of *Naim* (Gardens of Delight and Blessedness). Spirited and bright youths go around them waiting upon their service, they hold in their hands ewers, cups, and goblets effervescing with the *Kawthar*. Neither have they any headache nor any intoxication and above their heads are abundant fruits such as they choose... Flesh of fowls such as they desire, hazel-eyed spouses untouched like pearls in their shells... cherry trees laden with fruit... banana trees with fruit piled high... elongating shadows... cascading and flowing streams... fruits of every other kind never-ending and not forbidden..." (See Surah al-Waqi'ah). Bent on goodness always, these people "recline on such thrones that they find there neither scorching sun nor biting cold. The trees of Paradise ever throw their shade on them and their fruits hang down low within their reach" (See Surah al-Insan). "On that Day, there are such faces beaming with delight, they are well-pleased in that lofty

---

[293] The clear-flowing spring and drink of Paradise especially connected to Muhammad's dwelling in Paradise.

Garden on having been rewarded with the fruit of their endeavor... over there they hear no idle talk... and there are gushing springs, couches raised high, goblets placed ready to drink from, reclining cushions arrayed and gorgeous carpets spread out" (See Surah al-Ghashiyah). "And these are the Gardens of *'Adn* (Gardens of Eternal Bliss) through which rivers flow. Moreover, God is well-pleased with them and they are well-pleased with Him; this station of *rida* (resignation) is exclusive only for those who stand in awe of their Lord. Yes, "their reward is the Gardens of *'Adn;* they enter there adorned with armbands of gold and pearls, and their garments are of silk. (While entering they say): "All praise and gratitude are for God, Who has removed sorrow and grief from us; surely our Lord is All-Forgiving and All-Responsive; He rewards us by far and away of what we did" (See Surah al-Fatir).[294]

It is a New Beginning that is certainly worth living for in this life. In the life journey to that new beginning and its transitions through the worlds and Dunya, Gülen sees men and women in deepening fellowship with God and with one another.

## SUMMARY AND TRANSITION

Gülen's vision of the New Beginning embraces his visions for the Beginnings and the Endings. His vision certainly looks forward through the veils and tests to the future promised by God. Yet he directs our attention to this world and God's will for the present. In that effort, he is genuinely eschatological without being apocalyptic. He joins the spiritual dimensions with the rational aspects of experience in order to unite not only human endeavors but to unite the factors of body, spirit, and soul in order to take action towards resolving the dilemmas of ignorance, poverty, and division with universal education, justice, and dialogue. He gives these efforts and challenges the encouragement of a preacher and the practicality of experience through Hizmet and those who are influenced by the works and activities of the movement. We met him as a man of hope and expectation – and always as

---

[294] Gülen, "The Other Side of Death," "Ölümün Öteki Yüzü" in *Işığın Göründüğü Ufuk* (The Horizon Where the Light Appeared). Istanbul: Nil Yayınları, 2011, pp. 264–269. Text and translation provided by Yusuf Alan.

a devout Muslim. Now we turn to his challenges for those who have ears to listen and eyes to share the vision. He wrote about the new women and men:

> These new people will conquer their selves, thoughts, and hearts, and those of others, and they will discover the unknown. They will regard any time spent in not taking a new step into the depths of the self and the universe as being wasted. As they remove, through faith and knowledge, the veils covering the face of reality, they will become even more eager to advance further. With the messages and answers received from the Heavens, the Earth, and the seas, they will continue to journey until they return to their Creator.[295]

---

[295] Ibid, *Toward a Global Civilization of Love and Tolerance*, p. 83.

## CHAPTER FIVE

---

## Gülen's Challenges
## for Today's World

In his speeches and writings, Fethullah Gülen stresses the role of democracy, peace, dialogue, and tolerance in the development of peaceful coexistence between Muslim and non-Muslim populations. Some Western concepts of national identity connect tolerance with submission to the values of a majority. However, as Gülen…explains, "Tolerance [*hoşgörü*] does not mean being influenced by others or joining them; it means accepting them as they are and knowing how to get along with them." As Gülen repeatedly stresses, to over-come violence and hate, people of different religions and faiths must develop an atmosphere of mutual respect and peaceful coexistence and engage in dialogue.[296]

We have started to meet Fethullah Gülen. For many of the forty years (1959–1999) he was posted by the Turkish government's Directory for Religious Affairs as a preach-ing-teaching imam with administrative responsibilities in some of Turkey's large cities. While in his initial posting, he was introduced to and studied the thought and writings of Said Nursi. His renown as a preacher open to discussion, especially with youth, his dedication to education especially for the poor and those of modest means, and his in-person and tape recorded lectures gained thousands of supporters. More importantly, he has inspired persons to be dedicated and active in carrying on proposals he has generated and inspired. The rhetoric of

---

[296] Karina Korostelina, "Dialogue as a Source of Peaceful Coexistence," in *Islam and Peacebuilding*, Esposito and Yilmaz (eds.), p. 103.

the devout, enthusiastic preacher informed by his knowledge of philosophy and science comes through clearly in his writings and speeches.

We also meet him as a person thoroughly informed about the world around him. His first assignment was to the major urban center, Edirne, in Turkish Thrace. Close to the border of Orthodox Greece and Soviet-dominated Bulgaria, he knew of the ethnic-religious animosities between Greeks and Turks and the tensions of the Cold War between the USSR and the United States. He was well acquainted with the claims of atheistic materialism and the brutality of the Stalinist regime. At the same time, he also experienced the policies and practices of the determined ultra secular military authorities in his own country. Gülen tends to regard the glory days of the Ottoman Empire (from the fifteenth to beginning of the nineteenth centuries) as a time of religious pluralism and acceptance, cultural and intellectual brilliance, harmony, vibrant faith, prosperity, and peace. By the same token, he often looks upon the twenty-first century Turkey with alarm and hope. Indeed, alarm and hope may be seen as the twin themes of the challenges that I suggest Gülen points to in present situations and persons.

The first challenge is to the Turkish people and the several authorities that govern the Republic. Gülen favors neither a theocratic state nor a secular society that marginalizes religion and expressions of religion. He claims that Turkey and its people have a great heritage and an important future if they revive religious values, human dignity, and insure justice based on religious principles, all within the context of democracy. His 1998 *The Statue of Our Souls*, published the year before he left Turkey for the United States, is an appeal to Turks to see themselves as one people, not as mutually suspicious fragmented ethnicities. The way to achieve that goal is to revive Islamic consciousness and to put into action the Islamic values of seeking peace, merciful action, treating others with respect – and service to God. He understands Turkey to be the coming leader in helping to move the world toward the telos-eschaton because it has been a major home of religions and the birthplace of philosophy, and it is the cultural-political bridge between Asia and the West. His sense of alarm includes the prospects that old ethnic or ultra nationalistic animosities could become more aggressive and violent than at present, that militant Islamists might generate disorder and a skewed understanding of Islam, or that a resurgent anti-religious secularism might capture the loyalties of youth to the undercutting of genuine piety. He wrote:

> I must point out that this noble nation, which has been compelled to suffer blasphemous and arbitrary oppression for years, has never been completely subdued, and the aspirations to the eternal life in its thoughts have never been extinguished. These thoughts are at the same time a red hot ember, a spark that crackles with life when it stirs and a source of light which is able to illuminate the worlds.[297]

Gülen's second challenge is to his fellow Muslims. He was among the first to condemn clearly, firmly, and persistently the use of violence "in the Name of God" for political purposes. Terrorism, such as that sponsored by Al-Qaeda, and extreme national policies, such as those in Iran, distort the essential message of Islam as a religion of moderation, justice, and peace. He has denounced terrorist attacks and made clear his hatred for persons such as the late Osama bin Laden:

> I regret to say that in the countries Muslims live, some religious leaders and immature Muslims have no other weapon to hand than their fundamentalist interpretation of Islam; they use this to engage people in struggles that serve their own purposes. In fact, Islam is a true faith, and it should be lived truly. On the way to attaining faith one can never use untrue methods. In Islam, just as a goal must be legitimate, so must all the means employed to reach that goal. From this perspective, one cannot achieve Heaven by murdering another person. A Muslim cannot say, "I will kill a person and then go to Heaven." God's approval cannot be won by killing people. One of the most important goals for a Muslim is to win the approval of God, another being making the name of Almighty God known to the universe.[298]

Terrorism aside, Gülen complains that rampant individualism is sapping the vigor of Muslims. Disunity within the Muslim community is a critical problem that must be addressed by a revivification of the Islamic ideals of patience, reliance on prayer, and selfless efforts to

---

[297] Gülen, *The Statue of Our Souls*, p. 8.
[298] Ibid, *Toward a Global Civilization of Love and Tolerance*, p. 184.

develop spiritual unity and life-affirming groups among Muslims. In addition, he stated that there is not an Islamic nation or Islamic world but rather places where Muslims live and where they develop a cultural climate that may use Islamic terms and occasionally practice an external Pillar more out of habit or weak intention. The key is in education that blends science and Islamic values. Among those values is his conviction that human beings are the clearest type of mirrors of God's Names, and that Muhammad is the Pride of Humanity, the person who is the closest Friend and Beloved of God. Gülen challenges fellow Muslims who live in Muslim majority lands:

> Should they think in a totally different way when electing their leaders? Or should they carry out fundamental reforms? For the growth of a well-developed younger generation, Muslims must work to solve their problems. Not only their problems in the issue of terror, an instrument that is certainly not approved by God, but also those concerning drugs and the use of cigarettes—two more unlawful habits. Dissension, civil turmoil, never-ending poverty, the disgrace of being governed by others, and being insulted after having put up with government by foreign powers are all problems that could be added to the list.[299]

The third challenge is to the People of the Book. Gülen holds the Qur'anic and traditional Muslim position that the Bible has been mistranslated, misunderstood, and corrupted in the long course of history. Gülen recognized that relationships with Jews could be politically problematic. He held that dialogue and cooperation between Muslims and Jews who have not oppressed Muslims is appropriate. Clearly, the Jewish and Muslim insistence on the One-Only God, and denial of the Trinity, provide the groundwork for dialogue and collaboration. Nevertheless, the clear message of the One-Only God and the roles of the Prophets of God must resonate with Jews:

> God sent Prophets to teach their people the meaning of creation and the truth of things, to unveil the mysteries behind historical and natural events, and to inform us of our relationship, and that of the Divine Scriptures, with the universe....The Prophets guided

---

[299] Ibid, p. 187.

people through personal conduct and the heavenly religions and Scriptures they conveyed, to develop their inborn capacities and directed them toward the purpose of their creation.[300]

Since Christianity is the largest religion in the world, Gülen deals mostly with its adherents. The history of the relations between Christians and Muslims is freighted with misunderstanding, conflict, and hostility, yet there have been times of amity and cooperation. As indicated in the course of Chapter Three, Muslims and Christians share some understandings, at least on the semantic levels, about Jesus and part company on matters such as the forgiveness of sins, Jesus' death and the atonement, the Trinity, ritual acts such as the Eucharist and baptism, inspiration of Scripture, and so on. He warns, gently, that Christians ought to think more deeply about what the Bible says about the ministry of Jesus to heal, forgive, and avoid violence. He believes that the destructive problem that Christians must correct is the penchant of governments to seize power to control other peoples while invoking Christianity as a justification. As many Christians believe that Jews and Muslims will convert to Christianity before the final end, Gülen hopes that Christians will become Muslims when the spiritual messianic aspect of the mission represented by Jesus will be given prominence in conveying the Truth to people throughout the world during the End of Times. Because of the prominence of Jesus in both types of the End and the numbers of Christians and Muslims in the world, Gülen urges Muslims and Christians to collaborate in facing the challenges of ignorance, poverty, and disunity. Interfaith dialogue is absolutely necessary:

> Religion reconciles opposites: religion-science, this world-the next world, Nature-Divine Books, material-spiritual, and spirit-body. It can contain scientific materialism, put science in its proper place, and end long-standing conflicts. The natural sciences which should lead people to God, instead cause widespread disbelief. As this trend is strongest in the West, and because Christianity is the most influenced, Muslim-Christian dialogue is indispensable.[301]

---

[300] Ibid, *Essentials*, p. 165.
[301] *Essays, Perspectives, Opinions: Fethullah Gülen*, p. 32.

The fourth challenge addresses the rest of humanity. Gülen's dark analysis of the current state of the world is a warning that conditions may well worsen as humans continue to pollute the world, exploit creation, and refuse to show gratitude to the Creator by explicitly and implicitly denying God's ownership of the cosmos and that they are to govern their conduct by Divine law. Gülen realizes that each person is created by and is in a primordial covenant with God. Families and cultures are what obscure the person's perceptions. The hope is for God's religion to be purified and returned to its pristine purity so that its reason and compassion will attract the cooperation and partnership of persons of many different ideologies towards eliminating the triad of ignorance, poverty, and disunity.

> Today there is an interest in religion all over the world. In my opinion, representing faith with its true values has gained an even greater importance than before. Today there is a need for people who are virtuous, self-possessed, cautious, sincere and pure of heart, people who do not steal or think too highly of themselves, and who prefer the well-being of others to their own, and who have no worldly expectations. If society can educate people with these characteristics, then it means that a much better future is imminent.[302]

Gülen's fifth and final challenge is to the affiliates of Hizmet. The preacher-teacher-poet developed a story about a small group of dedicated persons who bravely and unselfishly embarked on a mission to bring light, understanding, and peace wherever they went. They were motivated to act for the cause of God in God's world. Although they had to endure arid stretches, criticisms, temptations, and their own shortcomings, they persevered because of their love for God and their ambition to meet Him. Wherever they went, they spread light, transforming dross into treasures. Obviously, Gülen offers a metaphor for the women and men of Hizmet. He concluded his tale with images and references that we may recognize as part of the telos-eschaton:

> A flood of love among people has started overflowing in almost every place that these bearers of mission visit. There have been breez-

---

[302] Gülen, *Toward a Global Civilization of Love and Tolerance*, p. 72.

es of happiness and gladness, one after another, that can be felt all around. Moreover, islands of peace, which we can call invulnerable castles of harmony and stability are forming near and far. Who knows, maybe in the near future, thanks to these volunteers who devote themselves to letting others live, the mind and soul will embrace each other again....And everything will find the opportunity to express the beauty in its own nature through its own language...people will regret having fought each other, ...an atmosphere of peace that was not previously established in the marketplaces, in the schools and homes will be established, ...no one will envy others, their property or their reputation, the powerful will treat the weak justly, the weak and the poor will have the chance to live humanely...nobody's blood will be shed and the weak will not cry, everybody will adore God and love humanity. It is only then that this world, which is the hallway to Paradise, will become an Eden that is fascinating to live in.[303]

Gülen has been at the forefront of those figures described in the story. The journey he has undertaken with those who have already joined him has the Hereafter as its ultimate end. Yet the way to that reality leads through this world, a world that God will bring to its telos-fulfillment, even for a brief time, as not only a collection of peace islands but also a globe of justice, mercy, unity, and peace.

The love of God is the essence of everything and is the purest and cleanest source of all love. Compassion and love flow to our hearts from Him. Any kind of human relation will develop in accordance with our relation to Him. Love of God is our faith, our belief, and our spirits in the physical body. He made us live when we did. If we are to live today, it is only through Him. The essence of all existence is His love, and the end is an expansion of that Divine love in the form of Paradise. Everything He created depends on love and He has bound His relationship with humankind to the holy pleasure of being loved.[304]

---

[303] Ibid, pp. 211–214.
[304] Ibid, p. 11.

# EPILOGUE

Even if the world is not in a process of renewal, and it is clear today that it is not, it definitely is in a process of reconstruction. When the correct time arrives, this reconstruction will certainly be realized. When this happens, instead of having a world that has been shaped with malice and hatred, a surprising world that has taken its form in a climate of love, tolerance [*hoşgörü*], and forbearance will appear before us. The collective conscience will gladly welcome and place it in its heart, not neglecting those who have a share in this reformation. These people will leave permanent tracks and, even if they have physically left this world, their tracks will remain for centuries. I believe with my whole heart that the only thing to do today in order to realize these spring fragranced dreams is to perform this kind of service for humanity. For this reason, instead of temporary, fleeting, and unpromising efforts, I would advise a type of movement that is lasting and fully beneficial in every way. I think that as long as I am alive I will not hesitate to repeat these recommendations.[305]

We have started to meet Fethullah Gülen. He has greeted us as a preacher-teacher-lecturer; organizer-administrator; advocate for educationally-deprived youth; critic of spiritual lethargy; facilitator for the development of educational, publishing, and media enterprises; patriotic Muslim Turk; pioneer in dialogue among the followers of various faiths; poet; author; man of hope and reflection; and spiritual guide. His absorption of Sufi spirituality has revealed him as a man of deep reflection in understanding the Divine Plan for all the worlds and for humanity. He is a man with a vision for what this world will be before it is terminated and an eternal new beginning opens in the Hereafter. As he describes the "Golden Generation" that is rising to end ignorance, poverty, and disunity,

---

[305] Ibid, *Toward a Global Civilization of Love and Tolerance*, p. 253.

we are able to discern his personal presence and leadership in the very activities in which he encourages others to participate.

The vision he has for the present world is a profound and fruitful Islamically-based reading of the three books revealed by God. The Book of the Universe, as one of these three books to be read, discloses the Divine arrangement of spiritual realms and the dimension of our world. The entities in that arrangement, whether animate or not, are regarded as willingly and promisingly in fellowship with their Creator. The entire universe is so ordered that it mirrors and witnesses the One-Only God's Names and Attributes directing the attention and action toward the fulfillment of the universe in the present world in anticipation of the Resurrection and the following eternal life of the Hereafter in a completely new world. The second book is the Qur'an. Gülen is eloquent in describing the Muslim belief that the Qur'an, along with its first and foremost practitioner—the Prophet himself, is the criterion and guidance for worship, servanthood, individual ethics, communal life, and relations with the whole of humanity. His interpretations of the Qur'an describe the influences of important figures such as Muhammad, Jesus, and many spiritual guides on life in the present and near future. Humanity is God's third book to be read. As the most highly polished mirror of the entire creation, humans are also the index, the referential key through which we may have access to understanding the Divine Plan's beginnings and endings as well as the duties, responsibilities and joys, and the tests and discipline God expects from us.

On the basis of his readings from and studies of these three books, Gülen meets us as a man of devout and informed hope. That hope is seminal in that it is planted in the aspirations, determinations, and actions of thousands of persons, many of whom affiliate with the Hizmet movement while others cooperate in its programs and activities. The seeds of that hope are planted in and start to germinate in this dimension, and, as he foresees, will be harvested in the future world. In the present, Gülen and those whom he touches at the deepest level rejoice in the advances that are made toward fulfillment, yet they feel deeply the pain and anguish of people who are still in turmoil and need.

At this juncture, I hope that you will agree that Gülen's vision of the creation's beginnings and endings determine his theological, anthropological, and social-ethical visions for a just and peaceful world now. We have met a man who mirrors the Divine Names and Attributes, to the best of his ability, to enlighten a Golden Generation among us. Meeting and continuing to engage with him, we may find him a Muslim friend, a person of *khullah*, or sincere friendship:

> Sincere friendship is pure loyalty. As for love, it is a passion, yearning, and consumption of burning. For this reason, sincere friendship is primarily marked by enthusiasm and thankfulness and then with sadness or sorrow. In other words, while it is enthusiasm and thankfulness that prevails in most people of sincere friendship, the people of love are known with remembrance, reflection and continuous sorrow. How interesting it is that the Master of creation [Muhammad], upon him be peace and blessings, lived in continuous sorrow marked with hope, prayer and entreaty…, having an established position of friendship, loyalty, and love in God's Presence.[306]

We end with our beginning:

In the Name of God, the All-Merciful, the All-Compassionate
All praise and gratitude are for God, the Lord of the worlds,
The All-Merciful, the All-Compassionate,
The Master of the Day of Judgment.
You alone do we worship, and from You alone do we seek help.
Guide us to the Straight Path,
The Path of those whom You have favored, not of those who have incurred (Your) wrath nor of those who are astray.

Surah *al-Fatihah* (The Opener)

---

[306] Ibid, *Key Concepts in the Practice of Sufism*, Vol. 3, pp. 265, 267.

# BIBLIOGRAPHY

## BIBLICAL, QUR'ANIC, AND HADITH SOURCES

Akgül, Muhittin, *The Qur'an in 99 Questions*, NJ: Tughra Books, 2008.

Al-Bukhari, Muhammad ibn Ismail. *The Translation of the Meanings of Sahih al-Bukhari*, Volumes I–IX, translated by Muhammad Muhsin Khan. Riyadh: Daru's-Salam, 1997.

Abu Dawud. *Sunan Abu Dawud*, translated with notes by Ahmad Hasan, Volumes I–III. Lahore: Sh. Muhammad Ashraf, 2004 reprint.

*Holy Bible,* New Revised Standard Version. HarperCollins Study Bible, Harold Attridge, general editor. San Francisco: HarperCollins, 2006 edition.

Ibn Abu Talib, Ali. *Peak of Eloquence. Nahjul Balagha*, Translated by Ayatollah Murtada Mutahari. Elmhurst, NY: Tahrike Tarsile Qur'an, Inc., 2009.

*Meaning of the Holy Qur'an*, Interpretation based on the original by Abdullah Yusuf 'Ali. Beltsville, MD: Amana Publications, 1997 (Ninth Edition).

Muslim, Abu'l-Husain. *Sahih Muslim*, Volumes I–IV, translated by Abdul Hamid Siddiqi. New Delhi: Kitab Bhavan, 1986.

*Qur'an with Annotated Interpretation in Modern English*, Interpretated by Ali Ünal. Somerset, NJ: Light, 2007.

Tabrizi, Wali-ud-Din Muhammad bin Abdullah. *Mishkatu'l-Masabih*, Volumes I–II, translated by Abdul Hamid Siddiqi. New Delhi: Kitab Bhavan, 1987.

## WORKS BY FETHULLAH GÜLEN

Gülen, M. Fethullah. Interview with Mehmet Gündem, January 25, 2005. Accessed August 24, 2012 from htpp//www.fgulen.com.

--------. *Key Concepts in the Practice of Sufism. Emerald Hills of the Heart*. Volumes I–IV, Somerset, NJ: Tughra Books, 2006–2010.

--------. *Muhammad: the Messenger of God, An Analysis of the Prophet's Life*. (Translated by Ali Ünal), Somerset, NJ: Tughra Books, 2009.

--------. *Questions and Answers about Islam*, Volumes I–II. Clifton, NJ: Tughra Books, 2008 and 2009.

--------. *Reflections on the Qur'an: Commentaries on Selected Verses*. Clifton, NJ: Tughra Books, 2011.

-------. *Speech and the Power of Expression: On Language, Esthetics, and Belief.* Clifton, NJ: Tughra Books, 2010.

-------. *The Essentials of the Islamic Faith*, (Translated by Ali Ünal), Somerset, NJ: Light, 2006.

-------. *Toward a Global Civilization of Love and Tolerance.* Foreword by Thomas Michel. Clifton, NJ: Tughra Books, 2009.

-------. *Towards the Lost Paradise.* Clifton, NJ: Tughra Books, 2010.

-------. *Essays, Perspectives, Opinions.* Rutherford, NJ: Fountain, 2002.

-------. "Necisin? Nereden Geldin? Nereye Gidiyorsun?" in *Fasıldan Fasıla* (Considerations), Vol. IV. (Translation provided by Yusuf Alan), Istanbul: Nil Yayınları, 2011, pp. 41–42.

-------. "Ölümün Hatırlattıkları ve Ötesi" in *Işığın Göründüğü Ufuk* (The Horizon Where the Light Appeared). Istanbul: Nil Yayınları, 2011, pp. 199–206.

## GENERAL WORKS

Abu-Rabi', Ibrahim M. (ed.), *Theodicy and Justice in Modern Islamic Thought: The Case of Said Nursi.* Surry, UK: Ashgate Publishing, 2010.

Ahsan Khan, Maimul. *The Vision and Impact of Fethullah Gülen: A New Paradigm for Social Activism.* New York: Blue Dome Press, 2011.

Albayrak, Ismail (ed.), *Mastering Knowledge in Modern Times: Fethullah Gülen as an Islamic Scholar.* Somerset, NJ: Blue Dome Press, 2011.

Alexander, Paul. *The Byzantine Apocalyptic Tradition.* Berkeley: University of California Press, 1985.

Augustine, Aurelius. City of God, translated by Henry Bettenson. New York: Penguin Classics, 1984.

Al-Awlaki, Anwar. *The Hereafter*, Vol. 1, Denver: Al-Basheer Publications and Translations, undated. Audio Tapes.

Brockopp, Jonathan E. (ed.), *The Cambridge Companion to Muhammad.* New York: Cambridge University Press, 2010.

Büyükçelebi, Ismail. *Living in the Shade of Islam.* Somerset, NJ: Light, 2005.

Carroll, B. Jill. *A Dialogue of Civilizations: Gülen's Islamic Ideals and Humanistic Discourse.* Somerset, NJ: Light, 2007.

Çetin, Muhammed. *The Gülen Movement: Civic Service without Borders.* New York: Blue Dome Press, 2010.

Cook, David. *Studies in Muslim Apocalyptic.* Princeton: Darwin Press, 2002.

Dimashqi, Al-Hafiz ibn Katheer. *Book of the End. Great Trials and Tribulations.* Riyadh: Darusalaam, 2006.

Ebaugh, Helen Rose. *The Gülen Movement: A Sociological Analysis of a Civic Movement Rooted in Moderate Islam.* New York: Springer, 2010.

Esack, Farid. *The Qur'an: A Short Introduction.* Oxford: Oneworld Press, 2002.

-------. *The Qur'an: A User's Guide*. Oxford: Oneworld Press, 2005.

Esposito, John and Kalin, Ibrahim, (eds.), *The 500 Most Influential Muslims*. Royal Islamic Strategic Studied Centre, the 2009 and 2010 editions. Washington: Georgetown University, 2009 and 2010.

Esposito, John and Yilmaz, Ihsan, (eds.), *Islam and Peacebuilding: Gülen Movement Initiatives*. New York: Blue Dome Press, 2010.

Esposito, John, (ed.), *The Oxford Dictionary Of Islam*. New York: Oxford University Press, 2003.

-------. (ed.), *The Oxford Encyclopedia of the Modern Islamic World*, Vols. I–IV, New York: Oxford University Press, 1995.

Fakhry, Majid. *Averroës. Ibn Rushd: His Life, Works and Influence*. Oxford: Oneworld, 2001.

Fatoohi, Louay. http://www.louayfatoohi.com accessed November 21, 2012.

Filiu, Jean-Pierre. *Apocalypse in Islam*. Berkeley: University of California Press, 2011.

*Foreign Policy* and *Prospect* www.foreignpolicy.com August 3, 2008. Accessed November 25, 2012.

Al-Ghazali, Abu Hamid. *The Niche of Lights*. Provo, Utah: Brigham Young University Press, 1998.

-------. *The Ninety-Nine Beautiful Names of God*. Cambridge: Islamic Texts Society, 1995.

-------. *The Remembrance of Death and the Afterlife. Book XL of the Revival of the Religious Sciences*. (Translated by T. J. Winter), Cambridge: Islamic Texts Society, 1989.

Glassé, Cyril. *The New Encyclopedia of Islam, revised editon of the Concise Encyclopedia of Islam*. Walnut Creek, CA: Alta Mira Press, 2001 edition.

Harrington, James. *Wrestling with Free Speech, Religious Freedom, and Democracy in Turkey: The Political Trials and Times of Fethullah Gülen*. New York: University Press of America, 2011.

Huntington, Samuel, P. *The Clash of Civilizations and the Remaking of World Order*. New York: Simon and Schuster, 1996.

Ibn al-'Arabi. *The Bezels of Wisdom*, translated by R. Y. J. Austin. Mahewah, NJ: Paulist Press, 1980.

-------. *The Meccan Revelations*, 2 volumes. New York: Pir Press, 2005 edition.

Ibn Ishaq, Muhammad. *The Life of Muhammad*. Translated by A. Guillaume. Karachi: Oxford University Press, 1955 edition.

Journalists and Writers Foundation, *Understanding Fethullah Gülen*. Istanbul: Journalist and Writers Foundation, nd, after 2010.

Kim, Heon Choul. *The Nature and Role of Sufism in Contemporary Islam: A Case Study of the Life, Thought and Teachings of Fethullah Gülen*. Pro-Quest UMI Dissertation Publishing, 2011

Markham, Ian and Pirim, Suendam Birinci. *An Introduction to Said Nursi: Life, Thought and Writings*. Surrey, UK: Ashgate, 2011.

Mattson, Ingrid. *The Story of The Qur'an. Its History, and Place in Muslim Life*. Oxford: Blackwell Publishing, 2008.

McGinn, Bernard. *Antichrist: Two Thousand Years of the Human Fascination with Evil*. San Francisco: HarperSanFrancisco, 1994.

Michel, Thomas. *The Damascus Sermon, http//www.bediüzzamansaidnursi.org*, accessed May 1, 2012.

Nasr, Syyed Hossein (ed.), *Islamic Spirituality*, 2 volumes. New York: Crossroads 1991.

Nursi, Bediüzzaman Said. *Risale-i Nur Collection, Al-Mathnawi al-Nuri: The Seedbed of Light*. Somerset, NJ: The Light, 2007.

-------. *Risale-i Nur Collection, The Damascus Sermon*. Istanbul: Sözler Publications, Revised and Expanded Edition, 1996.

-------. *Risale-i Nur Collection, The Gleams*. Somerset, NJ: The Light, 2008.

-------. *Risale-i Nur Collection, The Letters*. Somerset, NJ: The Light, 2007.

-------. *Risale-i Nur Collection, The Rays*. Clifton, NJ: The Light, 2010.

-------. *Risale-i Nur Collection, The Reasonings*. Somerset, NJ: The Light, 2008.

-------. *Risale-i Nur Collection, The Words*. Somerset, NJ: The Light, 2010.

Palmer, Andrew; Brock, Sebastian; Hoyland, Robert, Introductions, translations and commentaries. *The Seventh Century in The Western-Syrian Chronicles, Including Two Seventh Century Syriac Apocalyptic Texts*. Liverpool: Liverpool University Press, 1993

Philips, Abu Ameenah Bilal. Ad-Dajjal. *The Anti-Christ*. Alexandria, VA: Sound-Knowledge, 2001.

Poston, Larry. "The Second Coming of 'Isa: An Exploration of Islamic Premillennialism" in *The Muslim World*. Volume 100, number 1, January, 2010, pp. 100–116.

Robinson, James Harvey, (ed.), *Petrarch: the First Modern Scholar and Man of Letters*. New York: G.P. Putman, 1898.

Saeed, Abdullah. *The Qur'an: An Introduction*. New York: Routledge, 2008 edition.

Sakr, Ahmad H. *Al-Jinn*. Lombard, Illinois: Foundation for Islamic Knowledge, 1994.

Schleifler, Abdallah, (ed.), *The 500 Most Influential Muslims. 2012 Edition*. Amman, Jordan: Royal Islamic Strategic Studied Centre, 2012.

Smith, Jane D. and Haddad, Yvonne Y. *The Islamic Understanding of Death and Resurrection*. Albany: State University of New York Press, 1981.

Stoneman, Richard, (tr. and ed.), *The Greek Alexander Romance*. New York: Penguin, 1991.

Trofimov, Yaroslav. *The Siege of Mecca*. New York: Doubleday, 2007.

Ünal, Ali and Williams, Alphonse, (Compilers), *Advocate of Dialogue: Fethullah Gülen*. Somerset, NJ: Light, 2000.

Ünal, Ali. *Islam Addresses Contemporary Issues*. Somerset, NJ: Light, 2006.

-------. *The Resurrection and the Afterlife*. Somerset, NJ: Light, 2006

Wagner, Walter H. "Journeying to God: Muhammad's Isra and Mi'raj," *Cithara* 36, no. 2, 1997, pp. 20–29.

-------. *After the Apostles. Christianity in the Second Century*. Minneapolis: Fortress Press, 1994

-------. *Opening the Qur'an. Introducing Islam's Holy Book*. Notre Dame, Indiana: University of Notre Dame Press, 2008.

Walls, Jerry, (ed.), *The Oxford Handbook of Eschatology*. New York: Oxford University Press, 2008.

*Webster's New World College Dictionary*, Fourth Edition. Cleveland: Wiley Publishing Company, 2002.

Winter, Tim, (ed.), *Classical Islamic Theology*. Cambridge, UK: Cambridge University Press, 2008.

-------. (ed.), *The Cambridge Companion to Classical Islamic Theology*. Cambridge: Cambridge University Press, 2008.

Yavuz, Hakan, M. and Esposito, John, (eds.), *Turkish Islam and the Secular State. The Gülen Movement*. Syracuse: Syracuse University Press, 2003.

Yücesoy, Hayrettin. *Messianic Beliefs and Imperial Politics in Medieval Islam: the Abbasid Caliphate in the Early Ninth Century*. Columbia SC: University of South Carolina Press, 2009.